A RETURN TO
ROOTS

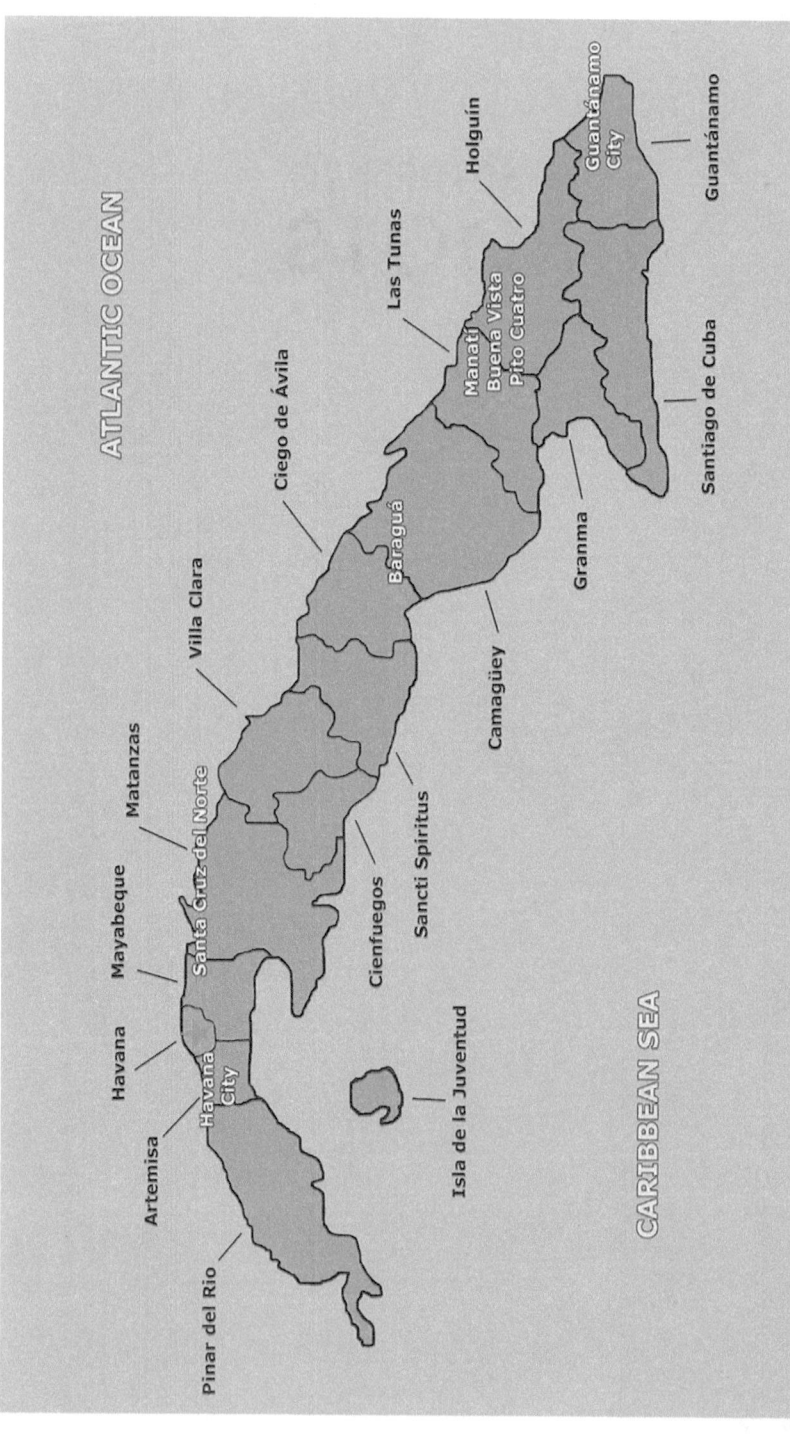

Map of Cuba

A RETURN TO ROOTS

"CUBAJANS" IN BARBADOS

Sharon Milagro Marshall

The University of the West Indies Press
Jamaica • Barbados • Trinidad and Tobago

The University of the West Indies Press
7A Gibraltar Hall Road, Mona
Kingston 7, Jamaica
www.uwipress.com

© 2022 by Sharon Milagro Marshall
All rights reserved. Published 2022

A catalogue record of this book is available from the
National Library of Jamaica.

ISBN: 978-976-640-881-7 (print)
978-976-640-883-1 (ePub)

Cover and book design by Robert Harris
Set in Minion Pro 10.5/14.2 x 27
Printed in the United States of America

The University of the West Indies Press has no responsibility for the persistence or accuracy of URLs for external or third-party internet websites referred to in this publication and does not guarantee that any content on such websites is, or will remain, accurate or appropriate.

CONTENTS

Map of Cuba ...... frontispiece

List of Figures vii

List of Tables ix

Preface xi

Acknowledgements xiii

PART 1: PROTECTORATE STATUS AND COLONIAL RULE

    Introduction: A Bajan Everywhere 3

1. Pre-1959 Revolution Cuba 8
2. Colonial Barbados 19
3. Ofelia Nicholls 52
4. Frank Philo 59

PART 2: REVOLUTION AND INDEPENDENCE

5. Post-1959 Revolution Cuba 67
6. Post-Independence Barbados 78
7. Nelson Goddard 87
8. Gilbert Rowe 94
9. Graciela King 103
10. Isabel Deane 110
11. Colbert Belgrave 116
12. Maria Thomas Ferrier 125

13.	Yolanda Nelson Springer	131
14.	Josué Ramírez Nelson	140
15.	The Yearwoods	151
16.	Pedro Hope Jústiz	160
17.	Pablo Atwell	169
18.	Roberto Trotman Brown	174

Conclusion 183

Notes 197

Selected Bibliography 209

Index 213

FIGURES

3.1. Ofelia Nicholls 52
3.2. Ofelia Parris married Clyde Nicholls in Curaçao in 1952 56
3.3. Ofelia returned to Barbados from Curaçao in 1960 57
4.1. Frank Philo 59
4.2. Frank in England in March 1957 63
7.1. Nelson Goddard 87
7.2. Nelson with his family 91
8.1. Gilbert Rowe 94
8.2. Sharon Marshall being serenaded along with other excited patrons by Barbadian saxophone virtuoso Arturo Tappin, at Jazz on the Hill in January 1996 100
9.1. Graciela King 103
9.2. Graciela with other members of the Niles family 105
9.3. Graciela and her sister Ydania at a picnic during their early days in Barbados 107
10.1. Isabel Deane 110
10.2. Isabel's parents, Eunice and Charles Willie 111
10.3. The Willie family 112
10.4. Isabel and her husband, Brian, sharing a happy moment at home 113
11.1. Colbert Belgrave 116
11.2. Young Colbert at school with teachers and other members of his class in Central Baraguá 117

11.3.	Colbert playing the organ at church in Barbados	122
13.1.	Yolanda Nelson Springer	131
13.2.	Yolanda with other foreign university classmates in the Soviet Union	135
13.3.	Yolanda surrounded by some of her students in the Primary Spanish Programme at Sharon Primary School	138
14.1.	Josué Ramírez Nelson	140
14.2.	Josué after his arrival in Barbados	144
15.1.	Florencia, Juana and Ernesto Yearwood	151
15.2.	Young Juana with her parents and brother Felipe in Cuba	152
15.3.	Florencia on her wedding day	155
16.1.	Pedro Hope Jústiz	160
16.2.	Pedro celebrating his graduation from the Warner Moro Institute of Foreign Languages with his mother, Irene Jústiz	162
16.3.	Pedro receiving his MA in linguistics (applied) degree at the 2015 graduation ceremony of the Cave Hill campus of the University of the West Indies	164
16.4.	Pedro conducting a choir from the Christ Church Girls Primary School	166
17.1.	Pablo Atwell	169
17.2.	Pablo on the job at the Radisson Aquatica Resort, Barbados	171
17.3.	Pablo received his diploma in tourism management at the 2017 BIMAP graduation ceremony	172
18.1.	Roberto Trotman Brown	174
18.2.	Roberto and Pedro enjoying the spirit of the Christmas season in Barbados	182
C.1.	Some members of the CuBajan community at the funeral service for Colbert Belgrave	194

TABLES

Table 6.1.   Cuba-Born Population by Sex and Year of Immigration **85**

Table 6.2.   Cuba-Born Population by Sex and Age Groups under-5 to 44 ...... **85**

Table 6.3.   Cuba-Born Population by Sex and Age Groups 45 to 85 and over **86**

PREFACE

MY BOOK *TELL MY MOTHER I GONE TO CUBA*: *Stories of Early Twentieth-Century Migration from Barbados* (2016) chronicles the movement of Barbadians – and other British West Indians – to Cuba in an era when the expansion of sugar cane cultivation there created work opportunities for the migrants.

At the official launch of *Tell My Mother I Gone to Cuba*, Francisco Fernández Peña, then Cuban ambassador to Barbados, said to me that I needed to write a second book about the Cuban-Barbadians[1] in Barbados. Since I was dealing with the stress of launching and marketing that first book, I did not pay too much attention to that proposal at the time. But little did I know that the seed had been planted then. It has since grown and evolved, seemingly of its own volition.

This book – *A Return to Roots: "CuBajans" in Barbados* – captures the narratives of descendants of some of those Barbadian migrants to Cuba – the sons and daughters, grandchildren and great grandchildren – who have settled in Barbados, closing the circle of migration. As the interviewer, I began this publication project with the idea of maintaining a professional distance from my subjects. I would soon come to realize that this would be difficult, if not impossible. Their stories are too closely linked with mine, some more so than others.

My late mother, Delcina Esperanza Marshall, was born in Cuba of Barbadian parents in 1927. She came to her parents' birthplace in 1936 at the age of nine, and returned to Cuba for the first time fifty-three years later in 1989. I accompanied her on that trip, my first to Cuba. Colbert Belgrave was the leader of that group of approximately thirty-five persons, which included Graciela King and her mother, Francisca Niles. Ofelia Nicholls, who – like my mother – also came to Barbados in 1936 with her parents, knew my mother and her siblings and was the neighbour of my late uncle Rupert.

After that first visit to Cuba in 1989, I would return many times. While on assignment there for the Caribbean Broadcasting Union in 1993, I went to Central Baraguá for the first time and interviewed some of the British West Indian descendants there. One of them was Joseph Atwell, the grandfather of Pablo Atwell. It was that interview which inspired the realization that my family story was part of a wider migration narrative. That set me on a course to discover more, and to enrol at the University of the West Indies and eventually earn a doctorate in history. That research was the basis for *Tell My Mother I Gone to Cuba*.

Yolanda Nelson is a dear sister-friend who was born in Baraguá. Her elder brother Elliot also became a friend who would chauffeur me around Havana on subsequent visits, and her sister Olivia would host me in her home in Baraguá when I was conducting research for my doctoral degree. It was there at Olivia's home that I first met Yolanda's son, Josué, although everyone at home and in the neighbourhood called him Pocholo. He was a ball of energy and continuous movement, surrounded always by four or five boys his age as they engaged in outdoor games and adventures. I am now considered part of the Nelson family, and family members have been entertained at my home on their visits to Barbados.

Gilbert Rowe grew up in the same neighbourhood as Yolanda and was her classmate in school. I have served as a courier for Gilbert, taking money to his uncle Hershel in Baraguá when I travelled there. Colbert performed a similar role on behalf of myself and my relatives in Barbados, taking envelopes to our cousins in Havana and Santa Cruz del Norte. Jenny Yearwood also lived in Santa Cruz del Norte, and was a neighbour to my relatives there.

On my various research visits to Cuba, I was fortunate to meet some more of the Barbadian migrants and their descendants. One of those Barbadian descendants – Pedro Hope Jústiz – was particularly helpful on my visit to the West Indian community in Guantánamo. Like me, his grandfather had migrated from Barbados to Cuba, and we soon discovered that we had other things in common. Pedro would eventually become my husband.

From 1993 to 2010, Gilbert produced the Barbados Jazz Festival, bringing major international artists to the island to perform on stage with local talent. It was a much-anticipated annual Caribbean event every January, attracting regional and international visitors. Pedro, my Mum and I, along with our friends and relatives, were frequent patrons at the various shows.

These are just some of the persons whose oral testimonies are recorded in *A Return to Roots*. Conducting these interviews between 31 October 2017 and 8 April 2018 has given me the privilege of connecting, or in some instances reconnecting, with these members of the CuBajan community in their homes, or mine. I'm the richer for the experience. I hope that you will also be enriched by reading their stories.

ACKNOWLEDGEMENTS

THERE ARE A NUMBER OF PERSONS WHOSE SUPPORT and encouragement nurtured the growth and development of this book.

First of all, I wish to acknowledge the role of former Cuban ambassador to Barbados Dr Francisco Fernández Peña, for suggesting that such a publication be produced.

To former Barbados ambassador to the Republic of Cuba Donna Forde, I shall be eternally grateful for your invaluable support and assistance in seeking recognition for this research.

To my friend Yolanda Nelson Springer, I am grateful for your constant and unwavering support throughout the entire period of my research both in Cuba and Barbados. Thank you for providing names and contact information for many of the CuBajans, and for readily agreeing to participate in this book project.

I am persuaded that the prayers and blessings of the phenomenal Ofelia Nicholls availed much. Thank you for your "token of love", Ofelia.

Staff at the Barbados Department of Archives, the Shilstone Memorial Library at the Barbados Museum and Historical Society, and the Barbados Public Library were very helpful in granting me access to the official documents which shed light on many aspects of bygone Barbados. This is much appreciated.

In particular, I thank Carlyle Best of the Sidney Martin Library at the University of the West Indies, Cave Hill, for going well beyond the call of duty to ensure that I had access to a microfilm document.

The late Professor Constance Sutton maintained a keen interest in the subject of Barbados's Cuba connections and encouraged my research. She would have been thrilled at the publication of this book.

Sir Woodville Marshall readily agreed to read an early draft of the manuscript, and for this I thank him, as well as for his comments about the work.

Special thanks to my husband, Pedro Hope Jústiz – the person who (to the

xiii

best of my knowledge) first coined the phrase "CuBajan" – for his enthusiastic support of the project and for participating in it.

And, most especially, to all the CuBajans who shared their wonderful stories and precious family photographs with me, so that I could share them with you, the reader, I say, *¡Muchisimas gracias! Que Dios los bendiga a todos ustedes.* Thank you very much! God bless you all.

PART 1

PROTECTORATE STATUS AND COLONIAL RULE

INTRODUCTION

A BAJAN EVERYWHERE

WHO IS A BARBADIAN? OR WHO ARE THOSE who have the right to call themselves Bajans?[1] The simple answer is, anyone born in Barbados. However, many whose "navel string"[2] is not buried in Barbados also lay passionate claim to that identity. Among these are Cubans of Barbadian descent.

However, Cuba was hardly the only place to which Barbadians migrated. The saying "Wherever in the world you go, you'll find a Bajan", is simply a reflection of the fact that the citizens of this small Caribbean island have been on the move for a very long time.

When Barbadians and other British West Indians began migrating to Cuba in the early 1900s, they were escaping the harsh living conditions and limited labour market prospects that had persisted in their home countries since Emancipation.

They were drawn to Cuba by the prospect of finding work in that island's expanding sugar industry. American investment in Cuban sugar plantations created opportunities in the labour-intensive cultivation and harvesting of sugar cane. When, in 1912, President José Miguel Gómez authorized the United Fruit Company to import labourers, the stage was set for large-scale migration.

Santiago de Cuba, at the eastern end of the island, was the main port of entry for most of the migrants as they completed the sea journey from Barbados and elsewhere in the Caribbean. The workers made their homes in settlements around sugar-growing plantations in areas such as Chaparra and Manatí in the province of Las Tunas, but they were also to be found at the easternmost tip of the island in Guantánamo and in places such as Central Baraguá in the central province Ciego de Ávila, just thirty-five miles from Havana in Central Hershey (now Central Camilo Cienfuegos) and the nearby municipality of Santa Cruz del Norte.

The ultimate aim of most of the migrants was to return home to Barbados eventually. If they could do so in a more prosperous state than when they left, so much the better. They maintained many of the cultural traditions of their homeland and immersed their Cuba-born children in this culture. They exposed them to the type of education which they themselves had received in Barbados and taught them English to prepare them for life "back home".

Many of these migrants were not able to fulfil that ardent desire to return to their roots in Barbados themselves, but some of their children, grandchildren and great-grandchildren have been able to achieve this dream. Some have been able to visit the island only for short periods, such as the group of twelve who were invited by the National Union of Public Workers in April 2006. The descendants' interviews with the local media were described in articles bearing headlines such as "Digging into Roots",[3] "Cubans Looking for Barbadian Relatives"[4] and "Cubans Looking up Roots".[5] The last article reports on their long-held desire to visit Barbados, stating: "They wanted to breathe the same air and walk on the same ground as their fathers, grandfathers and great-great-grandfathers did before them."[6]

Other descendants have settled in their ancestral homeland. Some of these reverse migrants were the beneficiaries of government assistance to make the journey from Cuba to Barbados, but many of them came of their own volition. This is their story.

These "CuBajans" have integrated themselves into Barbadian society, and despite their relatively small number and the resistance which some of them encountered, they have contributed significantly to the island's development.

Their personal histories of arrival and settlement in Barbados span from the 1930s to the 2000s, and so are told by persons ranging from ninety-four to twenty-seven years old. Nine men and seven women participated in the interviews. They have come from places as far apart as Havana in the west to Guantánamo in the east. But most were born and raised in the centrally located municipality of Baraguá. Their oral testimonies, told from a personal perspective, create glimpses of life in Cuba and Barbados over this period. They relate the adventure of travel to a strange yet familiar country, meeting relatives previously known only through letters, a chance encounter with a stranger who turned out to be a cousin, and the sheer delight of tasting an apple for the first time.

In conducting the interviews, the respondents were all asked a similar set of prepared basic questions, in addition to some prompted by their responses and unique circumstances. These interviews were recorded, and the audio-taped responses were then transcribed and compiled to form a narrative. The respondents were given the opportunity to check the transcripts for accuracy.

Taken together, these testimonies present an impressive picture of service in and to Barbados, particularly in the fields of education and music. They are survival stories of strength, struggle and success, with identity and belonging as common themes which will resonate with readers wherever migration has been present. They form the heart of the book. The work seeks to answer the question, "How did those who moved experience departure, migration and settlement?"[7]

A Return to Roots is divided into two parts. Part 1 looks at the Barbadian descendants who came to the island in the 1930s. At that period, Cuba was coming out of the US occupation and was a US protectorate, while Barbados was still a British colony. Part 2 deals with the stories of those who came in the 1970s and subsequently. This is the period following the 1959 Revolution in Cuba and the attainment of Independence for Barbados in 1966.

In their discussions of approaches to migration research in various academic disciplines, Caroline Brettell and James Hollifield state that "an initial contrast is between those who approach the problem at a macrolevel, examining the structural conditions (largely political, legal and economic) that shape migration flows; and those who engage in microlevel research, examining how these larger forces shape the decisions and actions of individuals and families, or how they effect change in communities".[8]

The introductory chapters for both parts of the book could be said to be more macro level, since they provide a brief historical insight into the economic, legal and political contexts within which the migration took place. However, it is through the micro level oral histories that we learn how individual and family decisions about migration were driven by these external circumstances. We learn too how these individuals were able to effect change in their new community.

Several of the interview respondents are, or have been, employed as facilitators in the Ministry of Education's Primary Spanish Programme. The programme was introduced in twenty-one primary schools as a pilot project in 1997. From its inception, the programme has been monitored by the education officer with responsibility for modern languages. As modern languages officer Peggy Agard explains, "The Ministry of Education entered into a contractual agreement with the government of Costa Rica to have some native speakers relocate and teach in Barbados."⁹ However, some of the Costa Ricans had to return home for personal reasons during the course of the school term. "Consequently, a decision was taken to use the native-speakers who were already resident on the island," says Ms Agard. "As a result, the Costa Ricans were eventually replaced by mostly descendants of Barbadians who had migrated to the Spanish-speaking territories of Cuba and Venezuela in search of a better life. They were indeed native-speakers but with strong Barbadian ties."

In 2006, eleven of the nineteen persons engaged by the Ministry of Education as facilitators in the Primary Spanish Programme were Cubans of Barbadian descent. As a result of retirements and engagement at other levels in the education system, that figure stood at seven in 2019.

When the Ministry of Education embarked on a comprehensive reform of the primary and secondary school curriculum in 2000, a Spanish programme for primary schools was formalized. A four-year primary syllabus was established. As the modern languages education officer states, "This meant that students from class one to class four would have a structured programme of study. Spanish had moved from a pilot project to a bona fide subject on the primary curriculum." On a phased basis, the programme was eventually expanded to all public primary schools in Barbados. The facilitators teach one Spanish lesson a week to each class in the schools to which they are assigned. Some are assigned to "as few as two schools while there are others who must visit as many as six schools".

Ms Agard describes the facilitators as "personnel with a passion to deliver" and "keen to do better". She reports: "They fully participate in the workshops which are designed to keep them current and are known to embrace new ideas and approaches." She states: "Some of the most engaging modern languages classes taught in the Barbadian classrooms have been taught by the Spanish facilitators. They have used graphics, manipulatives, music, dance, poetry, choral speaking and games to pique the interest of their young students."

This is regarded as one of the strengths of the programme and might account for the fact that the programme review lists "excited students" as another one of its strengths. According to Ms Agard, "The sheer delight that some students exhibit in and out of the Spanish classroom in response to the sighting of the Spanish facilitator is remarkable. Effusive greetings are accorded the teacher as the children try out what was learnt in the classroom in a real-life situation. Certainly, the authenticity which the current Spanish facilitators lend to the programme is one of the programme's greatest assets."

While it is possible to point to land, or a small shop or house in Barbados acquired with Panama money, it is less likely that similar claims could be made for those who ventured to Cuba. However, this text should demonstrate that the legacy of the Cuban migration is equally enduring, particularly in the lives of the children who have been taught by the CuBajans.

CHAPTER 1

PRE-1959 REVOLUTION CUBA

ECONOMIC AND POLITICAL DEVELOPMENTS

AFTER ALMOST FOUR HUNDRED YEARS OF SPANISH COLONIAL rule, Cuban nationalists were yearning for political independence from Spain. They had hoped that, having thrown in their lot with the Americans during the Spanish-American War of 1898, independence would be within their grasp. This was not to be.

The Americans had designs on the island and had hoped to annex Cuba to the United States. Even though this did not become a practical reality, the United States would still exert considerable influence on the affairs of the country. An armistice was signed between Spain and the United States on 12 August 1898, officially ending the war. But for almost four years after that, direct US rule followed under American military governor General Leonard Wood. At the end of that period, formal independence from the United States came for Cuba as the Republic of Cuba was born in 1902. However, as American troops prepared to withdraw from the island, administrative arrangements were put in place to ensure that the United States would still be effectively in control. The primary instrument denying Cuba full sovereignty was the Platt Amendment, which had been introduced in February 1901.

> According to one of its provisions, the US could intervene whenever it wished in order to protect life and property and to assure Cuban independence.... In effect, the amendment gave the United States the right to review and approve all treaties between Cuba and third countries and any loans the Cubans might wish to contract with third parties. Finally, Cuba was required to sell or lease coaling and naval stations to the United States.[1]

Despite widespread protest throughout the island, Cuban leaders reluctantly conceded to their more powerful neighbour to the north and accepted the amendment.

> With a protectorate status thus imposed on Cuba, the United States pulled down its flag on May 20, 1902. US military occupation was at an end. The newly elected Cuban authorities, headed by President Estrada Palma, took over the reins of government. But US impositions were only beginning. The US immediately demanded and got a reciprocal trade agreement with the new Cuban state, an agreement that Cubans felt clearly favored American interests. . . . The thirty-one years that followed can be described as the period of the full protectorate. They were characterized by corrupt Cuban governments which did what Washington demanded, and by growing US financial interests in Cuba.[2]

Cuba – at the height of the British West Indian migration in the early 1900s – was bustling with economic opportunity for migrants. This boom was driven largely by American investment in the island's sugar industry, particularly in the eastern part of the country. Between the end of the US military occupation and the beginning of the Great Depression, American investments in Cuba increased almost eightfold. Smith notes that "by 1929, the total reached more than $1.5 billion, almost 30% of American investments in all of Latin America. More striking, while American-owned sugar mills accounted for only 15% of Cuban production in 1906, by 1920 they accounted for almost 50%, and by 1929 for a staggering 75%."[3]

Cuba became an increasingly important source of sugar for the international market and required a ready source of labour to cultivate and harvest the crop. American sugar producers pressured the Cuban government to allow them to import cheap labour from nearby countries such as Jamaica and Haiti. In 1911, a group of landowners formed the Asociación de Fomento de la Inmigración, or Association for the Promotion of Immigration, with the objective of bringing in Haitian and Jamaican workers. With Presidential Decree number 23 of 14 January 1913, President José Miguel Gómez gave the Nipe Bay Company permission to import one thousand West Indian workers for Central Preston in Santiago de Cuba province. Another decree on 23 October of that year authorized the free entry of immigrants who had worked on the construction of the Panama Canal.

As a result of World War I, this immigration increased considerably when Cuba became the principal producer of sugar for the Allies and the demand for cheap labour grew. President Mario Menocal, successor to President Gómez, approved immigration legislation on 3 August 1917 which authorized the entry of foreign labourers, provided it was guaranteed that they would not threaten the public health of the country or become charges on the public purse.

It is estimated that 110,450 British West Indians migrated to Cuba between 1912 and 1927. The West Indian labourers, while welcomed by the plantation owners and managers to harvest and process their sugar crops, were not universally embraced by the general Cuban population. In some quarters it was felt that the West Indians were taking jobs away from Cuban workers and that the lower wages they worked for were driving down the earnings of those Cubans who did work in the industry.

The United States stock market crash of 29 October 1929 was the harbinger of the Great Depression of the 1930s which followed. Together they created the largest financial crisis of the twentieth century. In the shadow of this development, countries around the world were reeling from a severe drop in commodity prices and profits, a precipitous decline in international trade, and rising unemployment.

Overproduction by the world's sugar producing countries lowered the price of the commodity to such an extent that it was below the cost of production. From 1928 to 1932, the price of sugar fell from $2.18 per pound to an all-time low of 57 cents. Cuba's 1928/29 crop had been increased to five million tons, up from the four million tons of the previous year. But Cuba was not spared from the crisis.

> The years 1930–1933 registered the most dramatic fall in foreign trade that is known: the average is 143 800 000 dollars, always at the above prices, and the per capita of only 33,80 pesos. The fall had been brutal: from 89,30 pesos in 1929 to 32,20 in 1933, figures which despite their drama were only a pale reflection of the situation confronted by the agricultural proletariat, who in only five years had seen their real income reduced by 80%. . . . Unemployment affected more than half of the labour force. The 1933 harvest lasted only 67 days, half of that of 1926. Masses of hungry peasants fled towards urban centres in the impossible search for work.[4]

Another significant development of that era was political change. Barbadians in Cuba lived through the overthrow of President Gerardo Machado in 1931. The *Barbados Herald* newspaper did its part in informing the Barbadians who remained at home about what was happening in the country to which their countrymen and -women had journeyed. In its foreign news column, an article in the *Herald* on 15 August 1931 was headlined "Revolution in Cuba". It recounted that a manifesto issued by former president Mario G. Menocal had brought to a head the simmering opposition to Machado's government.

> A Revolution has been declared and the President had proclaimed a state of martial law. Fighting has taken place at the suburb of Luyano, and a more serious encounter has occurred in the Pinar del Rio province near Los Palacios. From Santa Clara come reports of increases in rebel strength and a rebel sortie in which 39 soldiers of the Government were killed and 29 taken prisoner. The situation remains tense, but the Government appears to have the situation well in hand in the capital.[5]

Machado would engage in a long struggle with opposition forces. After newly appointed US ambassador Sumner Welles arrived on the island, he attempted to broker an agreement that would see a provisional government headed by Carlos Manuel de Céspedes y Quesada. Machado resisted but was eventually forced to relinquish power after the crisis escalated and the army revolted. On the afternoon of 12 August 1933, Machado left Cuba on a flight to the Bahamas, "carrying five revolvers and several bags of gold".[6] He later settled in Miami, where he died in 1939. However, that was not the end of turbulent times in Cuba. Non-commissioned military officers led by Sergeant Fulgencio Batista staged a coup d'état one month after the collapse of the Machado regime. Batista had thrown his support behind Dr Ramón Grau San Martín, and de Céspedes was forced to resign.

UNWANTED FOREIGN LABOURERS

As Marc McLeod notes, "Whereas the Antilleans had been seen as essential to sugar production during the crop's halcyon days, their usefulness waned when the sugar sector went into decline."[7] In the aftermath of the 1920 crisis in Cuban sugar, the West Indians were regarded as unwanted foreign labourers. In what was known as the Dance of the Millions, the price of Cuban sugar reached unprecedented heights during that year's harvest. The world price for sugar had risen to 9⅛ cents by 18 February. As Hugh Thomas notes:

> This was well above any previous price ever obtained. Previously in Cuba it had been assumed that 5½ cents was enough to "stimulate the island to extreme prosperity". At this point a mania set in. The rest of 1920 was passed, day by day, in a dream-like atmosphere more reminiscent of a film comedy than real life. Up, up, up, went the prices. On 2 March, sugar sold at 10 cents; on 18 March, at 11 cents; on 27 March, at 12 cents; on 8 April at 15½ cents, and on 15 April, at 18 cents.[8]

The climax of this upward trajectory was reached during the week of 19 to 26 May, when prices rose to above 20 cents per pound. This resulted in a reduction in consumption. Then there was a sharp break in the price of sugar at the end of May. This was followed by a precipitous decline, particularly in August and September. When other sugar-producing nations released their stocks on the world market, it spelt disastrous consequences for Cuba. The sugar producers were heavily indebted to the Cuban banks, and when panic led to a run on the banks in October, the island's banking system crashed.

The Cuban government implemented a new policy towards the importation of West Indian labourers, and an early wave of deportations began. In keeping with this new policy, President Alfredo Zayas signed Decree 1404 on 20 June 1921. The decree mandated the immediate expulsion of the workers to their respective countries. In 1926, Cuba's secretary of public works declared that no more than 15 per cent of employees on public roadworks would be "Antillean workers"; he promised to employ "as many Cuban workers as possible or in their defect Spanish or other European laborers".[9]

In light of the global economic crisis of the Great Depression, the government of President Gerardo Machado y Morales had moved to protect the country's labour market by implementing a number of measures. In 1931, legislation was introduced to curtail the importation of labour altogether. This prohibition affected the immigration of foreigners, including British West Indian labourers. Those who broke the law faced a penalty of $500 and six months' detention. Then a draft immigration bill was introduced in the senate in January 1932. It sought to prohibit entry into Cuba of all classes of immigrants, regardless of their gender, occupation, character or nationality. The penalty for infraction was $1,000, six months' imprisonment, or both.

Following Machado's ouster, under the Provisional Revolutionary Government of Ramón Grau San Martín, efforts then turned from prohibiting immigration to obligatory repatriation. Decree 2232, published in the *Official Gazette* of 19 October 1933, authorized the forced repatriation of foreigners found to be without work or any kind of resources. A few weeks later, the Nationalization of Labour Decree was signed into effect on 8 November 1933. The law required that half of all employees in industry, commerce and agriculture be Cuban nationals. With these measures in place, large-scale migration to Cuba effectively came to an end by 1935.

However, these protectionist measures were not unique to Cuba. Elsewhere in the region, similar legislation was enacted to restrict the importation of labour and to protect the interests of local workers. In Panama, a 1926 law demanded that 75 per cent of employees of any enterprise be Panamanian nationals. By 1932, laws in Guatemala and Honduras reportedly required "all companies (native and foreign) to employ 75 percent native labour".[10] The Congress of the Dominican Republic passed laws in 1934, 1935 and 1938 demanding that all businesses employ 70 per cent Dominicans[11] and Venezuela's new *Ley de Trabajo* in 1936 required every company to employ 75 per cent Venezuelan workers.[12] In a similar vein, Elaine Pereira Rocha argues that the economic crisis of the 1930s affected the West Indian community in Costa Rica more than it did the rest of the country: "As unemployment rose everywhere the government passed laws limiting the number of foreign workers that could be hired in the banana industry and prohibiting companies from employing foreigners on the Pacific Coast. Government also instructed immigration officials to discourage West Indian migration to Costa Rica and to support the repatriation of those already in the country."[13] In these circumstances, many of the Barbadians in Cuba began to give serious consideration to returning home to Barbados.

Aware of the plight of who remained there during the 1940s, the Barbados government included the sum of £1,200 in the 1945 Estimates of Expenditure, under the head Subsidies and Grants. These monies were for a contribution towards relief of West Indians in Cuba. In response to a question from member of Parliament Wynter Crawford, Attorney General E.K. Walcott explained: "This Government wrote the Home Government stating that it would be prepared to recommend to the Legislature – and it was done last year – that in proportion to the number of Barbadians in Cuba we should pay 30 per cent of the cost of certain services and that amounts to £1,200."[14] Walcott explained that the number of British West Indians in Cuba at that time was estimated at 35,000 to 40,000. Of these, 10,000 to 12,000 were Barbadians. Crawford felt, though, that there was a better way of dealing with the situation: "I am not acquainted with all the facts but it does appear to me to be more advantageous if we repatriate these people to their respective island homes, provide the same social services and expend the money locally. The money would be circulated locally and, therefore, would be of some advantage to the island."[15]

LIFE FOR WEST INDIAN MIGRANTS IN CUBA

Large numbers of black West Indians had arrived in a landscape where there was an ongoing debate about the place of Afro-Cubans in their own country.

The island's economy was dominated by North American interests, while white Cubans were the leaders of the society. The Partido Independiente de Color had been formed in response to the 1908 elections in which not one single black politician had been elected to office, in spite of campaign promises from both the Moderate and the Liberal parties to end racial inequality.

However, the Partido Independiente de Color was disbanded in 1910 with the passage of the Ley Morúa, which prohibited the formation of political parties on the basis of race. With their political grievances unaddressed, social protest on the part of Afro-Cubans erupted two years later in Havana and Oriente province, which was known as the "black belt" of Cuba. Rioting erupted on 20 May 1912. This posed a threat to North American-owned sugar mills and mining companies, and the response from the United States was swift. Within three days, seven hundred marines were despatched from Guantánamo to crush the revolt. The Cuban army and the rural guard also launched an attack on the Afro-Cuban population. Thousands were killed in this bloody race war.

This was the nature of the society into which black labourers from Barbados and the other West Indian colonies had migrated. Migration to Cuba enabled many of them to earn wages which were much higher than those available back home, but their reception in Cuba was sometimes hostile. Some of the hostility towards them could be attributed to the fact that they were foreigners, but that they were *black* foreigners was an even greater contributory factor.

Some white Cuban intellectuals like Dr Jorge Le-Roy y Cassa were opposed to the importation of West Indian workers and "contended that they had introduced smallpox, measles, and typhoid fever into eastern Cuba, maladies which then spread to the rest of the island".[16] Santiago de Cuba was the main port of entry for the British West Indians. On arrival, they were subjected to quarantine of up to fifteen days and were required to pay a deposit. The deposit was to have been repaid if they were released before the expiry of the fifteen days, but this money was sometimes not returned. Additionally, there were complaints of unsanitary conditions where bath and toilet facilities were lacking. Governor Sir Charles O'Brien sought to warn prospective migrants from Barbados of the situation by way of a notice in the local press: "The Governor has been authoritatively informed that conditions in some of the quarantine stations are far from satisfactory, and intending immigrants to Cuba are strongly advised to assure themselves before departure that, if detained in quarantine, they will be properly housed and fed, and also to satisfy themselves as to the provision made for meeting the expenses of their detention."[17]

The housing accommodation available to the migrants was in segregated neighbourhoods, with white American employees at the top of the scale and agricultural workers at the bottom. This rigid housing segregation was particularly notable on the estates owned by the United Fruit Company. Some of the plantation owners paid workers in *vales*, or vouchers, which were redeemable only at the company store. There were several reports of incidents in which employers cheated immigrant workers out of money which they had worked for. In other instances, some of them were cheated out of property which they had bought. Others were imprisoned, beaten, shot or even killed by rural guards and plantation police who were the law enforcement agents of the day. On 22 May 1924, an unidentified Barbadian man was shot in the face by a Cuban policeman. The man lost an eye in the incident. He had reported that he had been stabbed by a Haitian man who then ran away. When the police came, they told the Barbadian to come to the prison. He said that it was while he was picking up a parcel to take with him that the police officer shot him and ran off.[18]

Complaints about the ill-treatment of the West Indian workers were lodged with the British diplomatic and consular officials in the country, since the West Indians were British subjects. On 3 January 1924, the British chargé d'affaires in Havana, Godfrey Haggard, filed a formal protest with the Cuban State Department. This would create some diplomatic tension between Britain and Cuba. It was not until August of that year that the Cuban government responded to the charges. They published a "grey book" containing the notes and correspondence exchanged with the British chancery. Haggard's successor, Thomas "T.J." Morris, suggested the real possibility of a break in diplomatic relations between the two countries, writing to London that "the attitude of the Cuban Government towards us is distinctly unsatisfactory. Unless I misjudge the temper of the people it would require but little to bring about a break in diplomatic relations."[19] Morris cited the "important interests" which Britain had in Cuba, namely the fact that the principal banks there were British, and their investment of over £16,000,000 in the railways. He noted pointedly that "without diplomatic representation these might suffer considerably. With the West Indian question therefore are involved other, and perhaps more important issues."[20]

This issue was one which was closely followed by the Cuban press. In its roundup of "Cuban Press on Events of the Day" column, the *Havana Post* reproduced *La Discusión*'s reporting on Anglo-Cuban relations: "England has traditional fame for always taking great care that the rights of its subjects are respected in every part of the globe; but in this case we consider that Albion has passed the customary limits and has acted indiscreetly and employed unjustified and undiplomatic proceedings."[21]

When Robert Vansittart of the Foreign Office wrote to the undersecretary of state at the Colonial Office in January of the following year, his view was that "it would appear that the policy hitherto pursued by His Majesty's Government has been pushed as far as it is capable of producing good results without risking an increase of Cuban obstinacy and possibly even a rupture of diplomatic relations".[22] The plight of the West Indians was deemed less important than Britain's commercial and diplomatic interests.

However, despite – or perhaps because of – the trying circumstances which some of them endured, the migrants themselves established several self-help organizations. These included fraternal lodges, friendly societies and welfare centres. They were also the principal supporters of Marcus Garvey's Universal Negro Improvement Association (UNIA), which had fifty-two chapters and divisions in Cuba by 1926. Schools, churches, social clubs and cricket clubs also formed part of life in Cuba for the Barbadians and other British West Indian immigrants. McLeod points to an advantage which afforded the British subjects a labour mobility which was largely denied their Haitian counterparts:

> While some British West Indian immigrants in Cuba continued to cut sugar cane, many others used their unique language skills, prior job experiences, and formal education to shift away from the sugar industry. Some worked as carpenters, as mechanics, or for the railroad. The ability to speak English led many British West Indians into the service sector – as chauffeurs, cooks, gardeners, hotel servants, and school teachers – especially for North American families and upper- and middle-class Cubans who prized English language skills.[23]

One locality in which Barbadian migrants settled in appreciable numbers was the municipality of Baraguá. The Baraguá Sugar Company, an American-owned entity, leased land in 1916 to start its operations in Cuba. At the time, the land formed part of the central province of Camagüey, but with the redrawing of provincial boundaries is now located in the province of Ciego de Ávila.

Immigrants began arriving there directly from the West Indies and some from Panama, where they had worked during the American phase of the construction of the Panama Canal. Estimates are that more than five hundred West Indians helped to build the factory in Central Baraguá. The first *zafra*, or harvest, lasted almost five months, beginning on 31 January 1917 and ending on 11 June 1917. At one point there were Barbadians in charge of the three shifts at the sugar factory. The three were Mr Lowe, Mr Maloney and Mr Roach, all members of the Christian Mission church.[24] Marc McLeod states that British West Indian migrants flocked to the Episcopal church in Cuba, and that West Indian laypersons and catechists proved essential to the formation and maintenance of stable congregations in the sugar zone. He cites one report: "The Episcopal bishop singled out the 'flourishing' congregations at Manati and Baragua for specific recognition; at the latter site, never less than 100 and often more than 400 persons attended services."[25]

Oliver Nelson – the father of Yolanda Nelson – was also a prominent Barbadian citizen in Baraguá. He had migrated to Cuba in 1920 and met and married another immigrant from Barbados – Clotell Springer. Nelson became a property owner, founded a newspaper and also became grand master of Cuba District Grand Lodge No. 1 of the Masonic Lodge. Nelson died in Cuba in 1959.

Maradell Greene describes the municipality as a place which offered hospitality to other Barbadians and West Indians seeing hardship elsewhere in Cuba: "People used to walk from Oriente to Baraguá. They were generally men. When people hear that men come in, everybody would push open their window to see the new men. They come up tired and hungry and so on, and Bajan people love to entertain. Everybody take in a few. People didn't rob and steal then. People used to try to accommodate people."[26] This hospitality was reciprocated in other West Indian enclaves throughout Cuba. Central Hershey, where Delcina Marshall was born and lived until age nine, was one such locality. She recalls that cricket was usually an occasion for the visits:

> Other West Indians used to come from Baraguá and different places. They came down on Saturday nights and played cricket on Sunday and then they left on Sunday nights to get back home to their jobs on Monday. And sometimes cricketers from Hershey would visit other provinces in turn. They came from Camagüey, Pinar del Rio, Matanzas, Santa Cruz and Havana. Almost every Caribbean island was represented. They stayed with different families.[27]

APPEAL TO THE EMPIRE

British consular and diplomatic officials in Cuba also had the responsibility of providing relief for those Barbadians and other British West Indians who found themselves in destitute circumstances and for arranging their repatriation. The British government had set up a fund of £20,000 per annum in 1944 to provide relief for the worst cases of sickness and destitution among the British West Indians in Cuba, "contrary to the normal policy of not maintaining British subjects abroad except on a limited and temporary basis".[28] This relief fund was still in operation in the 1949/50 financial year.

In the face of ill-treatment in their host country, the Barbadians and other British West Indians took refuge in their status as British subjects. Jorge Giovannetti writes, "It is important to note that most migrants used their affiliation to the empire as a survival strategy in Cuba, requesting support from the consuls, but also from the Foreign and Colonial Offices in London, the colonial governors in their islands of origin, and even the King and Scotland Yard."[29] Giovannetti notes: "They struggled in multiple ways (including the written word), challenging the Empire's racial understandings and power structure, and organizing themselves as part of a Caribbean community in rural Cuba. By the 1940s, most of the migrants had taken a decision to return to their islands of origin, stay in Cuba (where some of them had effectively made a life), or search for better opportunities elsewhere."[30]

On their return to their homeland, the Barbadian migrants who had come to question their status as British subjects in Cuba would still need to assess their place as citizens of the British Empire.

CHAPTER 2

COLONIAL BARBADOS

PERENNIAL IMPULSES TO EMIGRATION FROM BARBADOS

THE EMANCIPATION ACT WHICH CAME INTO FORCE ON 1 August 1834 legally liberated Barbados's enslaved population. However, the apprenticeship system which was to last for another four years effectively kept the former slaves tied to their previous "owners" as a source of labour in conditions not far removed from the days of slavery.

This state of affairs still obtained at the turn of the century, as Bonham Richardson observes: "A rural black Barbadian 'belonged' to a particular parish just as he 'belonged' to a particular estate."[1] The "located labourer" statutes bound individual workers to specific plantations. There was no abundance of Crown lands from which the workers could find alternative sources of generating income. Richardson describes the precarious nature of the workers' existence: "As long as a worker was in good health he could eke out a hand-to-mouth existence; but illness, drought, or any similar accidental departure from the routine often meant one's candidacy for pauper relief."[2] He states that in the labouring class housing enclaves in the capital, Bridgetown, and its suburbs conditions were even more dire.

In these circumstances of poor nutrition and squalid living conditions, it is not surprising that there was a high infant mortality rate. For example, "In 1906 half the infants of St Michael parish died before they reached twelve months of age."[3] While the 1878 Education Act had required school attendance for children under the age of twelve, "Throughout the island children of the poorer black families toiled on sugar cane estates along with their fathers, mothers, and siblings."[4] The planter class in this primarily agrarian society dictated terms of engagement in a market where cheap labour was abundant.

According to the *Barbados Blue Book* for 1909 to 1910, the average wage of an agricultural worker was eight pence a day. An able-bodied labourer was said to be capable of earning from eight pence to one shilling "within the ordinary working hours". Wages for skilled carpenters, masons and tradesmen were somewhat higher, between two shillings and two shillings, six pence a day. Domestic servants were always hired by the month, and their monthly wage varied from one shilling to eight shillings, four pence.

In addition to the economic privation, social exclusion extended to the franchise. Qualification as an elector or a representative in the House of Assembly was out of reach for the vast majority. This privilege was reserved for men whose land yielded £5 per annum, or who earned £50 a year, or who had benefited from a university education. Only 1,986 Barbadian citizens from a population of around 170,000 met these qualifications by 1911. It would not be until 1951 that universal adult suffrage was achieved.

Under these prevailing conditions, working-class people viewed migration as the only alternative for earning wages higher than those available in Barbados. Thousands of them left the island with hopes of improving their lot. It is estimated that between 1891 and 1909, 24,637 persons emigrated from Barbados. This figure was comprised of 15,820 males and 8,817 female emigrants.[5]

G.W. Roberts suggests that in the context of nineteenth century world migration, the movement of people from Barbados shrinks almost into insignificance: "The total outward movement during the 60 years following 1861 probably did not exceed 150,000. Yet despite the limited scale of this movement by world standards, it offers an interesting example of escape from disastrous overcrowding made possible by emigration."[6] Roberts posits, however, that were it not for migration on a relatively large scale from the already densely populated island, Barbados "might by now have reached a disastrous state of over-crowding, relief from which would have been possible only by widespread starvation, disease and death".[7]

Beginning in the 1860s, overpopulation was seen as the principal economic problem confronting the island, and from the late nineteenth century, the policy of successive governments emphasized emigration as a solution to the problem. Up to at least the 1950s, populist leaders such as Grantley Adams and Wynter Crawford were fervent advocates of emigration as the key to economic development. It was only from the 1960s that emigration was de-emphasized as a panacea for Barbados's social and economic ills. The *Barbados Herald* newspaper was an avid proponent of emigration from the island, principally because of overpopulation and the fact that remittances which workers sent from abroad benefited the Barbadian economy.

At the end of September 1919, a group of about one hundred men – mostly former soldiers who had served in World War I – left Barbados to work in the Cuban sugar industry. These men had been recruited by G.S. Archer, an agent operating in Barbados on behalf of the Cuban estate owners. At that time, there were no direct shipping links from Barbados to Cuba. The usual mode of travel between the two islands involved securing US transit visas and going via New York. So Archer had to make arrangements for the men whom he recruited to travel via schooner.

As sugar's fortunes waxed and waned in Cuba, so too did prospects for the Barbadians and other British West Indians. For example, they were affected when the price of sugar began to fall with the harvest of 1920, and President Zayas signed Decree 1404, mandating the immediate expulsion of foreign workers. News that the situation in Cuba was improving came to local readers by way of the *Barbados Herald* headline "Cuba Rapidly Returning to Prosperity".[8] Under this headline, the newspaper reproduced an item from the *London Financial News* to the effect that "the crisis brought about in Cuba by the huge surplus of sugar supplies following the boom which ended last year is now likely to pass and it is believed that within three or four months a normal state of affairs will exist". The article expressed confidence that several banks in the United States were prepared to assist the Cuban government, and "it is fully predicted that a loan of 50 million dollars will be raised to assist the sugar planters".

For Barbadians heartened by this news who wanted to get to Cuba and had the means to do so, transportation was available. The Xavier Rumeau Line had introduced a monthly steamship service between Bridgetown and the port of Santiago de Cuba in January 1921. This was a development welcomed by the migrant workers since it was an improvement on the overcrowded schooners. At least one other shipping line was providing service between the two countries by 1922. The Webster Steamship Company's passenger agent, George P. Harding, established offices at McGregor and Parry Streets in Bridgetown and offered twice-monthly departures for Cuba. The efforts of Archer, Harding and other agents to entice Barbadians to seek their fortune in Cuba would have been enhanced by advertisements in the local press describing idyllic working conditions. However, it was a far different reality which many encountered after their arrival in Cuba.

When the situation in Cuba improved following the 1920 crash, Barbadian workers were once again eager to try their fortunes. As the *Barbados Herald* reported on 21 October 1922, two batches of contracted labourers had recently returned home on the Webster Line's SS *Remelik* from Cuba, where they had been engaged with Chaparra Estates Limited, "one of the greatest sugar-producing organisations in the West". The writer lamented the fact that the steamship service had not been available earlier.

> Many Barbadians have, in the past, tried Cuba with benefit to themselves financially. Others who were unfortunate enough to be at work there during the 1920 crash in sugar prices and the ruination of the sugar trade, have suffered considerably. Could the latter have got out with their savings at the time of the trade slump suffering would not have been so great. But lack of steamship opportunity and the sudden restriction of employment completely eat up their little capital and reduced them practically to a state of pauperism and semi-starvation.[9]

The Webster Line, in the newspaper's view, had solved "the most acute problem of the situation" and filled a long felt want. The writer pointed out that conditions in Cuba were much improved, the sugar situation was being restored to normality, money was again being freely circulated and labour conditions were becoming attractive. These circumstances, the writer was certain, would provide the steamship company with "the patronage it justly deserves".[10] The writer's confidence was apparently justified, as an item in the 11 November 1922 edition of the newspaper reported on the numbers of Barbadian labourers transported over the previous three months:

> Since September the *Remelik* of the SS Webster Line, has made three trips from Cuba to Barbados and brought to the Colony 563 Barbadian immigrants who had been under contract with the Chaparra Estates Ltd. The batch of 110 which arrived here on Sunday, evidently closed the list of contracted labourers for which Chaparra is responsible, as we learn the *Remelik* will not be returning before early in December to continue her fortnightly service between the two countries.[11]

The article went on to explain that the Cuban crop season began in December, and in the interim the ship would ply between Cuba and Jamaica, from where large numbers emigrated annually to work on the sugar plantations. However, the *Remelik* was not the only ship which the company operated between Barbados and Cuba. The *Herald* of 6 January 1923 reported on the departure of nearly two hundred Barbadians who left on the *Wanderer III* of the Webster SS Line the previous night:

> Prices are good and might improve as the prospects of the crop are far brighter than they were last year, and sugar is expected to come back into a little of its own. Regular employment for about nine months is guaranteed to the emigrants who, should they desire, will be enabled to return home promptly at the close of the reaping season, thus avoiding the disabilities to which they were subjected in the past when inter-communication between the two countries was almost impossible to maintain.

The article stated that if the Webster SS Line maintained its services as promised, Chaparra and the other large plantations in Cuba would have no difficulty in sourcing the required labour. The writer was of the view that Barbados would also benefit as it usually did, "not only from remittances, but also from the direct expenditure of the immigrants who will be constantly on the move".[12]

The *Herald* returned to the theme the following month.[13] The newspaper suggested that the discouragement which the government was giving to would-be emigrants "ought to form grounds for searching enquiry into its motives with regard to the labouring people generally". The article reiterated that "it is only by the patriotic and self-sacrificing efforts of Barbadian labourers in foreign countries that the present low scale of wages to the stay-at-homes is made possible". The *Herald* was emphatic in the view that "to discourage emigration is madness". The newspaper argued that it was emigration which supported "the weight of local taxes" by way of "the large sums of money sent through the post office, and the still larger sums surreptitiously remitted". The writer issued a warning to the authorities: "If the people get no money from abroad, we are going to have trouble, for it is certain that there is no chance of living wages being paid in this island without some initial trouble. The Governor and his advisers are warned of this. It is no matter for trifling."

The writer acknowledged the difficulties which some of the migrants encountered in Cuba, but was of the opinion that as British subjects, Barbadians were entitled to the protection of the British flag wherever they were. It was the duty of the government, in the writer's view, to make representation to the Colonial Office with regard to any known abuses, and to call for adequate supervision of the conditions under which West Indians laboured abroad.

> We refuse to believe that a British subject cannot be protected in Cuba. If there are any hardships, the British Consul ought to deal with them. But there should be no

interference with the efforts of destitute and sometimes starving people to escape being supported from local poor rates. The man who wants to go to Cuba should make representations through their representatives in the House of Assembly to ensure for them the protection their nationality provides, but they should pay no heed to the people who tell them that they should stay at home and starve.[14]

In November 1923, the *Herald* once again took up the theme of emigration to Cuba.[15] This time the focus was on the conditions at home which made emigration from the island such an attractive prospect: "Nobody disputes the fact that there is or has been for generations a great surplus of labouring people in Barbados. The island has become accustomed to huge numbers of unemployed, but if the labouring class of the island was sufficiently advanced to demand a higher standard of living a solution would perforce be found." This article advocated that any method by which the congestion could be relieved should find ready acceptance, but the writer suggested that "unfortunately it had been decided that the welfare of the island depends upon a glut of cheap labour": "Excessive Poor Relief Rates, overcrowded almshouses and that class of criminal activity which always follows a low standard of living and idleness are calmly accepted. But the obvious remedy if and when it is possible is not to be applied."

The writer was adamant that no obstacle should be placed in the way of people desiring to seek employment in Cuba, despite acknowledging that "the situation is none too rosy at present". "The man who expects to find Cuba a land flowing with milk and honey will have a rude awakening", the article conceded. "Nevertheless, if there is a prospect of agricultural labourers obtaining employment during the Cuban crop season, we see that there is no honest reason why they should be prevented." The writer acknowledged that West Indians who had gone to Cuba during the sugar boom had suffered considerably when the sugar bubble burst, and accepted that under the circumstances responsible people would hesitate before advising their countrymen to risk another trip. However, the writer directly questioned the motives of planter and assemblyman Stanley Thorne, who was opposed to emigration of agricultural labourers: "But the source from which the chief opposition comes is so tainted that one can safely say it is no question of kindly feeling which prompts Mr Thorne to raise his voice in protest. To put it plainly, everybody knows that as a large employer, and being the man he is Mr Thorne's motive is a selfish one." The *Herald* suggested that "if Mr Thorne's statement about ill-treatment of W. Indians is correct then it is a case for official interference in another direction". Rather than refusing to grant passports, the article recommended, the government "should apply to the Colonial Office for instructions to the British Consuls in foreign countries to afford greater protection to W. Indians".[16]

Again, in a 1925 article entitled "Population, Unemployment and Emigration", the *Herald* made clear that "at the outset we must register a most emphatic protest against any attempt to restrict emigration".[17] The writer began the article by stating: "The chief production of Barbados is sometimes said to be population. . . . The distribution and direction and employment of our people is a problem, therefore, which should concern government in no slight degree." This situation was one which was clearly of concern to the newspaper: "The presence of a large number of more or less idle and undesirable young men and women on the streets of the town and open spaces of the villages has always been a source of concern to right minded people. The problem is made more intricate by the spasmodic complaints of estate owners of scarcity of labour."

The *Herald* argued that overpopulation was responsible to some extent for low wages, since there had always been a large field from which to draw workers, and questioned whether this situation had always operated "to the greatest good of the greatest number". The article made reference to the last report from the colonial secretary which estimated that Barbadians in Cuba, Panama and the United States had sent back more than £100,000 in cash and bank drafts: "Barbados relies to a great extent on the remittances from abroad, the product of emigration. Can it be argued that the £100,000 received from abroad, which is a rather conservative estimate, could be realised by preventing the free and uninterrupted emigration of our young people?" The writer added: "At the slightest rumour of properly paid labour in foreign climes the Wharf is invaded by hundreds of these same men willing to venture their lives abroad."[18] This eagerness among Barbadians to venture abroad to seek their fortune would persist for decades to come. However, some of them would need assistance in returning home.

GOVERNMENT'S POSITION ON EMIGRATION AND REPATRIATION

As working-class Barbadians ventured out from the island in the post-Emancipation period seeking to improve their fortunes, governmental attitudes towards emigration and repatriation varied, depending largely on economic circumstances at home. As Roberts states: "Throughout the West Indies planters feared that emancipation would in one way or another reduce their effective labour force."[19] Planters in British Guiana and Trinidad sought to pre-empt this development by promoting immigration of labourers. They appointed agents in Barbados and other islands to encourage workers to emigrate there and to facilitate their transportation. These agents were not always favourably regarded by the local authorities, but comparatively high wages on offer in these two countries would have been a main attraction for Barbadian labourers.

The Barbados House of Assembly, dominated by the planter merchant class, enacted legislation to restrict emigration in a calculated move to protect their own interests. The deterrent to emigration was not explicit in legislation enacted in 1838 entitled "An Act for the Government and better ordering of the Poor of this Island and the Prevention of Bastardy". But it threatened legal proceedings against a "mother or putative father of a bastard child" who left the country. Two pieces of legislation enacted in 1839 were more overtly designed to curb emigration. The first was "An Act to prevent the Clandestine Deportation of Young Persons from the Island", and "An Act to regulate the Emigration of Labourers from this Island and to protect the Labourers in this Island from impositions practised on them by Emigration Agents".

Roberts states: "By the middle of the nineteenth century the opinion was gaining strength that Barbados was over-populated."[20] This view was held by colonial authorities, and they began to assess colonies' claims to participate in African immigration schemes. It was a view which the authorities in Barbados were initially reluctant to accept, with Governor Hamilton maintaining that "sufficient employment could be found in the island for all its agricultural population and that emigration would then be inopportune".[21]

It was not until 1863, when a prolonged drought created great distress in the island, that the government of the day was forced to sanction emigration as a means of relieving the situation. That year, 2,500 people were allowed to go to Antigua and St Croix. By March of the following year, an act was passed to amend the laws relating to emigration with the objective of restating the conditions under which emigration agents would be allowed to conduct business. A significant feature of legislation passed in 1873 was that it "made provision, though on a very limited scale, for assisting certain classes to emigrate, a course of action never before taken in the West Indies".[22]

According to Roberts, "After prolonged disturbances and riots in 1875–76, interest in the problem of over-population heightened and the growing population came to be identified as the prime cause of increasing poverty and unemployment in the island."[23] What he characterizes as "the most significant phase in the history of emigration from the island"[24] began in 1904 when work on the Panama Canal resumed under the Americans. Between 1904 and 1913, the Canal Commission reported that the number of Barbadians under contract there totalled 19,900. Many others went on their own account to find work.

With regard to repatriation, the Barbados government had not always easily entertained requests for assistance from needy Barbadian citizens abroad. The government's attitude to assisting with the repatriation of its citizens from Panama had been less than enthusiastic. Velma Newton notes that soon after the movement to Panama began in September 1883 during the period when the French were in charge of the canal project, a notice placed in the *Official Gazette* warned Barbadian emigrants bound for Panama that the government would not refund any money spent on their behalf for relief, maintenance or repatriation. She asserts that while the legislature of Jamaica had been willing, before the crisis of 1889, to spend small sums of public money to assist Jamaicans on the Isthmus, this had never been the case in Barbados: "The government of that island welcomed the employment opportunities provided for Barbadians on the canal works, but felt that the emigrants left home at their own risk, and neither they, nor their dependants, should expect succour from government."[25]

However, in 1938 and 1939, various sums were approved to bring Barbadians back home from diverse places. For example, £7 was approved to repatriate Ephraim Francis from the Dominican Republic,[26] £25 for returning Mrs Hettie L. Jackson and her daughter, Adrianna, from Atlantic City, New Jersey, United States,[27] and £217 to reimburse the British consul at Caracas "for advances made by him for the maintenance and repatriation of the crew of the Schooner 'Lillian Barnes' which was wrecked off the coast of Aruba".[28] In 1942, there was another vote to reimburse the British consul at Caracas, this time for £43 "for maintenance and passages, etc. of crew of distressed Sch. Blomidon".[29] When, in 1943, E.K. Walcott brought a resolution for the sum of £240 for the repatriation of Barbadians, he gave a breakdown of how the funds would be distributed:

> In the Estimates £100 had been provided for the repatriation of Barbadians. This was supplemented by £200 under Resolution No. 19 of 1942. The available balance is £57, but there are two accounts outstanding, one for £43. 16. 5 being repatriation expenses of five distressed Barbadians from Surinam via British Guiana, and the other from the Government of St Vincent for £239. 16. 1, being expenses incurred on behalf of the fishermen from the boats which put in at St Vincent earlier in the year as a result of adverse weather conditions.[30]

Walcott said that it was estimated that this sum of £240 now asked for would be sufficient to meet expenditure to the end of the financial year.

After the schooner *Annie Eudora* was wrecked off Bonaire on 16 January 1944, £227 was voted "to refund to His Majesty's Consul at Curaçao the amount expended by him on the maintenance and repatriation of the crew".[31] During the years 1943–48, an annual sum of £30 was also voted for the relief of distressed Barbadians abroad.

REPATRIATION FROM CUBA

In the case of Cuba, the Barbados government's attitude to repatriation during the 1920s was similar to the position which had previously been taken with regard to Panama. Governor O'Brien's 1923 press notice regarding conditions at the quarantine stations also warned prospective emigrants what to expect should they leave for Cuba and wish to return: "The Governor also takes this opportunity of reminding those intending to proceed to Cuba to seek employment that the Barbados Government can take no responsibility for securing their repatriation to Barbados should they desire to return; they go at their own risk."[32] The notice advised them to satisfy themselves that they would be able to ensure repatriation, either at their own expense or at the cost of their employers. It ended with an emphatic statement: "The Government of this Island cannot promise help to any person wishing to return to the Island."[33]

This stance appears to have softened with the passage of time. A resolution was tabled in the legislature on 18 February 1936 to consider the grant of the sum of £16 "to meet the cost of repatriating Theophilus A. Browne and his wife, destitute Barbadians, from Cuba".[34] Colonial Secretary G.D. Owen moved the resolution, explaining that Browne and his wife had gone to Cuba from Panama in 1918. He added that "His Majesty's Consul General at Havana reports that Browne has had a stroke and is unable to work. His wife earns a mere pittance, and the Anglo-American Association has undertaken to pay half the cost of repatriation if this Government will provide the other half."[35] That resolution was passed.

In the Legislative Council on 17 November 1936,[36] another resolution was introduced by the acting colonial secretary, C.A. Reed, for the grant of a sum of £250 from the Public Treasury "to meet expenditure in connection with the repatriation of distressed Barbadians from Cuba". Reed stated: "This Resolution is the outcome of a communication from His Majesty's Consul General in

Cuba in which he describes certain appalling conditions prevailing in Cuba at the present time among natives of this country – conditions which could not possibly be ignored." In seconding the resolution, Dr J. Hutson expressed regret that the resolution was not for a larger sum. He told his council colleagues: "I believe I am correct in saying that a law has recently been passed in Cuba forbidding the employment of foreigners, so that thousands of Barbadians have been thrown on the rocks and are now starving. Some of them are kept alive by the people who formerly employed them."

In his contribution to the debate, S.C. Webster said that while he was not objecting to the resolution, the council did not know "if these particular cases were recruited here or whether they went to Cuba on their own". He recalled that when agents were actively recruiting labour for Cuba, a deposit was required for every recruit so that the company could repatriate him in case of need. Stanley Thorne queried what had become of that money, saying, "What I should like to know is whether somebody else, besides the Government, is not responsible for the repatriation of these people." J.D. Chandler, when he had the floor, made reference to Dr Hutson's statement regarding the passage of legislation in Cuba prohibiting the employment of foreigners. He stated: "I am not doubting his word, but it is only a few days ago that I saw in a reputable sugar journal that Cuba was perturbed over a great shortage of labour for reaping the coming crop of 1937. The two statements do not seem to tally, and I should like the Government to make some enquiries in the matter."

The acting colonial secretary had an explanation: "The sugar interests, as related in the sugar journal to which the Hon'ble Mr Chandler referred, are in need of labour but the Government, on the other hand, is trying to keep all the work for their own people." C.A. Reed told his colleagues that a perusal of the papers which he had in his possession would convince any honourable member as to the state of affairs in Cuba in relation to Barbadian labourers there. He said: "I may mention that there are, approximately, 15,000 Barbadians in Cuba – quite a large number, and it is a fact that certain laws recently passed now make it difficult for foreigners to obtain employment. It seems that before they can be employed they have to produce some certificate or other. This means many have not been able to get work." He added that there could be no doubt as to the seriousness of the situation in Cuba so far as Barbadians were concerned. The resolution was passed.

When the issue was brought up in the House of Assembly, Attorney General E.K. Walcott described it as "a matter which is difficult to be dealt with". He said: "We start with the idea that we cannot allow our own people to suffer as they are suffering in other countries, and yet we are faced with the principle that if we ever undertake to repatriate all Barbadians abroad who have served the countries in which they have lived faithfully and well we will be committing ourselves to an enormous expenditure in the future."[37] He explained that the executive, while not agreeing to the principle of repatriating persons because they needed repatriation, was merely asking that this sum of money be voted to meet extreme cases that were in dire need and distress. When the resolution was seconded by a Mr Elder, he said, "This is not only a serious question but a delicate one, and it is best to vote the money and say as little about it as possible." In his contribution to the debate, a Mr Kinch raised the possibility of another source of repatriation funds, stating: "It is quite probable that these people who are in such dire need and distress abroad have their relatives here who may be in a position to send for them and be willing to receive them."[38] However, Walcott explained that it had been the custom to investigate any special cases which had been put forward, but this had not been done in the present case because the matter had been represented as being very urgent. This resolution was also passed.

Governor Mark Young sent a despatch to the secretary of state for the colonies on 30 November 1936 regarding the vote of £250 by the legislature. In correspondence dated 11 January 1937, from Downing Street, London, the secretary of state acknowledged receipt of the governor's despatch. He took note of the fact that the money had been approved "for the purpose of enabling the most necessitous cases to be dealt with during the coming twelve months",[39] and expressed his appreciation of the action which had been taken in the matter.

At the meeting of the Legislative Council on 15 June 1937, the colonial secretary moved another resolution for a grant to meet expenditure in connection with the repatriation of distressed Barbadians from Cuba. This time it was for a sum of £2,000. He explained to the council the reason for the large sum:

> The British Consul General at Havana says that it is possible to repatriate these people, who are both sick and destitute, at a reduced cost if sufficient funds are provided to enable four or five hundred to be repatriated at the same time. The cost would amount to about twenty dollars a head, which is a good deal cheaper than they could be repatriated for if they came over in driblets.[40]

The consul general had stated that four hundred Barbadians had already applied, and further applications were expected. Preference would be given to the sick and destitute who were without prospect of employment. S.C. Thorne seconded the resolution. When Francis Godson spoke on the matter, he questioned the wisdom of returning the migrants to Barbados: "What are we bringing them back here to do? I was wondering whether it is not possible for us to find some place else – whether it is St Lucia or anywhere else – where those who are able-bodied can be sent to fend for themselves. This to my mind would be better than bringing them back here to increase the number of unemployed in this island." In response, the colonial secretary revealed that the consul general's report indicated that "consideration has been given to the possibility of some other solution but no one up to now has been able to think of a better way out of the difficulty". On the other point raised by Godson, he replied, "The question of settling these people in St Lucia cannot be considered now because the proposed Emigration Scheme has not yet been dealt with."[41] The money was voted.

A couple of months later – on 17 August 1937 – the colonial secretary brought yet another resolution on the same matter to the legislature, this time for the sum of £263.

> Members will recollect that by resolution 61 of the 15th of June, 1937, the sum of £2,000 was granted for the purpose of repatriating distressed Barbadians from Cuba on the understanding that this Government would have to bear the cost of their passages. The Secretary of State has since intimated by telegraph that the Cuban Government will bear the cost of the passages of the repatriates and expect to employ the Cuban military transport "Columbia" for the purpose.[42]

He explained that this offer from the Cuban government meant that Barbados would no longer need to expend the £2,000 previously approved, "But they ask that expenditure in the purchase of food and for the personal care of Barbadians while awaiting embarkation in the concentration camp and the extra rations on the journey should be borne by this Government, and therefore the Legislature is asked to vote £250 for the purpose." An additional sum of £13 was needed "to pay the port charges and the cost of conveying the repatriates from ship to shore",[43] so the sum of £263 was approved.

BARBADOS AND THE BRITISH EMPIRE

In the 1930s, when significant numbers of Barbadian migrants in Cuba were returning home to Barbados, the island was firmly in the fold of the British

Empire. On the occasion of Empire Day 1936, a writer in the *Barbados Advocate* opined:

> The Empire stands for all that is just, loyal, and harmonious in this shifting and difficult world of ours. Military, naval, and air defences merely act as police to guard our many shores, while economic prosperity adjusted on a mutual basis between both England and her colonies and between individual colonies ensures a feeling of confidence that is the *sine qua non* of international or any other form of prosperity. Long live the British Empire.[44]

On 21 January 1936, at a specially convened joint meeting of the Legislative Council and the House of Assembly, Governor Sir Mark Young had announced the death of King George V and special prayers were read. The governor's statement began with the following words:

> We meet to-day under the shadow of world wide grief in which this Island bears to the full its sorrowing share. It is my sad duty to announce to you the death of our beloved King. Shortly before midnight yesterday His Majesty King George the Fifth, who for more than five and twenty years reigned over this wide Empire, and through all that time reigned in the hearts of His loving subjects, passed away, by the will of Almighty God, from a life of service to His country and to His people.[45]

As part of the British Empire, Barbados was a country in mourning. Governor Young despatched a telegram to the secretary of state for the colonies: "I send at once on behalf of all inhabitants of the Island an assurance of the grief and sympathy which are universally felt in Barbados."[46] In addition to the telegram, flowers were later sent as well, as was stated in a notice in the *Barbados Herald*:

> His Excellency the Governor desires it to be notified for general information that on the death of His Majesty King George the Fifth, the Crown Agents for the Colonies were instructed to order a suitable wreath for the funeral on behalf of the Government of Barbados. A wreath was accordingly obtained and forwarded to the Lord Great Chamberlain's Office at Windsor Castle to be placed with the numerous other floral tributes to His Late Majesty. A photograph of the wreath has been received, and will be placed in the Council Chamber.[47]

All government offices in Barbados were closed on Tuesday, 28 January 1936, the day on which the funeral service of the late king took place, and the colony held its own memorial service on that day at St Michael's Cathedral. A notice issued by the colonial secretary in the *Official Gazette* provided details of the arrangements: "The service will commence at 11 a.m. with a silence of two minutes for which the signal will be a gun fired from the Wharf. . . . The Governor trusts that all classes of the community will unite in observing the occasion by a complete suspension of all normal business, work and locomotion for two minutes at the hour named."[48]

A MEMORIAL TO THE LATE KING GEORGE

With the king's passing, efforts were made to erect a suitable memorial to him. Acting Colonial Secretary C.A. Reed gave notice on 14 October 1936 that the governor had been informed by the secretary of state for the colonies that "a Mansion House Fund has been opened for the purpose of receiving subscriptions to a National Memorial to His late Majesty. This will take the form of a statue of His late Majesty in close proximity to Westminster Abbey and the Houses of Parliament, and a philanthropic scheme for acquiring fields for recreational purposes."[49] The public of Barbados was invited to subscribe to this fund, and to send their contributions directly to Mansion House in London. Reed added:

> It is also proposed that a memorial to His late Majesty shall be established in Barbados, but it is not intended to appeal to the Public for subscriptions towards the cost of this Memorial, which, if the Legislature agrees, will be met from public funds. The Governor therefore commends with confidence to the people of Barbados this invitation to them to subscribe in liberal measure to the Empire's Central Memorial to the late King.[50]

The Barbados memorial to the late king would become the King George the Fifth Memorial Park, established in the rural parish of St Philip. Major Herbert Walter Peebles was the driving force behind the effort. Peebles had served as administrator and colonial secretary of St Vincent – among other postings in the British West Indies – and had resided in Barbados since his retirement from the Colonial Service. Prior to this, he had been a visitor to the island, as one announcement in a 1932 edition of the *Daily Gleaner* revealed in its "Current Items" column: "His Honour Major H.W. Peebles, DSO, OBE, Administrator of St Vincent, left on Monday, Nov. 14 for Barbados on short leave of absence."[51]

The park was declared open by His Excellency the Governor on 24 May 1936. From a report carried in the weekly *Barbados Herald* the following Saturday, it could be surmised that it was an impressive affair. The writer extended his "warmest thanks and appreciation to Major Peebles for the splendid effort he has made to give the people of St Philip a Park".[52] He goes on to comment on the programme, which he described as "a varied one":

> I was one of those thousands that responded to the invitation to be present at the opening. I could not have wished for a greater success. I was fairly surprised at the arrangements which I know from experience must have involved a tremendous amount of organizing and work. . . . The programme was a varied one. The address by His Excellency was what it should have been. It had the note of encouragement to all concerned and implied that the movement would have his blessing at the proper time. His Lordship also struck the right note in his prayers. . . . The Chorus party that Father Hopkins brought to assist did yeoman service. His choir may be depended on to give splendid musical effects. . . . But the Scouts, the Guides and others that took part acquitted themselves quite good [sic] and I think the result should be very consoling to Major Peebles that all the trouble he took was not in vain.[53]

Clarence Roberts, a resident of St Philip now in his nineties, has fond memories of the park, and of the special occasion:

> It was the day that they generally gave us a treat. The treat was buns and lemonade and so, but this occasion when we went, they gave us four cents. We used to celebrate the King birthday and they took us there from all the nearby elementary schools for the opening. We wore red, white and blue; the boys were dressed in white pants, blue shirt and red tie. I think the girls were in the same colours too. At that particular time, I probably was about twelve years old.[54]

A bill incorporating the Committee of Management of the King George V Play Field Memorial Park was passed in the Legislative Council in December 1936.[55] Major Peebles was chairman of the committee. Up to that time, approximately $1,260 had been collected, and Attorney General E.K. Walcott introduced a resolution "for £312. 10s. od. to be granted to the King George V Play Field Memorial Park Committee as a contribution to the funds of the Memorial Park". During the debate which followed, a C.A. Braithwaite revealed how the colony had influenced developments in the mother country: "this scheme which has been brought into being by Major Peebles has been so well appreciated – though not to the extent that it should be in Barbados – it has been so appreciated in Great Britain that since the initiation of the idea here several playing fields of a similar kind have been established in Great Britain in memory of the late King George".[56]

CORONATION CELEBRATIONS

In the same way that Barbados mourned the loss of a king, the colony also celebrated when a new king was crowned.

The subject of King George's successor was a matter which came before the House of Assembly at the sitting of 24 November 1936. The House considered a resolution for the grant of the sum of £1,491. This sum was a preliminary grant towards expenses to be incurred "in connection with the celebration of His Majesty's Coronation"[57] in May 1937. E.K. Walcott explained that the Coronation Committee had decided at its meeting on 18 November to request this money early, since a portion was required to meet the cost of articles which had to be imported, and orders needed to be placed as soon as possible. He gave notice that more funds would be required: "It will be necessary to approach the Legislature later for a further sum to be used in feeding the poor, and for local festivities in the country parishes when a Parochial Coronation Sub-Committee in consultation with the authorities have fully worked out their proposals."[58]

These celebrations were being planned to commemorate the ascension to the throne of Edward VIII the following year, but he would abdicate the month after this meeting of the Barbados House of Assembly. The planned coronation on 12 May 1937 was held for his younger brother and successor, George VI, and his consort, Queen Elizabeth, instead. So that the following year, when the House took up the matter again on 13 April 1937, an additional sum of £1,330 was voted "to meet expenses in connection with the celebration of Their Majesties [sic] Coronation in May next".[59]

The members of the Legislative Council and the Executive Council had issued a proclamation on 12 December 1936 declaring that in "an instrument of abdication dated the tenth day of December instant His former Majesty King Edward the Eighth did declare his irrevocable determination to renounce the Throne for himself and his descendants, and the said instrument of abdication has now taken effect".[60]

The declaration also acknowledged that "the Imperial Crown of Great Britain, Ireland and all other His former Majesty's Dominions is now solely and rightfully come to the High and Mighty Prince Albert Frederick Arthur George", who, as George VI, had "become our only lawful and rightful liege

Lord". The gentlemen of the legislature also acknowledged "all faith and constant obedience, with all hearty and humble affection", and prayed "God, by whom all kings and queens do reign, to bless the Royal Prince George the Sixth with long and happy years to reign over us".[61]

Some months before the big event, a joint committee of the Legislative Council and the House of Assembly was formed "to prepare an Address of Loyalty and Congratulation to Their Majesties the King and the Queen on the occasion of Their Coronation".[62] The joint address of loyalty was passed by both branches of the legislature. Governor Young subsequently informed that it "has been laid before the King, who has commanded that an expression of his deep appreciation of the sentiments of loyalty and devotion contained in the Address may be conveyed to members of the Legislative Council and General Assembly".[63]

The sum of £173 was approved on 27 April 1937, "to provide for the payment of daily-paid employees of Government for the two public holidays in Coronation Week".[64] Commemorative postage stamps were issued in denominations of 1d, 1½ d, and 2½ d. The celebrations included a service at St Michael's Cathedral and a parade at the Garrison Savannah. But not all Barbadians were restricted to the local celebrations. Barbados was invited to nominate "two gentlemen" to represent the colony at the coronation in London. At a meeting of the Legislative Council on 1 December 1936, the acting colonial secretary, C.A. Reed, shared a message from the governor in relation to this invitation from His Majesty the King: "It is the intention of His Majesty's Government that the representatives selected shall be treated as distinguished visitors during the Coronation Celebrations and they, with their wives, will be given all possible facilities, including seats for the ceremony in Westminster Abbey."[65]

In accordance with this invitation, Governor Sir Mark Young nominated Legislative Council member Dr John Hutson, OBE, MLC, and Speaker of the House of Assembly, His Honour Harold Austin, OBE, to represent Barbados in London.

LITTLE ENGLAND

In *Double Passage: The Lives of Caribbean Migrants Abroad and Back Home*, George Gmelch writes: "The description of Barbados as 'Little England', a hackneyed phrase of the tourist trade, has some legitimacy. It has been coined in part from comparisons between the two landscapes, both green and rolling and everywhere showing the hand of humans."⁶⁶ Other comparisons could be, and are, made regarding similarities in place names – Worthing, Windsor, Bath, the Scotland District, and streets such as Prince William Henry Street, Queen Mary Road, Queen Victoria Road, Balmoral Gap and Buckingham Road. There is also the fact that the erection of Barbados's statue of Lord Horatio Nelson in Bridgetown predates that of its counterpart in London's Trafalgar Square. But the comparisons move beyond landscape.

Barbados – unlike its neighbours in the Caribbean – had only one colonial master for more than three hundred years. Gmelch posits that "Barbados' long and exclusive association with England"⁶⁷ had much to do with shaping the character of its people. While admitting that in trying to assess national characteristics "we need to be reminded that personalities range greatly in every society", he however states that "Barbadians, more than any other Caribbean people, are similar to the English in their reserve, civility, and having an unshakeable belief in their own superiority".⁶⁸ This might help to explain the confidence with which this colony backed the metropole during times of conflict.

SUPPORT FOR THE WAR EFFORT

Barbadians faithful to the empire volunteered to serve in the British Armed Forces during both World War I and World War II. During the first Great War, some Barbadian men left the island to sign up in Britain and Canada, but not all who wanted to go could afford the trip. In 1915, the Citizens' Contingent Committee was set up to provide funds "to enable young men of respectable parentage to proceed to England to join His Majesty's Forces".⁶⁹

> With this object in view the Committee opened a Fund, and issued a general appeal to the public, asking for subscriptions. The public responded readily and generously, subscribing in all £3,044. 12. 10. This amount was used to defray the expense of fitting out the men before departure, paying passages to England, expenses there before joining their Regiments and other incidentals, and later – at the close of the War – the upkeep of the men in London after discharge from the Army, while awaiting the departure of the Steamers to bring them back to Barbados.⁷⁰

The sum of money raised for this purpose was only a fraction of the thousands of pounds donated by private citizens in Barbados to support various funds. Percy Sinclair Leverick singles out one particular contribution: "Special mention should be made of the splendid contribution of Mr Alexander Ashby, one of our respected citizens – now numbered among the immortal dead – who added to the island's proud record by presenting to the Imperial Government his entire estate worth well over £50,000. The gift has been declared to be the most munificent benefaction recorded in the history of the island."[71]

However, it was not only private citizens who contributed directly to the war effort by donating money to enable soldiers to enlist and to the numerous funds connected with the war. The legislature also voted monies. "The sum of £60,000 was voted by the Legislature in three instalments of £20,000 each to the Imperial Exchequer towards the cost of carrying on the war, and £100 to the Lord Kitchener Memorial Fund."[72]

At the end of World War I, Governor Charles O'Brien seemed to offer excuses in a message to the Legislative Assembly for why more men did not volunteer: "The War is happily at an end, and the strain, through which we have successfully laboured, is passed. All could not proceed on active service overseas! Age, infirmity, business, the growing of essential crops, the feeding of the community, and the obligations of Government, of necessity kept many individuals in our midst, who earnestly desired to take a more active part in the Great War!"[73]

The first group of Barbadian soldiers arrived back home on 23 May 1919. This group consisted of 321 men, and they were soon followed by three other groups. They had returned with new experiences and new expectations. However, finding employment proved to be difficult. O. Nigel Bolland points to another factor that would have influenced the attitudes of the returned soldiers: "Bitterly disillusioned with the racial discrimination they had encountered during their war-time service for the 'mother country', and coming home to face unemployment and poverty, these men 'swelled the ranks of the discontented' and as ex-soldiers they were not easily intimidated by the standard show of force."[74]

It was in response to this situation that the Returned Soldiers Committee was formed to find work for the men. Alas, as David Browne notes, "the legislature's refusal to provide adequate funds resulted in the ineffective functioning of the committee". He writes that even before the war had ended, Governor Sir Leslie Probyn, "anticipating some possible discontent among ex-servicemen, embarked on a similar policy of urging the ruling elite, both privately and in the press, to provide employment for them as a matter of precedence during their demobilization".[75] Since opportunities on the island were limited, the committee turned to emigration as a solution. Browne suggests that emigration was perhaps the only option designed to assist the former soldiers which the ruling elite embraced with enthusiasm: "A small overpopulated island with a 'superabundance of labour', they argued, should pursue emigration like a 'safety valve' to relieve undue population pressure, and so avoid any possible social turmoil as a result of overcrowding and the lack of opportunity."[76]

Cuba offered possibilities. In fact, agents representing the Cuban sugar estates were actively recruiting in Barbados. One such agent, G.S. Archer, was seeking permission to recruit two thousand men. The governor gave his approval, "on the condition that he gave preference to any returned soldier who wished to go."[77] The first group left for Cuba in 1919. Glenford Howe writes: "By October 1920, no less than 422 had left for Cuba and many more went subsequently. Their departure was greatly facilitated by the desire of the authorities to get rid of them, so the committee contributed generously to their passage and ensured that they got first preference in the scheme to recruit labourers for Cuba."[78]

When conflict broke out again in Europe in 1939, Barbadians were ready and willing to enlist once more. The local government was also prepared to do its part to support the war effort. Browne lists some of the revenue raised from tax measures and other means which were approved by the Barbados legislature:

> An interim report prepared by a former assemblyman, Stanley Thorne, recommended, and it was later sanctioned by the House of Assembly, a gift of £100,000 to be met as follows: £50,000 to be taken from the surplus balance of the Public Treasury; £25,000 from monies levied and collected under the War Purposes Additional Taxation Acts 1940-21 [sic]; and the balance of £25,000 by a loan free of interest from the Sugar Industry Agricultural Bank. "An Act to impose additional taxation for a limited period for war purposes" was pushed through the assembly on 28 June 1940. It raised Income Tax by twenty five per cent, increased excise duty on rum and customs duties on tobacco, spirits, wines, beers, ale and snuff by twenty five per cent. An additional tax of 1½d per gallon was imposed on petrol and inland postage rates were increased by ½d per first ounce.[79]

However, government largesse to the imperial government did not end there, as Browne notes: "The local legislature went a step further and donated an additional £25,000 to the British Government. By 30 September 1942 the legislature boasted about the more than £125,000 which had been donated to the cause of the war, including the £100,000 of the colony's reserves which were 'placed at the disposal of His Majesty's government in the United Kingdom free of interest'."[80]

In addition to men and money, moral support was also said to be extended by Barbados to the mother country. This spirit of support would have been exemplified in communication reportedly sent by Grantley Adams to the king. A search at the National Archives failed to turn up official documentary evidence, but what appears to be an apocryphal tale still has currency in literature.[81]

Among the enlisted men from Barbados during World War II was future prime minister and national hero Errol Barrow. On 31 December 1940, Barrow joined the Royal Air Force and would fly forty-five operational bombing missions over the European theatre, a vast area where heavy fighting occurred. By 1945, he had attained the rank of flying officer, a junior commissioned rank. Among his other accomplishments, flying officer Barrow was also appointed as personal navigator to the commander in chief of the British Zone of occupied Germany.

Many years after the fact, Barrow appeared not to have approved of the gift of money voted by the legislature. As an elected member of the House of Assembly in the 1970s, he opined during debate in the House:

> During the war the Legislature of this Island passed large sums of money to send to England, and it was particularly wicked for Barbados to take up taxpayers' money and give to the United Kingdom when the United Kingdom needed money least of all. Twenty efficient pilots or navigators were far more valuable to the United Kingdom then than the taxpayers' money, or even the old moth-eaten destroyers that President Roosevelt made available, altogether were not worth £2,000.[82]

A notice from the colonial secretary carried in the *Official Gazette* of 23 December 1940 had urged members of the Barbadian public with relatives from Barbados serving in British units to supply their name, number, rank and unit, or ship. A similar notice published in the local press on 30 May 1940 had not yielded encouraging results. The colonial secretary said: "This information was required in connection with the arrangement whereby parcels addressed to men from the Colonies serving with British Forces are exempted from United Kingdom Customs duty." The information supplied would also be used to compile a register, since "it is known that there is a considerable number of men from Barbados serving in units of the British Forces in regard to whom the information has not yet been provided".[83]

In January of the following year, there was follow-up communication referencing the notice published in the local press on 19 December the previous year. This notice stated that "gifts sent to men from Barbados serving in the

British Forces or ancillary organizations may include gifts of alcohol and cigarettes, provided that the parcels are consigned to the Empire Societies' War Hospitality Committee". The gifts sent should "not exceed one bottle of alcohol and 500 cigarettes to an individual in any one month".[84]

At the height of the war, an order was issued prohibiting the application of imported fertilizers to land growing sugar cane. During debate in the House of Assembly, M.M. Greaves asked for and obtained permission to move the passing of the Address to His Excellency the Governor relating to the restriction. He stated that the House viewed such an order with concern "inasmuch as the shallowness of the soil of this Island renders necessary the continuous application of imported fertilisers in the growing of the sugar cane crop". Greaves noted: "The House realise that the exigencies of the time demand sacrifice by each and every country, but feel it their duty to advise Your Excellency that the enforcement of the above Order will and must of necessity cause a serious situation to develop in the Island which will adversely affect each and every inhabitant thereof."

Greaves and his colleagues feared that the imposition of the restriction would result in a reduction in the sugar crop, a decrease in the employment of labour and in the standard of living throughout the island. In his address he said, "The House respectfully ask that Your Excellency will take the necessary steps to communicate the views expressed in this Address to the Right Honourable the Secretary of State for the Colonies as soon as possible."[85] Chairman of committees D.S. Payne, spoke in favour of the proposed course of action and seconded the motion. However, there was at least one member who was not in agreement with the proposed measure. Wynter Crawford said emphatically:

> I do not think any useful purpose can be served by the passing of this Address. Certain people in this Colony seem to think the entire world must be run for Barbados, and that the sun and stars revolve around Barbados, and only shine to give Barbados light. How are we to expect the Imperial Government to rescind an Order which the exigencies of the present situation have made imperative purely because a few planters or sugar factory owners in this colony feel that their revenue for 1943 and succeeding years will be decreased?[86]

When the war came to an end, officials in Barbados received the news with joy. On 8 May 1945, E.K. Walcott laid the following message from Governor Grattan Bushe to the House:

> His Excellency the Governor has the honour to notify the Honourable the House of Assembly that Germany has surrendered unconditionally and that the Armistice will take effect from mid-night.
>
> His Excellency is sure that the people of Barbados will share with the people of the United Kingdom and of the British Commonwealth and Empire, and of the United Nations a deep feeling of thankfulness and gratitude that the first phase of the greatest of all wars against aggression has been brought to such a glorious conclusion and that Europe is once again freed from the hand of the oppressor.[87]

Naturally, this happy development would call for celebration. J.E.T. Brancker was appointed to a committee to plan victory celebrations. However, he was not impressed with the manner in which the commemoration of the war's end was to be marked in Barbados, as he told the House:

> I have the misfortune to be a member of one of the Committees, and like the honourable member, I looked for sympathetic Government co-operation. We had two meetings and made preparations for a celebration such as we thought the Government contemplated, but it now turns out that the Government is adopting its characteristic, parsimonious attitude. When one talks about the Victory celebrations in "Little England", one would not think that we would be behind the Mother Country in giving honour to the glorious day and thanks for the victory which has come to the United Nations. The Government has £700,000 in the Treasury, not knowing how to apportion it, and only proposes to spend £1,000 in the celebration of Victory Day, and is satisfied to broadcast to the world that it is doing something by way of celebration for the colony![88]

As had occurred at the end of World War I, this war's end had also brought with it a familiar anxiety; what to do about unemployment and a surplus population. This concern was expressed by Wynter Crawford in a message from the House to the governor:

> 2. The House regards with grave concern the return, consequent upon the end of hostilities, of thousands of Barbadians from overseas, in view of the fact that it will be impossible for large numbers to procure employment, thereby aggravating the unemployment situation.
>
> 3. The House is of the opinion that steps should be taken immediately by the appointment of a Commission of Enquiry to discover whether it is feasible to promote a large scale settlement scheme for Barbadians in British Guiana, British Honduras, or any other colonies in the British West Indies.[89]

This was also a concern for Governor Bushe, as he noted in his address on the prorogation of the legislature on 1 October 1946 that the First Caribbean Regiment had returned from overseas service on 18 of January of that year.

> All this, of course, has been accompanied by the discharge of a good many service men, and the task of finding suitable employment for them in this overpopulated Island has been a very difficult one. It has been made no easier by the fact that in the Services many of the men enjoyed a rate of pay and a standard of living greatly above that to which they had been accustomed in civilian life. Somewhat naturally few of them are anxious to return to their former occupations.[90]

The governor stated that during this period, vocational and educational training had been given priority. He reported that a rehabilitation committee had been set up in July 1945, and a grant of £5,000 made to enable it to assist persons demobilized from war service to re-establish themselves in civilian life.

> The Chairmanship of this Committee was at first undertaken by the Honourable J. H. Wilkinson and later by Major H. Peebles. Major Peebles has thrown himself wholeheartedly into his task and much of the success it has so far achieved has been due to his energy and enthusiasm. Of 1,125 men so far demobilised 790 have been placed in employment, and about 400 more remain to be demobilised. It is unfortunate that many men for whom employment has been found have refused it, considering it unsuitable or uncongenial.[91]

The various contributions of loyal Barbadians during the great conflict did not go unnoticed. Several prominent local citizens were conferred with the distinctions of Member of the British Empire and Order of the British Empire by His Majesty the King in recognition of their services rendered locally during the war. The Cenotaph War Memorial in Heroes Square, Bridgetown, commemorates the heroic local men who lost their lives during both conflicts. It was initially dedicated in 1925, "In lasting memory of the Barbadians who fell in the great war 1914–1918", and subsequently updated to include the words "To the enduring memory of those Barbadians who gave their lives in the Second World War". The names of the war dead are inscribed in the memorial obelisk, where wreaths are laid annually on Remembrance Day.

MERCHANT SEAMEN

One category of worker who found difficulty in securing employment during the war years was the Barbadian merchant seaman. Wynter Crawford brought their plight to the attention of his colleagues in the House of Assembly by asking, "Is the Government aware of the dire distress experienced by our 300 unemployed merchant seamen in Barbados who are eager not only to obtain employment but also to assist in whatever manner they can in the furthering of the Allied cause at sea?"[92]

Crawford was informed in the reply to his question that because of transport difficulties, His Majesty's Government had decided in 1940 that it was impracticable to send West Indian seamen to the United Kingdom for recruitment, but that efforts were made to secure the engagement of West Indian seamen by the shipping lines plying their trade in these waters. These shipping lines would subsequently discharge the men in the West Indies.

Crawford charged that the British government's policy was based on racial considerations, since it appeared that the government was not "prepared to run again the risk of having large numbers of West Indian seamen discharged in British ports when hostilities are over and the likelihood of their remaining there to create certain domestic problems". He described the policy as unfair:

> These colonies are supporting the war effort in every way that they can. As a matter of fact, they are contributing millions to the British war effort and to think of hundreds of seamen running around here doing nothing, – their families and themselves starving, with berths to be found on British ships and are being filled by Poles, Norwegians and other Europeans, – purely because the British Authorities do not want to have to deal with a so-called colour problem is not calculated to foster any sentiment of patriotism on the part of people who are suffering as a result.

He suggested that the local government "should make a protest and try to impress upon the Imperial Government its responsibility in this particular matter".[93] Hugh Springer, senior member for St George, said that as secretary of the Barbados Workers' Union, he had "come to know quite a good deal about the sufferings and hopes of the seamen and also a great deal about their personal and collective difficulties".[94]

> There is no question that since the war there has been a progressive diminution in the opportunities for employment. I do not think that there is any seaman who would deny that since the war, even before the submarine menace in these waters

became acute, there have been few trips to British ports and other places farther afield. As the Government has said, since the middle of last year, the bottom, so to speak, has dropped out of the employment market. It was bad up to then but it has since become really desperate.

Springer said, "Seamen have been employed only for a trickle here and there and there is no definite hope to be held out for the future."[95] In the Appropriations Bill for 1943, 1944–45, 1945–46, 1946–47 and 1947–48, the sum of £40 per annum was voted for the repatriation from Great Britain of distressed Barbadian seamen.

GROWING POLITICAL CONSCIOUSNESS

Manifestations of loyalty to the British Empire in Barbados co-existed with a growing political consciousness and labour agitation on the part of middle-class and working-class Barbadians.

Like several of those who had migrated to Cuba, some ex-servicemen who remained at home became active in Garvey's UNIA. The first branch was established in Barbados in 1919. Urban branches were set up at Reed Street in Bridgetown and in nearby Westbury Road. In the rural areas, there were also branches at Crab Hill, St Lucy, and Indian Ground, St Peter. David Browne notes: "By 1920, the UNIA was holding meetings regularly in Bridgetown and throughout the country districts, actively politicizing and mobilizing the black population. Around this time, the UNIA was boasting an active membership of over 1,800."[96] Members were recruited through advertisements in the local press. One such advertisement in the *Barbados Herald* of 7 April 1923 listed the association's aims as "race consciousness and race uplift in conjunction with practical schemes to aid members in sickness or distress, etc.".[97] The advertisement stated that the UNIA Limited was incorporated under the Companies Act 1910, and invited enquiries about "further particulars" at their registered office on Reed Street, near the corner of Suttle Street. Garvey himself visited the island in October 1937 and addressed an audience at Queen's Park, some months after the July disturbances.

Another critical organization was the Barbados Democratic League founded in 1924 and led by Dr Charles Duncan O'Neal. Their focus was on agitating for broader representation in the annual elections to the House of Assembly. The Barbados Workingmen's Association, an offshoot of the league, established in

1926, laid the foundation for a labour movement in the country. Browne notes their mass organizing activities: "The UNIA and the WMA [Workingmen's Association] resorted to a number of highly confrontational methods of political activity, such as holding mass political meetings and public demonstrations, and making attempts at industrial activity."[98]

UPRISING

In 1937, Barbados was rocked by a tumultuous rebellion which would ultimately be a catalyst for the movement towards independence thirty years later. As O. Nigel Bolland states: "The situation on the island was explosive. Unemployment and poverty were widespread, frustration was increasing and workers at the Central Foundry had come out on strike three days before the disturbances."[99]

Low wages and the poor working and living conditions of the masses were sources of a great discontent that was sweeping the region. In Barbados, the spark which ignited a major conflagration was the deportation of activist Clement Payne. Payne had been preaching a message which resonated with the black working class and had caused concern among the colonial authorities. He had been born in Trinidad of Barbadian parents and had returned to Barbados. Social unrest erupted in Bridgetown on 26 July 1937 and intensified on 27 July. The disturbances soon spread to some rural districts. This became known as the 1937 labour rebellion, or the 1937 riots. David Browne argues, "The July 1937 unrest in Barbados was a rebellion of the most profound form of political protest."[100] In his view, "The economic factors which surfaced during and after them must not be seen in isolation, but as part of a fundamental race and class struggle for control of economic resources and political power."[101]

Whether riot or rebellion, at the end of the uprising, at least fourteen people had died, while forty-seven had been injured and more than five hundred arrested. As Richard Hart states, "Payne's principal supporters were accused of creating 'discontent and disaffection among His Majesty's subjects' and of promoting 'ill-will and hostility between different classes' and prosecuted for sedition."[102]

F.A. Hoyos gives an account of his personal experience of that fateful Monday, which he says, "started calmly and promised to be as uneventful as life in Barbados had been for more than sixty years". He and his sisters had gone for "a drive in a little car with its hood rolled back".[103]

> We returned to the city by way of Bay Street. As we rounded a bend in the road we suddenly ran into a mass of people brandishing long wallaba poles in their hands. There seemed to be hundreds of them and they effectively blocked the road.
>
> We had no alternative but to bring the little open car to a complete halt. The people crowded around us and I remember thinking of the French Revolution and the pikes that were used to impale the heads of the aristocrats. I waited in silent helplessness, wondering whether we, too, like patricians of old, would endure the distinction of having our heads knocked off our shoulders.
>
> As the people crowded around us, however, one of them was heard speaking with the voice of authority. "Dem is alright," he said, "dem is coloured people. Let dem pass." At once I pressed the accelerator and drove through the crowd as they made way for us.[104]

Hoyos left the car at home and later returned to Bay Street. He writes, "I was soon able to discover what I had escaped. For Bay Street was thickly covered with broken glass. The men with the long poles had used them to smash the windscreens of the cars that passed through Bay Street that night." His eyewitness account of the disturbances included events of the following day:

> On the way back that morning I passed by Probyn Street and noticed the excitement that prevailed in Golden Square. The people were angry because of some incident that had occurred during the night between themselves and the police. They had erupted from Golden Square into Probyn Street and driven back the mounted police who were in the area. They took cars out of a nearby garage and threw them into the careenage. Then they proceeded to Broad Street where they smashed the show cases of the leading shops in the City.[105]

The Barbados Volunteer Force[106] was called out to assist in restoring and maintaining order in the city and the rural districts as well. While there were confrontations between police and the angry crowds and some destruction of property, the protest mainly took the form of raids on the plantations' sweet potato fields. Browne views this form of action as significant: "These potato raids, and the attacks on the plantation livestock, were purposeful acts perpetrated with revenge as well as, ultimately, to make a political point. The rural crowd, like their urban counterparts, seized the opportunity to attack the plantation, the symbol of oppression of the black labouring classes."[107]

Ofelia Nicholls was a young girl who had recently arrived from Cuba at the time. She still has vivid memories of her experience during that tumultuous episode in the island's history.

When they had the riots in 1937, the morning I went to school. I went to the Carrington Village School. Miss Springer was the headmistress. It start up around ten o'clock and there were gunshots and a lot of noise, and people running. I run and went up under a cellar. I was always afraid of frogs, and they had a lot of them in the cellar. The frogs start to move away from me, and I run and went home. It was an awful time.[108]

While for Frank Philo, another recent arrival from Cuba in the year of the disturbances, the recollections are less detailed. He says, "I don't recall too much about the '37 riots, because we were just young children. But I remember my mother pushing us back in the house. We were living in St Andrew."[109] Clarence Roberts remembers some of the occurrences in the rural parish of St Philip where he lived at the time:

I was living at the Crane as a young boy. I remember the volunteers at that time, which would be soldiers now, but it was volunteers that they used to call them, in station wagons they called the Mae West. They drove around keeping order, and they had rifles through the windows. Wherever they saw a crowd they would disperse the crowd. There were a lot of stories going around. At that time we didn't have no radio; Rediffusion[110] wasn't about yet. And it was just from one vicinity to the next that you would pass the word.[111]

Governor Mark Young had issued a memorandum on unemployment shortly before the disturbances had erupted. In it, he had drawn attention to "the absence of opportunities abroad, in places such as Panama, Cuba, the United States and other West Indian islands, where many Barbadian migrants had found work previously".[112] Governor Young appointed a commission of enquiry "under the chairmanship of Sir George Deane, a former Chief Justice of the Gold Coast, to investigate the causes of the riots".[113] The Deane Commission's report, published on 2 November 1937, "pointed to poverty and overpopulation as the prime causes of the riots". Since Barbados was only one of several British colonies in the region to experience this upheaval, the British government also appointed a Royal Commission under Lord Moyne "because of the scale and seriousness of the disturbances throughout the region".[114] The commission began hearings in Barbados at Queen's House on 17 January 1939. Reports from the hearings carried in Jamaica's *Daily Gleaner* newspaper disclosed discussion on, among other topics, the question of labourers' wages: "It was stated that the wages of labourers in this colony barely kept body and soul together. There were about 35,000 labourers whose average wage was between

8 [shillings] and 9 [shillings] per week. The Lord Bishop stated that it was in exceptional cases during the crop that a cane cutter could earn five dollars per week."[115]

Overpopulation in the island was another topic at the hearing. Naturally, the discussion turned to emigration as a means to "lessen the overpopulation". Major H.W. Peebles was among the witnesses. Peebles testified: "They say that the population is increasing by 2,000 a year, and personally I do not think that many of the people who live in this island would leave it if they had an opportunity. I think about 7,000 would be the amount who would go. I do not think 20,000 or so would go." When asked by the commission's vice-chairman, Sir Edward Stubbs, to state the reason for his belief regarding the numbers of Barbadians who would be willing to emigrate, Major Peebles responded by saying: "First of all, sir, the Barbadian absolutely loves his own country and he is very difficult to move at all. Many of them went abroad in the old days, but all those knew that they were coming back, and they also left their families behind them and sent money to them."[116] Sir Edward made it clear at the hearing that the commission's mandate was "solely to enquire and to recommend".[117] Among the commission's recommendations was alleviating the problem of overpopulation through emigration.

A resolution for the grant of £7,000 was introduced in the House of Assembly on 17 August 1937 "to provide for extraordinary expenditure in connection with the recent disturbances in this island".[118] And on 12 September 1939, Deputy Speaker G. Douglas Pile introduced a resolution at the meeting of the House for the grant of the sum of "nine hundred and seventy eight pounds sixteen shillings and three pence". These monies were to "provide for compensation in respect of the 1937 Disturbances recommended by the Local Forces Committee and for an honorarium to the Secretary and other incidental expenses".[119]

The uprising led to a number of changes in Barbadian society. Hoyos lists some of them: "Four significant events followed the disturbances of 1937 – the formation in 1939 of the Progressive League, now the Barbados Labour Party; the passing of the Trade Union Act in 1939; the entry into the House of the first Progressives as a disciplined party in 1940; and the formation of the Barbados Workers Union in 1941."[120]

The plantation owners' hold on the government was loosened when property qualifications were widened in 1944 and universal adult suffrage granted in 1951. This was followed by a full ministerial system in 1954 and cabinet government in 1958. Since 1961, when Barbados achieved full self-governance, the country's government has been chosen by general elections. These developments led to gradually improving economic conditions for working-class people. The culmination of this political trajectory was the achievement of independence from Great Britain on 30 November 1966.

Sir Frederick Smith is of the view that the Democratic Labour Party, in power between 1961 and 1976, achieved many great things: "Included in the list over the 15 years in power were independence, free education, economic and social progress, strong governance and embedding robust democratic institutions."[121]

From the 1960s, the role of emigration as the answer to Barbados's economic fortunes began to be de-emphasized. However, Barbadians were still attracted to foreign markets in order to better themselves. Apart from the large-scale migration to Panama and Cuba, Barbadians had ventured out to British Guiana, Brazil, St Lucia, St Vincent and Trinidad, among other places in the region. The Dutch colonies of Aruba, Curaçao and Surinam also proved to be fruitful fields of employment for venturesome Bajans. Their wandering ways would continue in later years, with migration to Great Britain, the United States and Canada.

CURAÇAO OPPORTUNITIES

Barbadian and other British West Indian men also found work in Curaçao's oil-refining industry. Curaçaose Petroleum Industrie Maatschappij oil refinery established itself in Curaçao in 1915 and later began recruiting workers from the British colonies.

Rose Mary Allen notes that the migration of this group came in different waves: "The first was in 1924, when men came from Jamaica, Barbados, but also from Haiti to help to set up the oil company. The West Indian immigration came to a halt during the Depressing [sic] years of 1930–1935, when immigration from the British West Indies temporarily stopped. During the Second World War, due to the increase [sic] need of oil by the Allied countries again workers were imported."[122]

The men also found work at the adjacent tanker company Curaçao Stoomboot Maatschappij, and the Phosphate Mining Company. However, Allen states that it was not only West Indian *men* who were recruited to work in the Dutch colony: "One noticeable feature of this migration is that it included a fairly large group of young single women (locally known as 'sleep-in maids'), recruited independently as domestic workers in and after the 1940s." She explains that they were called sleep-in maids because they worked and lived in the homes of the oil company's mainly Dutch staff, and those of members of the island's traditional elite class. Most of the women were brought into Curaçao by their employers, who were responsible for securing their work and residence permits.[123]

GREAT BRITAIN

World War II created overseas employment opportunities for workers from Barbados and other British colonies. After the war, labour shortages in Britain attracted many West Indian workers to assist in the rebuilding effort. This phase of the exodus from Barbados is well documented. The British Nationality Act of 1948 had given all Commonwealth citizens free entry into Britain. This open immigration policy and the scarcity of labour served to fuel this post-war migration. The peak period was between 1952 and 1962.

It is estimated that between 1955 and 1966, more than twenty-seven thousand Barbadians migrated to the United Kingdom. Many were recruited on contract directly by entities such as British Rail, London Transport, the British Hotel and Restaurant Association, and the National Health Service. Ceri Peach asserts that while Caribbean migration to Britain was essentially powered by free market labour forces, it had its origins in government-sponsored war time recruitment.[124]

It is in this context of continual outward movement from Barbados that the migration to Cuba had taken place. This book seeks to document the movement to Barbados of descendants of some of the Barbadians who migrated to Cuba in the early twentieth century.

The two oldest interview respondents – Ofelia Nicholls and Frank Philo – came to Barbados with their parents in 1936 and 1937, respectively. Like their parents who had travelled to Panama and Cuba during the height of migration to those countries, both Mrs Nicholls and Mr Philo would later leave Barbados in search of other economic opportunities – Mrs Nicholls in Curaçao and Mr Philo in Britain. Their stories are told in the next two chapters.

CHAPTER 3

OFELIA NICHOLLS

Hometown: Baraguá, Ciego de Ávila
Barbados connection: Mother and father
Occupation: Shop assistant and domestic
Arrival year: 1936

MY MOTHER WOULD TALK TO US ABOUT PANAMA. Her husband went there alone, so he send for her in Panama. His name was George Warwick Parris. My father get blow up in the Panama Canal Zone. He came from number 12 Station Hill, but my mother come from town. She was Gertrude Codrington.

Then they went to Cuba. I was born in Baraguá in 1924. But my father left my mother and went to another place to cut canes. I can't remember right at the moment now where it is. In Falla. He went to Falla. And then he went to Matanzas and different places cutting canes, because there wasn't much work in Baraguá.

Because what had happened, he had come from Panama, hearing that Cuba had money growing 'pon a tree, but when he get there he didn't find the money growing 'pon a tree, he find poverty. So then he left her.

They had a man named Mr Pelley was the administrator. He and his wife came to work in the administration office and my mother got a job working with them after they came from America. So after, things get so bad, and everybody was scrambling. But one thing, the West Indians lived together. They shared whatever they had. You will go with peas . . . You will go with yams. Because the land was very good to plant in. So whatever you plant seemed to grow . . . corn, whatever. The only thing we never had there in Cuba was breadfruit. But everything else. The Jamaicans, whoever they were, we lived together as one family.

We had a storm. The rain fall eight days, night and day. That was in 1932.[1] I think I was eight years old then. We were in a little house. But God is so good. The water was washing down the river and going, that even the cattle and everything was going. The *potrero* where the animals used to graze was flooded; they come up. The lagoon overflow. The snakes left for higher ground. Well that was an experience! Shops break open and the food and everything come floating down. And people had to get something to eat. That's the first time I ever see wet wood burn. My brother and the boys from the neighbourhood went and put on a kerosene tin, and whatever they get – yam, potato and everything . . . no meat . . . they put it on and they cook it. When they done, it taste very good. Everybody come and get a little bowl full that day. I'll never forget that. People used to live real good; whatever they had they used to share. Not much money; not much pesos, but they lived.

The night we had to put our feet in a sugar bag to warm ourselves. And lightning! When lightning come, you see it cut those barbed wires, or it cut down a banana tree. Cuba had bad, bad rain. That was the first storm that I ever know, and I don't remember any other storms. We used to sing a song:

El derrumbe mas fuerte en terror
El ciclón pasó pa' Cienfuegos
¡Ay, peligro para Cuba!

[The most terrifying landslide
The hurricane passed through Cienfuegos
Oh, danger for Cuba!]

I learn that song, and I'll never forget it. And everybody was so disturbed.

We had two churches. Mr Sayers was the Methodist church, and we had the Christian Mission. Then a man came with a Salvation Army, but he didn't last very long. He died quick. His body like it wasn't conducive to the atmosphere, so he died. They found him dead one day. My mother train us and bring us up in the church. I had to recite at the Sunday school, and my brother too. So when we come here, it wasn't hard to catch on.

A man named Mr Libert came from Jamaica and he opened a little school that the children could learn English and so, you know. And then they had a woman named Catana. She was Cuban. She used to do little handcraft work, and that's how I learned. My mother tried to let me do little things with my hands. My mother used to do flowers and paper hats and all those kinds of things. And she learn me and I remember those things. Sometimes when she had the work at Christmas, I helped her.

But then she said it was getting too hard. My father went away and she didn't know . . . Then suddenly one day he came. It was just too hard to handle. In 1936, then, my mother get a few people together and said that they couldn't take it anymore. She wanted to go home. So Mr Pelley tell her that if she can get at least twenty-five people that he would . . . I don't know where he was getting the money from, America or where . . . that he would help them to go. So we came on a boat then from Cuba here to Barbados. We came on a cargo boat; it was awful. The boat was carrying timber, coffee and cotton. So you had to wait until it go different places. Before we get here, it stopped in Dominica or Guadeloupe. And then my mother said, "This voyage was too rough, and I'm not going back on that boat." She was the speaker for the group. We had to wait three or four days in Dominica until a passenger boat was coming.

But she had her family here. Her husband family lived in number 12 Station Hill. So them didn't even know we was coming. When the boat land out there, and then they bring us. At that time they had the police vehicles that you used to call a "Doris". It was like a taxi. They had two. I remember I was hungry, and I told my mother, "*Tengo hambre*" ["I'm hungry"]. The policeman asked my mother what I said, and when she explain, he stop at a shop in Roebuck Street and bought turnovers, flat jacks and rock cakes and a drink for me.

They brought us there in Station Hill. Although they never know that we was coming, they just accepted us and opened the door. So then later in the day they had then to go down to the harbour. That time it was behind Manning Wilkinson out there. It was just a little thing; nothing like what we have now today. And the tide high. They went the next day and take up their little trophies or "trumphies", or whatever, off the boat and then came here. We didn't have chairs or tables or anything like that. That's how it really happened.

I was twelve years old. I came with my mother, my father and my brother. It was thirty-six of us that came on that boat. The Greaves was there, the different people, the Stanfords. We still correspond with each other and so. Well, some have passed away. The first place that my father rented in Carrington Village was one and six – thirty-six cents!

When they had the riots in 1937, the morning I went to school. I went to the Carrington Village School. Miss Springer was the headmistress. It start up around ten o'clock and there were gunshots and a lot of noise, and people running. I run and went up under a cellar. I was always afraid of frogs, and they had a lot of them in the cellar. The frogs start to move away from me, and I run and went home. It was an awful time.

Then after, my brother Ruben went to work then at the Purity Bakery, and then he work at the Swiss Bakery. The gentleman there said, "But you are a nice, fine young man. I don't see why you should be selling bread." He said, "Over there want policemen. You think you would like to go?" He said, "I'll try. But I know more Spanish than English." The gentleman give him a letter of recommendation, and he get the job. He used to run the airport[2] – Grantley Adams [International Airport].[3] He retired from the police force as a sergeant. After he retired from the force, he then worked at Rockley Resort as chief of security. And they were so proud of him. Then he had cancer and he died.

When I went to work, I was about sixteen years old. I worked there [with a lady] in Tenth Avenue, Belleville. You know how much I used to get? Six shillings a month! You know what that is? A dollar and forty-four [cents]. That time I was young and strong. But her mother was a slave driver. When I done all the work, she put me to pull nut grass. Twelve and one o'clock before she let me go home, she put me on a bench out there to pick every nut grass from out of there. One Saturday, I'll never forget, she cooked breadfruit and curry something. I ate some of that, it must have been stale. I was so sick. I was so sick that I didn't know myself. I went home and was vomiting, vomiting, and everything was happening to me. I told my mother, "I'm not going back there. Go and tell her I'm not coming back." She said, "Don't let her rule you." Because she was getting good work for nothing. I told her, "Mama, if you want to go and do it, you can go, but I'm not going back there."

I picked up myself and walked to the Second Avenue, and I saw an old lady under a shed. She was Rev [Basil] Ullyett wife. I went and said to her, "Good morning." I asked if she wanted anybody. She said, "Yes." And she paid me ten shillings. From six I get ten. And all I know, that woman learn me. On Saturday nights she used to have dinner for the Reverend. He was at St Paul's Church, an Englishman, Rev [A. Harold] Bartlee. And she would have nice things ... cold salads, pickled beets, meatballs, different things mixed up. And I stayed with her for a *long* time. And after I thought that that ten shillings was not enough, I tell her that I going. She said, "But why you going?" I told her that I going, and I went and learn to despatch shop at Sam Gibbs in Suttle Street.

But you know I always wanted to better my condition. When somebody show me two times how to fold, I done know how to fold. But the money used to beat me, but they would take the money and so. Then I was working at M.L. Seale. I used to get fifteen dollars a week. But I just wanted to work and help myself. Above all, God has been very good to me. Then I left here in '50 to go to Curaçao.

I spent nine years in Curaçao. A young man had said that he liked me; Clyde Joseph Nicholls. I knew him from here. We got married in Curaçao in 1952. I was only nineteen when I know him. He came on a vacation and saw me working in the shop. He said he would send for me, if I could do any kind of work. I said, "Yes, I can." He asked this doctor, Dr de la Fuente [if he would employ me], but he had to pay the surety. Curaçao was very, very good. I had no regrets in Curaçao. People from Brazil, Portugal, name it. Everybody you could have find, and [they] lived together. But you had to learn the Papiamento language. But because I could speak Spanish, I was able to learn the Papiamento quickly. Although that I can't speak Dutch, I know most of what you say. But I can't reply, you understand?

Figure 3.2. Ofelia Parris married Clyde Nicholls in Curaçao in 1952. Courtesy of Ofelia Nicholls.

I worked with Dr de la Fuente and his wife. I did all the work. Well those people generally cooked their food. So when I got there, she was a young woman too, with just two little children. They could go away to Suriname . . . anywhere, and leave those two children with me.

The whole house was almost glass, and you had to keep that glass clean all day. I used to live in. So one day she went out and she didn't come back in time. So when she came back I had cooked some peas, potato chips, some steak and a potato salad. And when she came she said, "Ofelia, you put on something for me?" I said, "Yes." She said, "I smell it." And quick so, the husband came in behind her. She start playing she fussing 'round. But when he taste it he said, "You ain't cook this." Right so. "You didn't cook this." And she didn't answer. But I know from that day I had to cook. They never know how to cook peas and rice. They cook the peas by itself. I cook peas and rice, everything I knew, I cook. I had no problem. They treated me very well. So many little things they gave me when I married. I can look and see things that I still have from those people. They treated me very nice. They wanted to take me to Holland with them, but I had already married. They were disappointed that I had to go.

I came back in '60. The CPIM [Curaçaose Petroleum Industrie Maatschappij][4] was laying off people. They start laying off men. The oil wasn't selling so much then. Everybody start laying off. It was a multitude of people from left, right and centre. Wherever in the world you think somebody could have come from, they were in Curaçao.

My husband and I had gone to a church service in Aruba. And Mother Jackson said, "Let her spend some time here." And I spend a week in Aruba then with them. Everybody like me because

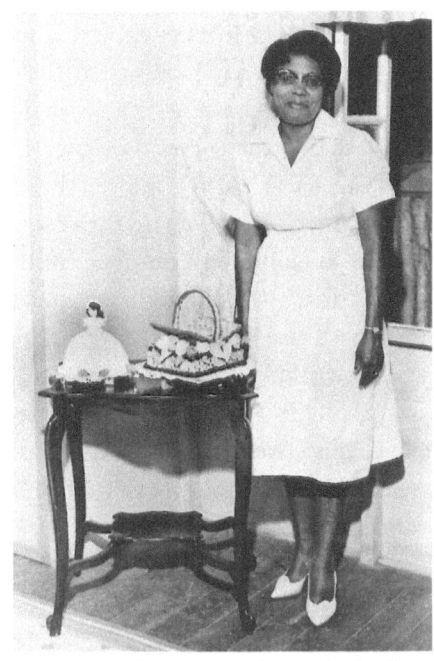

Figure 3.3. Ofelia returned to Barbados from Curaçao in 1960. Courtesy of Ofelia Nicholls.

I like to get up and work and do something. I can't sit down idle. When I come back then he tell me, "We going home you know." I said, "You get laid off?" He said, "No. But everybody I know going and I going to be here my one, and those chimneys I have to climb, it getting too hard." When he go up in those chimneys, he up in the clouds. "I going to take my money, and I'm going to go." So I started to buy my little things. We came and went to live with his mother in St George. Glebe Land, St George.

I remember one day he told me, "I will always love you." He really kept his word. Well now this is seventeen years that my husband died. I'm here with my two sons, Timothy and Samuel.

Barbados has come from a far place. Those who went away try and send money and build homes and elevate themselves. The little roads were so narrow, dirt roads. I think they have done very well. God has been good. I consider myself a child of God, because if he didn't help me, I wouldn't be here now.

Although it was hard in Cuba. And as for Machado. Political things is bare trouble. Afterwards he [Machado] get overthrow. He had a jetty going out on the sea. And when you get there and they leave you out there, you drop down in the sea and the sharks eat you. This man Mr Libert was in his house with his wife. He was a schoolteacher. They come and carry him away, and he was gone. You know how they know where he went? The fishermen catch a shark, and when they cut it open, the signet ring was in the shark. That's how we know.

In Cuba, you had to mind your business. You couldn't say who you were for. Even your children. One time they say you couldn't keep no fowls, and people used to go and inform on their family. Don't know if their head was bad or what. So that's why my mother wanted to run. But Cubans are nice people. They are honest, and if they're for you, they're for you. They are not no two-timers. Very nice people. That's all I can say.

When Fidel Castro came here, they invited me to a reception at Government House. We were there waiting to see when he would arrive, but we didn't see when he came in. All of a sudden he appeared and shook some hands. We didn't notice when he left either.

I never went back to Cuba. I travelled throughout the Caribbean, to St Maarten. I went to Israel, Canada, England, Germany and the United States. I had an opportunity to go back to Cuba, but no thanks. I had enough. But my son Timmy went.

This interview with Ofelia Nicholls was conducted at her home in Bank Hall, St Michael, on 31 October 2017.

CHAPTER 4

FRANK PHILO

Hometown: Baraguá, Ciego de Ávila
Barbados connection: Mother
Occupation: Electrician
Arrival year: 1937

MY MUM HAD FOUR BROTHERS OVER THERE IN Cuba – Uncle Dolphus, Milyard, Thomas and Samuel. Another brother, Aaron, had migrated to America. She was a young girl when she leave home. She was only fifteen years old when she went to Cuba. But her brothers were over there. My grandparents had twelve of them, eight boys and four girls. A very big family. I think they said my grandmother had a shop in the early days. A person who had a shop in those early '20s was pretty well off.

When her brothers see her over there, they wanted to know what she was doing there. She said, "Well you all over here, so I come too." What she did then, she decided to wash their clothes, cook their food and so on. Eventually she meet my dad, William Philo. His father, my grandfather, was from Antigua. I was born in Central Baraguá, the fifth of August 1927. I celebrated my ninetieth birthday this year.

I came from Cuba a baby in arms because there were four of us, three boys and one girl. I'm going according to what my mum tell us. Apparently she left Cuba in 1927 and came to Barbados. She had four of us – Estela, Everton, Pasin and myself. So I was a little baby. She came to Barbados and stayed for about two years. After the two years then, she went back to Cuba. She left the two oldest – which was Estela and Everton, and took back me and Pasin. After my mum went back to Cuba, apparently my dad and her disagreed and they parted. Then she had another gentleman named Mr Lee, and she bore four children for him in Cuba. That was Caleb, Caroline (we call her Cissy), Eugenia and Colvin. So that was eight of us then.

That time my dad was living with another lady called Mary. She was from Jamaica. Mary had two children then for my dad. My mother never said too much about him because, you know, mothers always have something bad to say about the other partner. One day she called me and showed me him walking across, and she pointed to him and said, "*Es tu papa, un payaso.*" "That's your father, a clown." And I gone back playing with the boys. But I never see him to say that he is a dad who could come and hold me. So I never did know my dad at all. I really didn't know him. I have a picture of him. I think they said that the majority of his life my father was an engineer working in the factory. They called them engineers, but when I went to England, I realized that engineer is something totally different. You have to have blueprints and that sort of thing. Those chaps I think just greased the engines and did all sorts of odd jobs, but they weren't really engineers.

Life in Cuba I think was very good in those days. We used to have what you call an *almacen*; what you call here a supermarket. The person who owned it was named Viscaya. I grew up with a chap called Papasito, and Coya, and Mario, as boys playing together. We had a nice time playing cricket and baseball. Well we used to go to school. We used to go to the ice factory. When the *tiempo muerto*, the dead season, came in we used to go and get syrup from the sugar factory.

I remember there was a girl we used to call one-arm Carmen, and Mr

Sayers, Mr Knights, Mr Berkley and Ms Barker, who used to take us to Ciego de Ávila. In those days, as children growing up, things were so nice. We had water toilets. We had the *barracon* where the people used to live. I can say that in those days, in the '30s, before you ever exist Sharon, it was beautiful. No two ways about that.

So then my mum leave Cuba again . . . my mum was a travelling woman . . . and came back to Barbados in 1937. I was just nine years old. We were sad to leave Papasito and our other friends. But we were very happy to be coming back to Barbados, because Cuba was getting hard, and we're going to a paradise place now. We left from Santiago de Cuba. My mother had this trunk, and a woman named Juanita was holding on to it saying it was hers. And we know it can't be her trunk, so we children were just like little rats all around. All I know is that we came over on a cargo boat and stopped in Guadeloupe and Martinique. Because my mum said that she didn't know if she would be able to take us about again, because she loved travelling. And St Lucia, I can remember. And then, Barbados.

Here, my brother and I went school in a place called Airy Cot. That's in St Thomas. Others went to St Simon's School, where "Sleepy" [Sir Frederick] Smith's father was the headmaster. You had to go through Turner's Hall Woods to get to St Simon's, but because I was asthmatic, my mother didn't want me to pass through the woods.

It was very difficult, because remember as I said, it was only my mum. Well, she was bilingual, but we only knew a little bit of English, because we only went school for a short while over there. So the English was virtually non-existent, so to speak. We spoke more Spanish than English, so we had to learn quick to speak English properly. She should have taught us English more over there. But seeing that we were so young, she never thought of it. I can even remember that she spoke with some of the other West Indians in Spanish. Very rarely I ever heard her speaking English.

In Cuba, when the *tiempo muerto* came in, I remember they had corn, and we had a mill that you used to press with your feet like that to feed the corn. It was very coarse cornmeal. So she would make like bakes, and she make pap. And when we come in from school, it is bake or it is pap, and cou-cou. And we had a dog named Mancero, and he refused to eat it. But things were so hard in those times. So she told us how nice things were in Barbados and she was going to bring us back to Barbados.

Well when we come here then, it was a different story. I came back here as a young boy and had to go to my grandparents. And the first thing I can remember that my grandmother put on the table for us when we came back was cou-cou. We cried! Because remember, we just left Cuba with the same kind of meal that we got. So we cried our eyes out. But even my mum when she brought us back to Barbados said it was one of the biggest mistakes she had made. Because in those days when we came back to Barbados you had a lot of people who still had outside toilet pits and you had to bring water and things like that. And it wasn't like that over there. We had piped water in the house over there. So as far as we were concerned, we left good living and come back to poverty. And that was why at the time my mum regret that she did bring us back.

I don't recall too much about the '37 riots because we were just young children. But I remember my mother pushing us back in the house. We were living in St Andrew.

Then my mum died in 1945. As kids, we used to say that my mum broke her heart.

As we say in Barbados, I went from pillar to post after I left school. I leave school early when I was in fourth standard. My mum passed away; I don't have a dad. I was from here, there and everywhere. I decided that I want to be an electrician. I used to play about with batteries and making little cars. Eventually, a cousin of mine who had a couple of kids, he teach me to drive. But by teaching me to drive then, I then applied for a job as a driver. They used to pay us next kin to nothing. But it suit me because I got more practice. I didn't mind the pay so much. Eventually then I start to drive buses. Those were the general buses. Around the time of Hurricane Janet[1] in 1955, I was driving buses. We had to stop work. My sister's wooden house got damaged.

Around that time, the British had this massive immigration from the West Indies. I emigrate to England. I determined that now I'm over there, I would learn the trade that I liked. So I became an electrician, and I worked for British Rail for forty years. I never moved from British Rail. I went there in '56 and came back to Barbados in '96. I travelled to Russia, Yugoslavia, Holland and different places with British Rail. Even now they still send me my pass. When I go up to England now, when I get off the plane, I catch a train and I don't have to pay.

I had got married over there. My wife, she was from Barbados. But, regrettably that didn't work out, so we parted. Then I met my old-time sweetheart from Barbados, and eventually I married her. But she passed away. Both of my wives were nurses. I have two daughters, one in England and one in

Barbados. I had two sons, but one of them passed away. And I have a nice granddaughter in England. In Cuba, I still have a brother from my father's side. I had a sister there, but she went to America. She died. My dad had those two children – a girl and a boy. I have a lot of cousins over there too. My uncle had kids over there. The Jordan family is all there in Baraguá.

I've been back to Cuba nine times. I love going back. I have my brother over there, Sammy. I think he's eighty-four. I have a niece, Sammy's daughter, Janet. Since I've been travelling to Cuba, I brought three of them over here to see what it is like.

I was asthmatic from birth. I was the sickliest child out of the ten children that my mother had. So she spend a lot of money on me. But I've lived to this age, and I still go dancing. I go to *Q in the Community*.[2] I enjoy life. I thank God for life. To see that I am nine-zero [90]. I can go for a walk, go dancing. I don't smoke, I don't drink, I don't gamble. Well, I buy the Lotto. I say if I win, I'll take care of my family in Cuba. I'm more Barbadian than Cuban, but I love Cuba so much. Cuba is a beautiful country. A beautiful country. No two ways about it.

Figure 4.2. Frank in England in March 1957. Courtesy of Frank Philo.

Frank Philo's interview was recorded at his home in Silver Hill, Christ Church, on 31 October 2017.

PART 2

REVOLUTION AND INDEPENDENCE

CHAPTER 5

POST-1959 REVOLUTION CUBA

ECONOMIC AND POLITICAL DEVELOPMENTS IN CUBA

WITH THE SUPPORT OF SYMPATHIZERS IN THE ARMY, Fulgencio Batista seized power in 1952, three months before scheduled elections. His return to Cuba from exile in Key Biscayne, Florida, would mark his second period at the helm of the country. Wayne Smith says of President Batista:

> Although never above pocketing government money, after coming to power in 1952, Batista carried corrupt practices to the extremes of the Grau and Prío presidencies. Corruption under Batista took on a more sinister form as organized crime from the United States was sold an expanding piece of the action in Cuba. By 1957, American gangsters controlled most of the nightclubs and casinos in Havana, and they were moving into other business sectors as well.[1]

In the wee hours of New Year's Day, 1 January 1959, Batista fled back to Florida. He was accompanied by members of his family, some members of his regime, and the ill-gotten wealth which he had managed to plunder from the Treasury to finance his retirement. The guerrilla forces led by Fidel Castro in the Sierra Maestra had prevailed.

Just a couple of months later, on the floor of the Barbados House of Assembly, Errol Barrow gave his perspective on this development in Cuba: "Batista got away with $5 million a month for five years, that is $300 million, and when the Revolution came in Cuba, it came with such suddenness that every major power in the world was taken by surprise including the Government of America which kept the closest watch over Cuba." In assessing the Cuban revolution, Barrow questioned whether the people of Barbados had "set their targets high enough". He pondered, "Are they not contented until the end of time to be hewers of wood and drawers of water, living in somebody else's house, sleeping on the floor and bumming a meal here and there." Barrow made it clear that he was not advocating violence in Barbados, but warned that "if we go on ignoring the plight of the masses of people in Barbados, something will happen. Do not be misled by their present complacency and acquiescence."[2]

> I am telling you that if they had the *aura vitae* – you will forgive me for using a foreign phrase because we are not to debate in a language other than English in this Chamber, but I cannot think of any equivalent word in the English language which would express what I want to bring out – if they had the zest for life that people in Cuba had, they would have dug a deep ditch, blind-folded all of them over there and let them stand over the same ditch, shot them down and covered them with mould. That is the only way, apparently that you are going to get progress in Barbados.[3]

When Fidel Castro triumphantly entered Havana to join the other fighters of his rebel army from the Sierra Maestra, it signalled a major turning point in the life of the country. Max Azicri states: "The revolution was now in power. Uncertainty about its meaning and direction loomed in Cuba's future. The people, however, joined in a massive celebration of Batista's fall, welcoming Castro and his fellow guerrillas as true liberators. Unknowingly, Cuba was about to embark on a new, uncharted path. That path would soon lead Cuba to start building a socialist regime, the first one ever in the western hemisphere."[4]

The new revolutionary government set about transforming the existing social and economic structures by introducing policies to effect improvements in areas such as land tenure, trade, banking and housing. Education and public health were major beneficiaries of the new policies and served to improve opportunities for low-income workers. Azicri points to one positive impact of the change in government: "The revolution's socioeconomic policies addressing the needs of marginal and traditionally dispossessed groups had the direct effect of improving the living conditions of black Cubans. They had lived in poverty in colonial times, so blacks made substantive gains under the new egalitarianism."[5] However, while these developments were to be lauded, Azicri notes another significant aspect of life under the new revolutionary regime: "Strong pressure was exerted upon the population to show 'oneness' with the revolution not just in words but in action. From the government's side it was particularly urgent to enlist the population in the works of the revolution, creating a close identification between the leaders and the masses."[6]

He asserts that a negative by-product of this was that the government considered those who were not bona fide participants as disaffected and capable of harming the revolution either by action or omission. He argues that for those who chose not to integrate themselves into the revolutionary process but remain in Cuba, it alienated them further from the newly emerging value system. The West Indians living in Cuba were not exempted. Andrea Queeley observes: "At the same time that many Cubans rejected the changes and left the country, there was a process of investment in revolutionary society. This investment was due to, among other things, opportunities for social mobility created by the redistribution of the society's resources in the effort to eliminate social inequality. For some people of English-speaking Caribbean descent, this meant becoming fully Cuban."[7]

With regard to discomfort with the new regime, Azicri adds, "For some, it provided an additional reason to emigrate to the United States, or elsewhere."[8] For some of the Barbadians and West Indians in Cuba, that "elsewhere" was their home country. Their governments had been providing financial assistance to help them cope. For example, in 1961, the Barbados government increased its contribution towards the relief of West Indians in Cuba by $11,520. Provision was also made to remit to the Foreign Office, contributions due for the years 1958–59 and 1959–60 at the rate of $5,760 per annum. At that time, Barbados was part of the West Indies Federation. Premier Sir Grantley Adams had left to become the first prime minister of the federation, and Dr Hugh Cummins had succeeded him as premier of Barbados on 17 April 1958. J. Cameron Tudor expressed some concern during debate on this vote in the Barbados Parliament, stating: "I understand now that there is on a very large scale a certain amount of persecution of those West Indians who for one reason or another cannot come to terms with the Castro Regime. I regard it therefore as a very serious matter, the idea that there should be West Indians, especially Barbadians, in Cuba who are suffering any sort of disability."[9]

He asked whether the government had any information on the point, and what either the government by itself or in consultation with the other units of the federation was doing. Tudor also wanted to know "whether any applications have been received from Barbadians who are now resident in Cuba, who may be suffering in consequence with their disagreement with the present regime". He disclosed that he had "been informed from correspondence that the plight of the West Indians in that territory is not at all to be envied and that some very serious and heart-rending appeals have come out from West Indians living in Cuba to the various Governments of the Federation". Not only had Tudor been informed by the correspondence which other persons had received, he disclosed that he himself had been a recipient of some correspondence from people who had had contact with refugees coming out of Cuba. This information revealed that "the plight of West Indians in Cuba is very severe indeed".[10]

F.E. Miller, minister of social services, explained that there had been an increase in the number of requests for repatriation and that in recent years, the repatriation of people from Cuba was being done by the individual territories rather than at the federal level: "Two or three years ago it was down to a trickle of one a year and sometimes less; but quite recently there is a sudden upsurge of applications bordering on about fifty. It is for that reason that we find it necessary to increase this Fund from $10,000 to $21,000. At the moment I would say that there is tremendous movement."[11]

Tudor had another question for the minister; this time in relation to whether there had been complaints from the Barbadians resident in Cuba about ill-treatment by the Cuban government and, if so, how those complaints were being dealt with. He suggested that if there were in fact such complaints, "that would be a matter which we would have to let the Federal Government or the British Government take up for us". He acknowledged that "some time has to elapse before everybody who wants to be repatriated gets repatriated, but we would like the assurance from the Cuban Government that during that period there would be no ill treatment of our nationals in Cuba".[12] It was, however, Premier Cummins who opted to respond to Tudor's question. He said that he had not personally seen any complaints and did not know whether the minister of social services had seen any. He explained why this would be unlikely: "The complaints from Barbadians or any British subject resident in Cuba come through the British Consulate, so much so they are the people who put out to the various islands the complaints from West Indians or other British subjects resident in Cuba. These complaints would hardly therefore come directly to the Government of Barbados; they would have to be processed through the British Consul."[13]

In 1949, British consular officials had listed Gilbert Rowe's father, Cyril A. Rowe, among Barbadians under sixty asking for repatriation to Barbados. He was thirty-nine years old at the time. At that time, Cyril's mother, Martha Hunte, was seventy-six years old and was listed among the Barbadians over sixty willing to be repatriated to Barbados. It is not known what delayed Cyril's departure until 1970. Even though he was a young boy, Gilbert vividly remembers the immediate consequences of the moment when his father was finally given permission to leave Cuba with his family: "But I can remember when that cable came, as a child. Because a man on a motorcycle used to come up, deliver the cable to you; you were given permission to leave. You had to leave the house. Instantly! Not tomorrow; you leave the house, and they seal it. It was now the property of the government."[14] Gilbert and his family slept at the house of his grandmother, who was called Coley Cain and who had been born in St Philip.

In 1973, Colbert Belgrave's father, Cleophas, returned to Barbados with his older son, Eddy. Colbert explains, "At that point in time, growing up in Cuba, we had this law that when you reach a certain age, you could not leave the island. You had to go to military service. Seeing that my brother was going to complete his fifteen years shortly, my father did not want the military service to catch up with him. So what he did, he brought along my brother first."[15] Colbert's own escape from military service would come six years later, when he and his mother came to Barbados and the family unit was intact once again.

> I was born being an asthmatic, and my father knew that and he said that he never wanted me to go through the military service. So what he did, which was very tactful and helpful, he made sure that by the time I was fifteen years old, I had a British passport. So that would have meant that I could not go to military service. But you still had to do the theory part at university or college.[16]

For those who stayed, there were testing times ahead. In the early 1960s, the Cuban economy began to undergo some difficulties. Various commodities were in short supply and rationing was introduced in order to meet the basic needs of the whole population.

Clotell Springer was preparing to return to Barbados with her younger children in 1976, but fate intervened. Her daughter Yolanda Nelson Springer was eleven years old at the time.

> She could not travel with us because we were Cuban citizens, and at that time you could only travel to another country if you were leaving to go and live there. In order to do that, you were required to have a passport from that country that allowed you to live there. She had to get our papers in order to apply for Barbados passports and wait on the government to give us permission to leave the country. During that process, she had surgery for kidney stones, and she died during surgery as a result of internal haemorrhage.[17]

Yolanda's elder sister Gloria was of age to travel on her own, and she came to relatives in Barbados. One of her visits back to Cuba was the catalyst which brought Yolanda to join her Barbados in 1994. This was during the Special Period, when Cubans experienced severe economic hardship. Gloria saw the toll that daily life was taking on her sister and arranged for her to leave. Yolanda recalls, "It was really stressful, and life became really stressful in Cuba at that time. It was a real crisis, 1993–1994. It was a period when people started leaving en masse, on rafts and anything they could find. I left Cuba the seventh of September 1994."[18] It would be five years before her young son Josué could reunite with his mother:

> Cuba would not allow him to come until Barbados Immigration gave me a paper saying that he was allowed to come and live here. Immigration here was telling me, "He's your son; bring him. We'll give him a permit to go to school until the papers are ready." But Cuba was saying, "No." I needed something legal that said he is allowed to live in Barbados. At that time, the policy in Cuba was that children under eighteen years could not travel. Eventually I got him here in 1999.[19]

The economic deprivation of the Special Period also prompted Florencia Yearwood to write to her father's relatives in Barbados. She says: "In my letter I talked about the economic situation in Cuba. Because I went to university, I had a good salary. But I didn't have the money when my son Yanier was to graduate to buy his clothes to go to the graduation. And the family here understood."[20] As a result of her letter, Florencia's Barbadian relatives travelled to Cuba. They invited her to come to Barbados, and she made the journey to her father's birthplace in 2000.

CUBA AND THE UNITED STATES

The Castro regime's relations with the United States would have a lasting effect on the Cuban economy. Cuba nationalized industries and companies, notably the Texaco, Esso and Shell oil refineries in 1960. On 19 October 1960, the United States – under President Dwight D. Eisenhower – imposed a partial economic embargo on the island, though medicine and food were excluded.

On 3 January 1961, the United States severed official diplomatic relations with Cuba, and a few months later, Fidel Castro formally declared that the revolution was "socialist" in nature. Louis A. Pérez Jr asserts, "After 1961, one of the key elements of US policy against Cuba was to isolate Cuba economically as a way to disrupt the Cuban economy, increase domestic distress, and encourage internal discontent – all designed to weaken the regime from within."[21]

On 7 February 1962, US president John F. Kennedy extended the trade restrictions imposed by Eisenhower to a ban on all trade with Cuba, except for the non-subsidized sale of foods and medicines. This ban was broadened further a month later to include the importation of all goods made from or containing Cuban materials, even those manufactured in third countries. It was that same month, March 1962, in which food rationing began in Cuba.

In February 1964, an incident at sea would have further long-term consequences for Cuba–US relations. It would also have implications for some of the British West Indian workers in Cuba. A group of Cuban fishermen whose vessel had drifted into US territorial waters near Key West, Florida, were detained by the US coast guard and accused of espionage. The Cuban government responded by cutting off the aqueduct supplying water to the US naval base at Guantánamo Bay. As tensions escalated, both sides increased their military presence in the area. There was further confrontation in July 1964 in response to an accusation from Castro that "Marine sentries at the base had killed a Cuban soldier and wounded two others".[22]

The US naval base had been a major source of employment for West Indians. Tim Reynolds argues that these employment opportunities came at a price, since "Base officials and private contractors used the workers' diverse origins to stifle collective organizing":

> Workers hailed from around the Caribbean, and in a country still reeling from the Great Depression, labor tensions split along racial and national lines. Workers leveraged their citizenship, language, and race to obtain positions with more security and responsibility, and bosses seemed happy to oblige. English-speaking workers secured full-time administrative and skilled labor roles – the most coveted positions – while the rest were left to compete for manual labor jobs, the majority of which were part-time or temporary contract positions. At the bottom – in terms of pay, benefits, and prestige – were women of color in domestic roles, who earned far less than both white women in the same positions and their male peers on the rung above. And of course, no one enjoyed the same benefits as US civilians working the same jobs.

Reynolds notes, however, that these workplace disparities at the naval base were eventually addressed: "The local press invoked FDR's language of good neighborliness to push for more Cuban employment (most of the full-time workers were Jamaican or West Indian, due to their English language skills) and, in 1950, base workers successfully organized a fledgling union, aided by a joint effort from Cuban anticommunist unionist Eusebio Mujal and the American Federation of Labor's Serafino Romualdi."[23]

As the quarrel between the United States and Cuba escalated, the US Navy suspended the pensions of Cuban retirees and fired approximately two thousand of the 2,750 Cuban workers at the base: "The Navy gave these terminated workers an ultimatum: return to Cuba, or stay at GTMO [Guantánamo]. Roughly fifteen hundred of them chose Cuba, where they were mostly placed in comfortable bureaucratic positions. Another 448 workers – most of whom ultimately emigrated to the United States – opted to live on the base."[24] Several hundred Cuban workers kept their jobs, commuting from Cuban territory in Guantánamo to work on the base. The last two elderly commuters – Harry Henry and Luis LaRosa – retired in December 2012.

CUBA AND THE SOVIET UNION

Diplomatic relations between Cuba and the Soviet Union had been established at mission level during World War II on 14 October 1942, but had been broken off ten years later on 2 April 1952 after the military coup by Fulgencio Batista.

Following the triumph of the 1959 revolution, the Castro government would look to renew the association. Tad Szulc asserts that Castro, "entered into the first conversations with a Soviet emissary over caviar and vodka in his INRA[25] office in the autumn of 1959".[26] Three months after that meeting, Deputy Premier Anastas Mikoyan travelled to Havana to consolidate the relationship. H. Michael Erisman argues, "Cuba's main concern throughout the whole of this early period was its deteriorating relations with the United States."[27] The United States had succeeded in persuading all the countries in the Western Hemisphere, except Mexico, to sever ties with Cuba. Erisman asserts, "In partial response to this Yankee hostility, Havana established its Moscow connection and received economic and military assistance from the USSR."[28]

The island's economy came to rely heavily on this support from the Soviets. "Not only did Cuba conduct 85 per cent of its trade with these partners before 1989, it also received preferential prices equivalent to several billion dollars of aid annually."[29] These economic subsidies were estimated to be worth approximately $6 billion a year. When the Soviets reduced petroleum deliveries to Cuba, the government introduced petroleum rationing on 2 January 1968. The dissolution of the Soviet Union came in December 1991. At the time of the collapse of communism in Eastern Europe and the Soviet Union, considerable damage was inflicted on Cuba's economy. "Without these subsidies, Cuba's capacity to import shrank by 75 percent, causing severe shortages of energy, raw materials, and food. The resulting depression slashed gross domestic product (GDP) by at least 35 percent, led to the closure of hundreds of factories, and left tens of thousands of Cubans unemployed. By one estimate, real wages shrank 80 percent between 1989 and 1995." Eighty per cent of the island's exports were lost as well.[30]

Cubans experienced deprivation, having to do without basic goods that they had become accustomed to having. This era of economic hardship for Cubans was known as the Special Period in Time of Peace, which was at its most severe in the early to mid-1990s. In addition to severe shortages of fuels such as gasoline and diesel, food and medicines were also scarce. However, in the words of Fidel Castro, there was a silver lining to this dark economic cloud:

> The current circumstances made new things, new ideas, new formulas essential. Also, the current circumstance helped us to discover that we were coming out of an era of fat years, very fat, of abundance, of a great abundance of resources, and into an era of very great scarcity, a lean period, very lean, and this helped us to discover the form in which the resources were being used or in which many resources were even being wasted.[31]

Renewed diplomatic relations had brought not only economic and military benefits to Cuba, but also scholarship opportunities for Cuban citizens to study in the Soviet Union. Barbadian descendant Yolanda Nelson Springer was one such beneficiary. She was awarded a four-year scholarship in July 1978 to attend the Alexander Ivanovich Herzen University in Leningrad. She specialized in pedagogy and psychology for pre-schoolers. Her story is told in chapter 13.

CUBA, THE CARIBBEAN AND AFRICA

Cuba's 1976 constitution provided a new legal and political framework for the country; it was now officially a socialist state. There was now also a new administrative division of the island. From the latter days of Spanish colonial rule, there had been six provinces – from West to East: Pinar del Río, La Habana, Matanzas, Las Villas, Camagüey and Oriente.[32] Following a resolution from the first Congress of the Communist Party of Cuba in December 1975, this number was expanded in 1976 to fourteen provinces: Pinar del Rio, La Habana, Isla de la Juventud, Matanzas, Cienfuegos, Villa Clara, Sancti Spiritus, Ciego de Ávila, Camagüey, Las Tunas, Granma, Holguín, Santiago de Cuba, and Guantánamo. The objective was to facilitate the planned economic and social developments by establishing more direct links between the party leadership and the population. Then, in 2011, the vast province of Havana was divided to create two new provinces – Artemisa and Mayabeque.

This new socialist state aligned itself with like-minded regimes around the globe and took on an active role in liberation struggles on the African continent. However, Carlos Moore is of the view that this foreign policy shift had its genesis in the October 1962 Cuban missile crisis, which left the island unprotected without the deterrent of Soviet missiles: "Pushed by events totally unrelated to African affairs, in 1964 Havana resolved to expand its influence in black Africa. As a result, Cuba's foreign policy would shift from merely moral support for the liberation movements and 'progressive' regimes in Africa to a more dynamic stance."[33] The Cuban government started sending troops to Angola in support of Dr Antonio Agostinho Neto's Popular Movement for the Liberation of Angola in late 1975.

The movement of troops from Cuba to Africa would have implications for a few countries in the Eastern Caribbean. As Moore states, "In case of a major crisis in Africa, the eight- to nine-hour nonstop flight to Sierra Leone and Guinea could be perilous for heavily laden aircraft. Landing and refueling facilities were necessary at some intermediary point."[34] Moore is of the view that this practical consideration prompted diplomatic overtures: "The states of the Caribbean therefore became the next target for the solicitude of Cuban diplomacy. Setting aside its long-standing lack of interest in its neighboring islands, Cuban leaders including the Caudillo himself went to work. By September 1974, agreements for airport use had been reached with Guyana, Jamaica, Trinidad and Tobago, and Barbados."[35]

Barbados, the most easterly island of the Caribbean archipelago, would become a refuelling stop for Cuban aircraft before they made the journey across the Atlantic Ocean to the African continent. Sir Frederick Smith, a member of the Barbados cabinet at the time, describes such use of the country's airport as "one of the most profound contributions we have ever made" and "one of Errol Barrow's finest hours as a leader".[36] Barrow – the country's first prime minister – explained to his Cabinet colleagues that he had allowed the planes to refuel at Seawell Airport because "the support was helping to destroy apartheid" and that "the troops going to Angola was really about holding back South Africa".[37] The refuelling stops continued for three months until diplomatic pressure from the United States brought them to an end. After a rejection by Dr Eric Williams to the Cuban proposal to use Trinidad's airport for the purpose, the flights to Africa were made via the Azores, Gander, Guyana and the Cape Verde Islands.

Azicri outlines the escalation process: "The deployment of Cuban troops in Angola was incremental, and it followed a fast pace: from eighty-two men departing from Cuba to Angola on 7 November, the numbers increased rapidly to 4,000. Later, 5,000 to 7,000 additional troops were flown in using Soviet transport, increasing to approximately 18,000 strong, their numbers varying as some returned home and others were replaced."[38]

There is a school of thought that Castro was acting as a proxy for the Russians when he initiated the incursions of Cuban troops in Angola. Tad Szulc refutes this notion:

> Contrary to widespread belief, it was Fidel Castro's idea – certainly it was not the Russians' – to engage Cuban combat troops in the civil war in Angola on an absolutely open-ended basis. The year 1986 began the second decade of the large-scale Cuban military presence there. Over 200,000 Cuban troops rotated through Angola during the first decade, and Castro has pledged to rotate 200,000 more Cubans, if necessary. But contrary to Fidel's own assertions, it was *not* South Africa's armed intervention in the Angolan civil war that forced him to rush his forces to Angola. The truth is that Castro beat everybody to it, entering first the conflict in an impressive display of instinct, imagination, and daring.[39]

Cuba's engagement with Angola and Guyana would provide the son and grandson of two Barbadian migrants with the first glimpses of their father's and grandfather's homeland. We learn in chapter 15 from Ernesto Yearwood and chapter 16 from Pedro Hope Jústiz that it was while in transit at the Grantley Adams International Airport that the hope was sparked to eventually visit, and perhaps live in, Barbados.

CHAPTER 6

POST-INDEPENDENCE BARBADOS

CITIZENSHIP RIGHTS

AS MIDNIGHT APPROACHED ON 29 NOVEMBER 1966 AND a new day dawned, the Union Jack was lowered and the Barbados flag raised during a moving ceremony at the rain-soaked Garrison Savannah. The new national anthem was played for the first time, replacing "God Save the Queen", which would have been familiar to Barbadians of that era. It signalled the birth of a new sovereign nation.

With the Barbados Independence Act 1966, the UK Parliament granted Barbados independence with effect from 30 November 1966. In addition, the Act provided for a new constitution to take effect at independence. This was achieved through the Barbados Independence Order 1966. The 1966 Independence Constitution conferred Barbadian citizenship on specific categories of persons, including those born in Barbados and outside the country. According to section 4 of the constitution, "Every person born in Barbados after 29th November 1966 shall become a citizen of Barbados at the date of his birth." It also states: "A person born outside Barbados after 29th November 1966 shall become a citizen of Barbados at the date of his birth if at that date his father is a citizen of Barbados." This section would be applicable even if the father had acquired Barbadian citizenship. There is also the provision that "a person born outside Barbados after 29th November 1966 shall become a citizen of Barbados at the date of his birth if at the date of the birth at least one of his parents is a citizen of Barbados who was born in Barbados".[1]

This latter provision has particular relevance for Cubans of Barbadian descent, since it allows first-generation Cuban Barbadians to claim citizenship in their parents' birthplace. There was another means through which Barbadian citizenship could be acquired. "Any woman who, after 29th November 1966, marries a person who is or becomes a citizen of Barbados shall be entitled, upon making application in such manner as may be prescribed and . . . upon taking the oath of allegiance, to be registered as a citizen of Barbados."[2]

In the case of women who were Barbadian citizens, the Independence Constitution did not confer them with the equal right to convert their foreign-born husbands into Barbadian citizens, or even to take up work in the island. This fact was lamented by Edwy Talma during debates in the House of Assembly. During the session on 3 February 1970, Talma highlighted an aspect of the 1952 Immigration Act which he found to be discriminatory. He said that there were cases where people of foreign origin lived in Barbados and were granted citizenship. However, he pointed to the fact that

> in the case of a man he is granted citizenship, but in the case of his wife she is not granted citizenship although they were both foreigners. As far as Barbadian women bringing in foreign husbands go, a lot depends on the contribution which the husbands can make. If he is sitting around and becoming a beachcomber, his case will have to be reviewed.
>
> In the case of a man bringing in his wife, if she can teach French, or make some big contribution educational, social or otherwise, then she is being well received and will be able to work.[3]

His colleague, Neville Boxill, declared in response that there was a point which Talma had overlooked. Boxill stated, "There is no Queen that can make a man a King, but a King can make a lady a Queen. If a man marries a Queen, he does not become automatically a King. That is why you get the disparity between a woman bringing her husband and a man bringing in his wife." To that retort, Bernard St John described Boxill's concept as "an antediluvian and mediaeval one", and questioned whether the honourable minister was "in favour of perpetuating this shameless system of discrimination between a man and a woman".[4] St John took up the matter with his colleagues once again later that year on 28 July 1970, during debate on the Immigration (Amendment) Act, 1970:

> Now there are certain aspects of this matter on which I would like to hear members of the House express their views, particularly in relation to what I regard as the most flagrant form of discrimination against women that could be conceivable. On many occasions I have found that a Barbadian woman who marries someone other than a Barbadian finds herself in a very discriminatory position *vis-à-vis* her counterpart, a Barbadian man, because his wife is automatically allowed to come

in; but her husband has to walk to the door of the Ministry of Home Affairs and beg for a work permit.[5]

Prime Minister Barrow corrected St John, pointing out that it was not necessary to go to the Ministry of Home Affairs, since "no one wishing to get permission to reside and work in Barbados has to do any more than fill out a form and file it at Central Police Station".[6] However, St John was firm in his position:

> I believe that if you are a citizen and have a claim here; and if your husband comes here, so long as he behaves himself, does not commit any criminal offence, so long as he is not a charge on the Treasury, he should have a right to live here in Barbados, and I hope that it will be the unanimous decision of this House that all members on both sides feel that this discrimination should stop.[7]

Barrow had a retort for both the members who had spoken on the motion. He was of the view that

> they should appreciate that it is a legal provision according to the law of the most civilised countries, amongst which for this purpose we must number ourselves, that a husband is responsible for his wife and not that the wife is responsible for the husband. It is the duty of the husband to find a matrimonial home for the wife, and it is not the duty of the wife to find a matrimonial home for the husband.[8]

The anomaly was eventually corrected in 2000 when the legislation was amended to accord Barbadian women the same rights as their male counterparts in relation to residency and citizenship for foreign spouses. The language regarding the conferring of citizenship and nationality is now gender neutral. Those who also have the right upon application to be registered as citizens of Barbados include, "a person who has been married to a citizen of Barbados, and has cohabited with that citizen, for such period as may be prescribed immediately preceding that person's application".[9] The Immigration Act, cap. 190 (last amended 1979) included the husband of a person who is a citizen by birth or by descent as qualified for the status of permanent resident.

In what was described as "the most sweeping changes in the pathway to citizenship since Independence in 1966", the Barbados government announced its intention to introduce legislation amending the Immigration Act to expand the categories of persons who would be eligible for Barbadian citizenship. Among these, "Citizenship will be available to a grandchild or a great grandchild of a Barbadian citizen." This move was prompted by "a declining population, a growing elderly group that imperils National Insurance Scheme funds, and a need for economic growth".[10] Prior to this, only children of Barbadian parents were granted citizenship by descent.

BARBADOS-CUBA BILATERAL RELATIONS

A booklet produced by the Barbados Ministry of Foreign Affairs in 1987 describes relations between Barbados and Cuba as "cordial and correct".[11] The publication states that "Barbados, in concert with the three independent Commonwealth Caribbean States, opened formal diplomatic relations with Cuba in December 1972. It took this action in recognition of a fundamental geographical reality, of the need to expand relations with the wider Caribbean, and of the concept of ideological pluralism."[12]

At the October 1972 Heads of Government Conference in Trinidad and Tobago where the leaders agreed to the establishment of the Caribbean Community and Common Market (CARICOM), the four leaders announced that they would be establishing diplomatic relations with Cuba. They proceeded to do so simultaneously on 8 December 1972, and this day is celebrated annually as Cuba-CARICOM Day. Sir Frederick Smith hailed the regional effort to end the diplomatic isolation of Cuba: "The Caribbean prime ministers, in particular Errol Barrow of Barbados, Dr Eric Williams of Trinidad, Michael Manley of Jamaica, and Forbes Burnham of Guyana showed decisive and pro-active leadership on this; indeed they genuinely led the Western Hemisphere on the issue."[13]

Smith disclosed that prior to formalizing the diplomatic relationship, Barbados and Cuba had begun low-level trade and agriculture exchanges in 1971. A special mission from Barbados had gone to Cuba in October 1971 to discuss future cooperation in agriculture and trade, and in turn Cuba sent a technical mission to Barbados in 1972 to view the country's achievements in sugar cane technology. Smith gave the reasons for these overtures: "Barrow considered that it might be useful to explore cautiously the possibilities of trade and functional cooperation with Cuba, especially since Barbados, acting through the British embassy had been for some time helping older Barbadian immigrants to Cuba to resettle in Barbados."[14]

One tragic consequence of embracing Cuba was the bombing of Cubana Airways Flight 455 off the west coast of Barbados on 6 October 1976. All seventy-three persons on board were killed in the terrorist act – fifty-seven Cubans, eleven Guyanese and five Koreans. The Barbados government erected a monument at Payne's Bay, St James, to honour those who died. It was unveiled on 1 August 1998 during a visit of Cuban president Fidel Castro to Barbados. Smith states: "It is important to remember as Barbadians that it was not just Cuba they were targeting. Barbados and all of the Caribbean territories that had welcomed Cuba back into the fold had been the focus of the terrorists."[15]

The Ministry of Foreign Affairs booklet states that "the two countries exchanged non-resident diplomatic Ambassadors in 1973, and since that date have enjoyed a relationship based on mutual respect for the differences in national political systems".[16]

Bilateral relations developed further with the establishment of a Cuban embassy in Barbados in May 1994, with the non-resident status of Lázaro Cabezas converted to that of first resident ambassador. This was later followed on 16 September 2010 by the setting up of a Barbados Resident Mission in Cuba, where Donna Forde served initially as chargé d'affaires. She was subsequently promoted to ambassadorial rank in 2017.

Since the establishment of the Barbados embassy in Havana, Cuban Barbadians have been appealing to the good offices of the embassy's consular services to apply for official documents such as birth certificates. Between 2010 and 2017, fifty-eight applications for birth certificates had been dealt with by the embassy. The Cuban Barbadians also submitted applications for Barbados citizenship by descent. During this same period, fifty-five such applications were received. These citizenship requests are no doubt motivated by the applicants' desire to ultimately take up residence in their parents' birthplace.

RETURNING TO ROOTS

However, well before the establishment of the mission at Havana, Barbadians and their dependents were interested in returning to their roots. In the year 1969, thirty-seven Barbadians were repatriated from Cuba by the Barbados government, ten in 1970, eight in 1971 and four in 1972.[17]

During debate on the Appropriation Bill in the House of Assembly on 17 March 1970, there was an item under the head of Ministry of External Affairs which provoked a query from member of Parliament Burton Hinds. He requested that the prime minister "tell us about these Barbadians under Item 64, which is for relief of Barbadians in Cuba – $6,000 – and then Item 65 – Old Peoples' Home at Panama".[18] When Prime Minister Barrow rose to respond, he chose to deal first with the Panama situation. He disclosed that he had first-hand knowledge of the home, since he had visited it. He explained that the home was jointly run by the governments of Jamaica and Barbados.

> As you know, the Panama Canal was built substantially by Jamaican and Barbadian labour, and because of the peculiar arrangement of the Canal Zone, if you are in the Canal Zone you are entitled to the Social Security benefits. The people who live outside the Canal Zone, when they got to retiring age, were in an extremely disadvantageous position compared with people who lived in the Canal Zone who would be entitled to go to the United States on emigration without any great difficulty; but not many West Indians were left in the Canal Zone when the US Administration carved out the belt and said that the United States Government had exclusive jurisdiction over that.[19]

Barrow explained further that the home was not on the Panama side, but at the other end of the Isthmus of Panama in Colón. When he had visited, there were about seventeen or eighteen Barbadians resident there. In relation to Cuba, Barrow stated that many of the Barbadians had gone there from Panama around 1913 to work in the sugar industry mainly in Oriente province, and that a lot of them were still there. Some of them had appealed to the Barbados government to bring them home:

> The number of requests that we get every year is between thirty and forty. From 1913 until 1970 is a matter of 57 years, and even if these people went there in their prime and youth, they are now old and most of them are very indigent and may not be supporters of the regime; but a lot are finding it very difficult to make out under the arduous conditions which exist. I would like to say that even in the former regime under Batista they were not any better off. For some reason they did not make provision for migrants to enjoy the same kind of welfare services as the people who were natives of the country itself; so the number of requests we still get every year for repatriation is between thirty and forty.[20]

For some of those who succeeded in making the journey back home to Barbados, Barrow revealed that the reception was not always warm and welcoming. He said that many of them came to live in Bridgetown and some had to be accommodated at the infirmary when their relatives could not be located.

> Even before they got here they asked the City Council if they could make any provision for them when their families could not be found. A lot of these people sent back money to their relatives, and then when you went to find their relatives you could not find them because they do not want to be bothered with old people; but

we regard them as being our responsibility because this is our country. The British Ambassador in Cuba and the British Consul in Havana are the people who make arrangements for these people to fly back home.[21]

Nelson Goddard's father Ethelbert had settled in Oriente province. He was one of the Barbadians who returned to his roots that year, with assistance from the government. Goddard recalls: "I came with him in 1970 when he came as a repatriate. The Barbados government sent for him. Our journey to Barbados was from Cuba to Mexico, then from Mexico we went to Jamaica, and then Barbados. That was the flight path they arranged so that we could get out."[22] There were no challenges in locating relatives to receive the Goddards. They went to live with Nelson's uncle on Welches Main Road, St Michael.

During debate on the following year's Appropriation Bill, the question of repatriating Barbadians from Cuba came up once again. On 18 March 1971, Barrow informed the House about a case which had cropped up at his office at six thirty that very morning. He explained that it had to do with the repatriation of a family, namely the four grandchildren of a Mrs Josephine Maxwell of Christ Church who was returning to Barbados. The cost of passages and incidental expenses would be $2,520. He told the House that the Ministry of Finance had advised that head 24, item 62 – Repatriation of Barbadians from Cuba – was not the proper item from which the amount of money necessary to bring the four Maxwell children to Barbados could be advanced, since they were not born in Barbados. Therefore, another scheme had to be worked out. The Ministry of Finance had no objection to the money coming from head 16 – Prime Minister's Office (1) – Item 15 Contingencies – to bring Mrs Maxwell's grandchildren to Barbados. Barrow explained:

> She will not come back without her grandchildren; she says she will not leave her grandchildren to be exposed to destitution in Cuba; so we have got the nephews in Christ Church to guarantee repayment of a loan of $2,520 to the Barbados Government, and we have recommended that Mr George Eliazar Maxwell should enter into a legal undertaking to repay to the Government the amount advanced, the first payment to be made immediately after return of the relatives.[23]

He said the assistance from Barbados was necessary since "these people are denied social security and everything like that by the Castro government, and are treated like dirt after their grandparents worked in the sugar plantations. This is not a political accusation against Castro; these are the facts of life."

Barrow added, "The Ministry of Home Affairs said they had no objection in the peculiar circumstances, because I think they are entitled to be registered as Barbadian citizens when they get back here."[24] The Maxwells would add to the number of CuBajans already in the island. In 2007, Constance Sutton wrote, "An estimated 136 to 150 Cubans are currently living in Barbados of which some 35 to 50 are said to be of Barbadian descent. The majority of the latter are first generation Cubans of Barbadian descent who came with their parents when they returned."[25]

Barbados's 2010 Population and Housing Census estimated the population at 277,821 persons. Of that number, 133,018 were male and 144,803 were female. This resident population consisted of 32,825 persons (14,833 males and 17,992 females) who had given their place of birth as a country other than Barbados. Only fifty-six of these persons (twenty-eight males and twenty-eight females) listed Cuba as their country of birth.

Table 6.1. Cuba-Born Population by Sex and Year of Immigration

	2010	2009	2008	2007	2006	2005	2000 to 2004	1990 to 1999	Before 1990	Not stated
Total	–	2	5	1	2	1	16	10	16	3
Males	–	–	3	–	–	1	11	5	7	1
Females	–	2	2	1	2	–	5	5	9	2

Source: Barbados Statistical Service, *2010 Population and Housing Census*, vol. 1, 117.

Table 6.2. Cuba-Born Population by Sex and Age Groups under-5 to 44

	Under 5 years	5–9 years	10–14 years	15–19 years	20–24 years	25–29 years	30–35 years	40–44 years
Total	1	1	2	4	3	4	5	4
Males	1	1	1	2	3	–	1	1
Females	–	–	1	2	–	4	4	3

Source: Barbados Statistical Service, *2010 Population and Housing Census*, vol. 1, 101.

Table 6.3. Cuba-Born Population by Sex and Age Groups 45 to 85 and Over

	45–49	50–54	55–59	60–64	65–69	70–74	75–79	80–84	85 and over
Total	4	6	7	2	2	–	3	3	5
Males	3	4	4	1	2	–	–	2	2
Females	1	2	3	1	–	–	3	1	3

Source: Barbados Statistical Service, *2010 Population and Housing Census*, vol. 1, 106.

The following chapters represent the oral testimonies of children, grandchildren and great-grandchildren of Barbadians who migrated to Cuba in the early twentieth century. These CuBajans who came to reside in Barbados between 1970 and 2003 share stories of their lives in Cuba, their journey to their ancestors' birthplace and their experiences on returning to their roots.

CHAPTER 7

NELSON GODDARD

Hometown: Pito Cuatro, Oriente/Las Tunas
Barbados connection: Father
Occupation: Entrepreneur
Arrival year: 1970

I was born in Oriente province. At the time we used to call it Oriente province. It was in a little countryside place there called Pito Cuatro in Oriente where I was born on the second of May 1955.

There were six of us siblings. The eldest one was Leonard (he's passed away); the second one was a girl, Mildred; after Mildred, there was Lisle (we call him Cyril); after Cyril was Lemuel (he lived in Barbados, then migrated to Miami); then Evelyn and then me.

In Cuba at the time, life was very nice. I liked it very much. We had Barbadian folks living there in Pito Cuatro who were still living there when I left.

87

Childhood days were nice days, especially around Christmas. The Cubans celebrate the twenty-fourth of December, and Barbadians, we always celebrate the twenty-fifth. So we used to celebrate two days as Christmas. Being that we were in the countryside, we used to go to Chaparra by my grandfather's place and meet with about thirty or more grandchildren. My grandfather – my mother's father – was David Brooks, and he was from Anguilla. My grandmother was Margarita Richardson, and she was also from Anguilla. He had a big house. That was our fun every Christmas, to go up by him and spend the holiday season. They had a big pot they used to cook the food in for everybody. They would kill a goat, or a lamb or a turkey, or chickens. But it had to be something big, because there were a lot of us. That used to be what it was like in those days, until I came to Barbados in 1970.

My mum, Beatrice Goddard Richardson Brooks, their daughter, was Cuban born, but an Anguillan descendant. My dad – Ethelbert Beresford Goddard – was Barbadian born. He used to tell me, "With the head that you have, I would like to take you to Barbados. I wouldn't want you to waste the privilege of studying and doing the things that you like to do." I think he said that when he saw that I was playing with batteries and generators and making electricity. So he said, "This child, we have to take him to Barbados and see if he makes something of himself."

I came with him in 1970 when he came as a repatriate. The Barbados government sent for him. Our journey to Barbados was from Cuba to Mexico, then from Mexico we went to Jamaica, and then Barbados. That was the flight path they arranged so that we could get out. It was interesting seeing the different countries and their style of living. We got to Mexico the Friday, spent the Saturday, and the Sunday we went to Jamaica. We spent the Sunday in Jamaica, and then we left for Barbados the Monday morning.

We went to live with my uncle on Welches Main Road, near the post office. I think right now it's a constituency house. My uncle died and the children moved from there. They sold it and went down to Cave Hill. I only spent about two months, or three months, at my uncle. We had a house that my uncle bought for my father in Bank Hall. When the folks moved out of the house, we went there. Then I bought Bank Hall from my uncle. I still own it now. My oldest son, Orlando, lives there. He also built his own house in Sunbury Tenantry.

I felt great about coming to Barbados; I always wanted to. My mum and them were fixing papers to come to Barbados back down in the '40s. And every time the ticket came, it always came with someone missing, and my mum didn't want to come and leave anyone behind. Well she could have, because there were two that never wanted to come over to Barbados. They remained in Cuba. But they have been to Barbados and back. They like the Spanish ambience.

The English that I thought I knew, I would say was a little broken English. I used to call it Spanglish, because we used to mix the two. We start off speaking in English and then we throw in a little piece of Spanish in between. Like certain words you can't remember. We could have done that because we knew what we were referring to. English is quite a difficult language. I tried to do English while I was at school down there, but the teacher said that I was getting confused with the two languages. And being that I was living in Cuba, she advised me to forget the English and learn the Spanish. So most of my education was in Spanish. We spoke English with my father. But when he came back to Barbados he had to start learning the English again because certain words that were used, he wasn't aware of them. Certain words they used to say to him, and he would ask, "What is that?" They would ask, "You are Barbadian?" He would say, "Yes, but what is that?" Then he would say, "Oh, oh, oh. When I left here, they didn't use that word."

In Cuba, he worked in the sugar cane industry. Being in the countryside, that would have been the only job offered to him at that time. He worked on a plantation. But then he built his home after that. My mother had remained behind in Cuba with three boys and two girls. When we got here, it was easy to get them out. We went and claimed for my sister who is here now, Evelyn. She came a year or two after me. So it was my sister, my mum and me.

When I came here, I went to the Seventh-day Adventist Secondary School. But I only went there for one term. My dad was already in his sixties and he couldn't get any work, and I had to venture out and go and learn some trade. I learned carpentry. When they were building the National Stadium, I went there as an apprentice at a construction firm. We put up a lot of the security bars, boxing and different things. They kept us on staff at the stadium when they were doing the grounds, and we took care of any little thing that went wrong in the VIP stand, a little paint, a little touching up here and a little touching up there.

Then we were laid off. A lady named Mrs Redman was the secretary in the office. She asked me, "Where are you going now? There's no more work. What are you going to do?" I said, "I'll find something somewhere around." She said, "Alright, I'm going to call my husband. He's in charge of urban development.

I'm going to speak to him." Then she told me, "Go on Monday and speak to this guy. He's my husband." I went there as they started building Ideal Homes. I started to work there. They made me a handyman. So I would do the finishing touches and I would hand over the keys.

The manager was Derrick Williams. So he told me, "I have something to do. Would you come with me and work with me?" I said, "I'm working with you already." He said, "I don't mean so. I'm going to open Homex Constructions, and I want somebody like you." So I was in charge of building the first sample house. And then I left them and went on my own. The electronics field is something that I always wanted to do and experiment with. While I was building houses, I did a radio and TV electronics repair course.

After I got through with the course, I was self-employed. Now I was mixing the two. I had a guy who was receiving the stuff during the day, while I was doing construction work. And when I came in, I would fix the TVs and radios that the guy collected for the day. It went on and went on. I then worked with West Indian Suppliers, installing and servicing elevators and escalators. I did Marine House, I did the old Hilton hotel, I did the Treasury building and a hotel named Tropicana. Then I learned how to install satellite receivers. The first satellite receivers which were installed on the domestic side, I was the one who pioneered that. My boss was a man named Malcolm DeFreitas, who owned Chubbie's Video. From there, he made me a part of the management. Afterwards, I left again and went on my own.

Now I'm self-employed again in the photovoltaic industry. In 2010, I went and did a course in Boston. But the industry is not doing as well as people think. My side of it hasn't taken off as it should have. I did the installation for my home, and so far I've done five other installations in Barbados. A lot of people would like to do it, but it's costly. There are a lot of benefits though. For instance, I didn't even know at first that we had an island-wide power outage yesterday. The electricity went off and my daughter called and asked me, "Daddy, you know the power off?" I said, "No." She said, "Well look outside and you're going to see how dark outside is." So when I looked out, I asked her, "When it went off?" She said, "About two thirty in the afternoon." I said I didn't know, because I was on solar power.

I mentioned my daughter. My wife Stephaney and I have three children. The eldest is a son, William Orlando. He's an engineer at Pine Hill Dairy. He went and studied in Cuba. He speaks Spanish. He did electrical engineering and mechanics. He worked at Cable and Wireless for about thirteen/fourteen years.

Figure 7.2. Nelson (*seated left*) with his family; (*clockwise*) son André, daughter, Lilia, son William Orlando and wife, Stephaney. Courtesy of Nelson Goddard.

The second boy, André, he works at the Treasury. My daughter, Lilia, is the last. She's working with a computer firm. She and Orlando studied computer science at the University of the West Indies. Stephaney and I were married in 1977. December the eighteenth, 2017, makes it forty years of marriage. She is a graduate teacher. She's a senior teacher at Bayley's Primary School.

When I go to Cuba, it's a lot of scrutiny I have to go through. Because under the era when I left Cuba, you were supposed to leave for good and couldn't come back. So I made that decision. But then they changed the policy and said, "Yes, you can come back."

I am under a different immigration status than the average Cubans who are here now. Any of those who came out after 1970, it's a different agreement than before 1970. I came out in 1970, so I'm right on the cusp. Any time I'm going to Cuba, I have to ask for permission. For me to go to Cuba, I have to get permission. I can't just go to Cuba, like take up and buy a ticket, catch a plane and go to Cuba. I can't. Because when I get to Cuba, they can turn me back. I cannot stay as long as I want. I have to give a specific time that I'm entering the country and exiting the country. I was in Cuba in 2016, and came back in 2017.

Now when I go back, it reminds me of my childhood days. There's something that when you go back you feel – how can I put it? – the ambience. It's different. I feel at home, yes. But still certain things make me not feel at home. There's still the joy to go back and see where you were really born and where you spent your childhood. I mean a lot of things have changed, but I like to go. It's just the red tape, paperwork that I have to go through to visit. I feel that I was born there, so I should have the freedom to stay there. They tell me yes, I can do it, but I would have to take back my citizenship, and then I have to give up this one. But I could still live in Barbados, as they say. It's only two siblings right now who are over there, because the other two came out. One was living here, but he went to Miami. He has American citizenship now.

But I like it here. I feel comfortable here, I work here. I make my living here. I built my house here. I feel like a Barbadian; although the Barbadians don't accept me as a Bajan. April this year will be forty-eight years that I'm living in Barbados.

There are a lot of opportunities that I lost, and I know that I did not get them because I'm not Barbadian. A certain Barbadian looked at me already and told me that I would never make it in this country. He is a black businessman. I said, "Before I met you, I was making it." My own colour told me, "I going to make sure that you don't get anywhere." The reason for it was because I gave him a price and he wanted me to change the price. I said, "Well that's my price. If you have other people out there that are offering a different price, try them." He said, "But I want you." I said, "But this is my price!" He said, "You with that attitude, you'll never make it in this country." I told another one, "I am not working for no one anymore. I'm working for myself." It was a white man; he didn't like that. He asked, "What do you mean by that?" I said, "If I can do it for you, I can do it for myself." He told me, "You're not going to make it out there." They call you a foreigner. They hear the accent, they don't know. I've done a lot of things for free. But I keep a low profile.

I always tell my children that I thank my father for bringing me here. Because my being here too is [because of] Errol Barrow. My father wrote Errol Barrow and told him he wanted to come back home. They claimed us as repatriates. They paid for everything. They paid for the airfares; they paid for the accommodation. They picked us up at the airport when we were in Mexico and took us to a hotel. It was the same thing when we got to Jamaica. We didn't know who these people were. They just asked, "You're so and so? Come with me." When we got to Barbados, my family was there with Immigration, and they said, "Okay. Everything is alright."

Mr Barrow said, "The only thing is if you want to leave Barbados, you've got to repay us. If you stay here, you don't have to repay anything. If you leave to go anywhere else, you'll have to pay." But all that's finished with now; I can just come and go as I like. At least when I come back to Barbados, they generally tell me, "Welcome back."

Nelson Goddard's interview was conducted at his home in The Crane, St Philip, on 9 January 2018.

CHAPTER 8

GILBERT ROWE

Hometown: Baraguá, Ciego de Ávila
Barbados connection: Mother and father
Occupation: Promoter and entrepreneur
Arrival year: 1970

MY MOTHER TOLD ME THAT I WAS BORN in 1956 on September the eighteenth at ten-thirty the night. It was a moonlight night, so I was told. That was in Central Baraguá.

You know I left there at thirteen, so I remember Cuba as a little boy. And a strange thing happened when I went back. I remembered Baraguá as a bigger place, because your perspective as a child is different from when you become a man. I remember playing with Pupi, who is Nelson Mello, who used to live right across from us. Pupi is still my friend. I've got fond memories of Baraguá.

As a matter of fact, when I went back to Cuba in 2004, the first person who was by my uncle's house to meet me was Pupi. So I put down my bags and we went walking, hugging up. And this chap, I can't remember his name, but he must have known us from when we were small. He said to us, "Look at you two; just as when you all were young." Because we used to rule the roost; we weren't easy.

I remember playing also with Alfred Carty, Alfredo who is now living in New York. He used to live right behind us. I remember all the boys. I remember Dominguín. It was really a fun childhood. I remember that I had to go church every Sunday. Because Grandpa was the boss of the Episcopal church. I remember having to go to morning service, Sunday school and evening service. You don't forget those things.

Baraguá was our world. I don't remember going to Ciego [de Ávila] more than maybe once. I don't remember going to Colorado, which was just next door, at all. You know when I hear "the wrong side of the track", I remember Baraguá. Because the track, the train track, used to divide Bajan Town – which was basically the black people quarters and the poor white quarters. And the other side of the track, that was where . . . you wouldn't have recognized that then, but when I went back I realized that . . . that was where the Americans who used to control the sugar factory used to live. Strange enough, our life was Bajan Town, not that side of the track. I think I went over that side of the track once, because there was a swimming pool over there, and you used to learn to swim there (not me; I never learned how to swim). But that's my memory of that side of the track.

I got my leg broken playing baseball. I must have been no more than about nine or so. And I know that the baseball field that I got my leg broken on was on that side of the track. I don't know how far on that side of the track, I don't remember. But it could not have been far. I've got good memories. I remember the folks still. I remember a friend of mine who died. He was older than me. Growing up, he had a strong will. Years after I got here, I found out that he was killed in the army. And how he was killed, based upon what I heard then, was that he was rebellious. You can't be rebellious and in the army.

The mere fact that you would hear Bajan Town, that would tell you. It was Barbados away from Barbados. There was no question about it. As a child, I would not have remembered much that my parents would have spoken about Barbados, but one thing I know, it was Barbados. You've been to Baraguá, you would see that the houses look a lot like the houses that were here in those days, still are, Bajan chattel houses. But I knew that there was a place named

Barbados. I knew that my grandfather Joseph Gaskin... a strong man if there was ever one; strong features and everything... was a Barbadian. There was no question about it. And when you were going to church, you knew that the majority of people who lived in Baraguá were Barbadians, or Barbadian descendants. Mind you, there were some Jamaicans living there. Because I remember as a boy eating flat jacks. Flat jacks is what we would call here turnovers, but they were done differently. They were flat, and they were done by a Jamaican woman. They used to taste real good.

There's nobody that I look up to more in this world than [my father] Cyril. He was a good man, and a quiet man. If I'm half the man that my father was, I'm a good man. My father was really good. My father was an angel. He taught me how to look after your family through thick and thin. My father was a tailor. He used to leave Baraguá and walk the train tracks to Colorado... when my mother told me so I couldn't believe it... to deliver a pair of pants to get money to feed his family. My father was a unique man.

My being in Barbados today is because of an accident of birth. My father's mother, Martha, was in Panama. His father died building the Panama Canal. The story of my father is unbelievable. It is a story of strength of character. I could not have been here if it was not for my father's story. His mother got pregnant in Panama and she insisted that her child must be born in Barbados. She brought Cirilo here to be born. He was born, and three months after, she moved him from here and went back to Colón. That's where he grew up. But it's because of those three months that he spent here that made him a Barbadian. That provided us with the opportunity to come to Barbados. It was nothing to do with my mother or her family. It was because of Cirilo, Cyril, and that accident of birth.

There was this gentleman who used to tell my father, *"Cirilo, esta aproximando el viaje"* [Cyril, the trip is getting closer]. Because they knew that we had applied to leave, and he would always tell my father that. I'm yet to know whether it was pulling his leg or what. But I can remember when that cable came as a child. Because a man on a motorcycle used to come up, deliver the cable to you; you were given permission to leave. You had to leave the house. Instantly! Not tomorrow. You leave the house, and they seal it. It was now the property of the government. So we slept by Granny, my grandmother that born in St Philip – Coley Cain, as they used to call her. Her full name was Georgina Coulthrust Cain.

She has a really interesting story that I discovered. Because I always wondered, "How did she get from Barbados to Cuba?" And my consciousness, because it happened to my family, that the route to Cuba was Barbados to Panama, Panama to Cuba. So I assumed that that was the route. Only last year I realized that it was not so. She left here and went straight to Cuba. You can imagine the courage that would take in those days, as a young woman, by herself. Picking up and rolling. But that's where we stayed after they sealed the house.

It was not a sad moment; it was good because we were travelling. And we were coming to this place named Barbados, which would have offered you, in those days, an opportunity to become whatever you could be. And I'm always grateful for that. I don't know what was more interesting – travelling overseas, or that first ride from Baraguá into Havana. Remember you go under a tunnel at some point. That's what I remember at that age. As a young child living in Baraguá, you didn't go to Havana. You didn't go to Ciego [de Ávila city] often, furthermore Havana. It was hard, it's still hard after all those years. Because you're leaving your friends, your real friends that you grew up with. Leaving Pupi, leaving all my boys.

I came to Barbados in 1970, at age thirteen. We came as a family. It was my dad, Cyril Adolphus Rowe, my mother, Elsie Melvita Rowe, me and my brother, Calvert, and my two sisters, Adela and Wilma. We took a very interesting route. People always ask, "You came by boat?" But no, we travelled by plane from Cuba to Mexico, a place named Mérida. And we spent some time in Mérida. That's the first place I saw a supermarket, a place full of food that you could go and buy what you wanted. Then we left there and we went to Jamaica. We spent a little time in Jamaica, and then came to Barbados.

My family was at the airport to meet us. That's the interesting thing; there was always this bond between our family, those who were in Cuba and those who were in Barbados. That link was never allowed to break. It was not by accident, because Granny used to write her family. And when we came here, it was Aunt Leotta, Leotta Taylor who is Granny's sister. We were picked up at the airport and taken to Leotta's house in Union Road, St Philip. That was the root; St Philip was the root from my mother's side. My mother was a Gaskin who married into a Rowe. But you know how we are as Spanish people; having Granny as a Cain, and Grandfather was a Gaskin, she becomes a Gaskin, but she's also a Cain. My grandfather Gaskin also came from St Philip. He come from Clarke's Hill in St Philip. Remnants of the house in which he was born are still in St Philip. And I still have family up there.

On my father's side, the Rowes in St Philip are our family. We've got some family in St Andrew. I'm actively trying to follow up my father's family. He has a lot more family in the States. The majority of my father's family are living in the States. Panama Canal Zone was administered by the Americans and once the canal was finished you had a choice either to go to the States or follow the money to Cuba. His sisters and older brothers chose to go to the States. He was the youngest and had to go to Cuba with his mother.

My first impression when I came to Barbados was shock. It is interesting, you know, history repeats itself. A lot of people don't remember that I come from Cuba, or they don't know. So it is always an interesting thing when they talk about foreigners, and this thing about the Guyanese when they were coming here. And I smile, because it isn't anything new. Apart from our family, that is the same reaction that we got. We experienced it at school, not from everybody, but from some of the schoolchildren.

Of course, I made friends. We spent a few nights in Union Road, and then Aunt Leotta had arranged for us to rent this house in Congo Road. And it's still there. I make it a habit to make sure that I show my son the house where we spent the first night, and the house that we lived in in Congo Road, because you must know your history. And you must be proud of your history, because that's what propels you. We didn't stay in Union Road long enough for us to have friends, not at that point. We subsequently made friends going back to visit Leotta. I remember the first night we spent at this house that was rented. The first thing I heard in the morning was, "Everton!" And that was a person by the name of Everton Hunte that was my friend and is still my friend. Then there were the Conliffes who used to live opposite to us. Mr Conliffe used to be a bus driver. The strange thing about that particular area of Congo Road is that I didn't feel that animosity. We were lucky in a lot of ways. That was not part of our experience in that area.

We had to learn English in Baraguá. Grandpa used to send all of us to school with an English teacher. She didn't used to play; she had a ruler. So we knew English. Of course, we would speak it with a Spanish accent. I still do, even though I fool myself that I don't. You only realize that the accent is still there when you hear a recording of yourself speaking. My spelling was not very good, and it's still not good. I'm very grateful to computers and spellcheck. We could speak English, and that was an advantage that we had.

I went to Princess Margaret Secondary School, and proudly so. I still call it "the university". I am proud to have gone to school there. It was an interesting period. There would be some children who would be most unkind to you, but we were a strong family. To know my grandfather Joseph Gaskin . . . strong . . . there's nothing weak about the descendants of Gaskin. Nothing! We were strong; mentally we were a strong family. And my father was a strong man, a man of few words. So we dealt with it.

The Princess Margaret years were interesting years. I thoroughly enjoyed Princess Margaret. I think it is a special school, and I wish that the students who go to Princess Margaret now would really know the history of that school, and the people that passed through that school. The first black general manager of Cable and Wireless, Trevor Clarke, went school there. He used to live in Brereton. Carlos Holder . . . the Lord rest his soul in peace . . . Central Bank deputy governor, went to school at Princess Margaret. And we can go on and on and on. Mac Fingall was one of my teachers there. When I tell people so, they can't believe it. I don't think he was that old, I believe he was young.

After I left Princess Margaret, I went to college for a little while, but I didn't finish Cave Hill. I became a teacher. I taught at Ellerslie [Secondary School] and at St George Secondary School. I taught science. Strange, I never taught Spanish. Ellerslie was my first job, and it was the best thing that ever happened to me. The headmaster there was a fellow named [Cuthbert] Brathwaite. He was known in Barbados as a disciplinarian. It was the best thing that ever happened to me. He taught you discipline. I could see Brath now; shoes always shining, impeccably dressed. You knew by his presence that he was the boss. And you had to go to Prayers. And he would tell you that there was really not a race between children and teachers to get to the door at three o'clock. Amazing!

Just like the teachers we had at Princess Margaret, we had Griffith, who is now a reverend. He was a reverend at St Barnabas. I think he started that senior day care centre – Busky [Bernard] Griffith. Then we had Carolyn Sinckler. Then we had Robert "Bobby" Morris, who was ambassador to CARICOM. Bobby Morris taught us history. Those years were years when learning and knowledge were in vogue.

After leaving Congo Road, I used to live on Six Roads. Before you got this roundabout, it was actually six roads, and we used to call it "University of the Square". Because to lime there, you had to have knowledge. You didn't speak unless you had knowledge. Freundel Stuart [former prime minister] is a product of the University of the Square, and a lot of other fellows. It was a beautiful experience. We used to discuss real stuff. We used to deal with [Frantz] Fanon, and with *How Europe Underdeveloped Africa* by Walter Rodney. We used to take pleasure in knowing these things. We moved away from *The Making of the West Indies* by [Roy] Augier and [Shirley] Gordon, a history book that the majority of schools used, and we went to Eric Williams, *Capitalism and Slavery*. We read *History Will Absolve Me* [by Fidel Castro]. We did *Das Kapital* [by Karl Marx]. We used to read all those things. We used to discuss *The Little Red Book*, Mao Tse Tung. Study was important; if you didn't know, shut yuh mout'. Go home and read it up, so that when you come back, you have some basis on which to speak.

Pete Lorde, who was in charge of the disaster management a while ago; there was a fellow named Puckus. Brilliant boys! These boys were bright. They didn't play, they were bright. Those boys were sharp! So education was in vogue. That's why I smile a lot of times. I didn't talk much; people didn't know much about me. You felt good. You didn't used to read for achievement; you just sopping up knowledge. You were reading about Patrice Lumumba and all those African boys, [Jomo] Kenyatta and them boys. And we used to enjoy reading the newspaper, because you had to read Gladstone Holder and Waldo Ramsey. I remember, "The mind boggles, to contemplate the tragic, calamitous consequences of a personal nature which would naturally flow from any such aberration." That was about the incident with the diplomatic dog.

Figure 8.2. Sharon Marshall (*seated*) being serenaded along with other excited patrons by Barbadian saxophone virtuoso Arturo Tappin, at Jazz on the Hill in January 1996. Jazz on the Hill was one of the most popular events of the Barbados Jazz Festival.

The Barbados Jazz Festival came about by accident really. Necessity is the mother of invention. GMR International Tours was never a production company, it was an incoming tour company. But it was undercapitalized. So out of necessity, the Barbados Jazz Festival was born with GMR International Tours as a production company.

A strange thing happens in life, when you do find what you're supposed to be doing, all of your life experience comes to bear on that. [About bringing some of the biggest names in music to Barbados for the jazz festival], I've never been one to stargaze, and it comes from my grandfather.

My mother gave me a story about this white fella that was in charge of the sugar factory. Something happened between him and my grandfather. My grandfather got up from by his machine and went and knocked on the man door and demanded respect. My grandfather was a strong man. So I am my grandfather's child. To people it seemed like it was all this, but to me it was the tools required to work. It never felt special that I attracted so many people. Some of them have become my friends, but to me it was a matter of getting something done.

I don't think that I'm sharper than anybody else, and I don't fool myself that I was the only person who could have done it. The idea was the right idea at the right time, and I happened to be the person at that time. It took a lot of guts, but I'm a Cuban. Your husband would tell you, when we put our mind to something, that is it.

I remember sitting at this establishment, and somebody . . . I would think that they didn't know it was me . . . but looking back now, I think they knew it was me. I heard, "Who Gilbert think he is? We tried doing this and we couldn't get it done." Don't tell me so; I'm a Cuban, ¡Caramba! Soy hijo de Fidel. [Heck! I'm a child of Fidel.] I'm a child of the Revolution. Don't tell me I can't do it. The mere fact that we left Cuba when we did, from a small place named Baraguá, where the streets are still dirt streets. Don't tell me that I can't do nothing. From the time I leave Cuba and come here, I was ahead of the game.

The jazz festival was about work; I don't think that you look at work as an achievement. There is an aspect of the jazz festival that I'm really happy about, but I don't talk about. Other people will have to talk about it. Let me adapt some of what Fidel said, history will deal with that, if history is fair.

At the end of my days, if I had to look at my successes and my failures, it would be gauged by my child and my grandchild. Whether I succeeded in teaching them well, whether I succeeded in making them outstanding people, as well as the fact that I kept my word to my mother who told me, "Don't forget the family in Cuba." I've got an uncle and cousins there. I've kept my word to my mother, that I look after Tío and the family. I still do. That means a lot to me. I promised my mother not to forget Hershel, not to forget Kelvin that passed away, God rest his soul. He was the backbone, because he came here before us with Granny. That was the backbone of our family when we first got here. There's always been someone in our family who took care of business. And I tell my son so all the time: his turn will come. And when his turn comes, don't ever say that the load is too much to bear. It's never too much to bear.

Barbados has been good to me; I wouldn't live anywhere else. All in all, I wouldn't change it [life in Barbados] for the world. I really would not, because my preferred place to be, apart from Cuba, is Barbados. Because I'm always a Cuban. I'm a Cuban. I don't ever want to deny that fact. Somebody born in Israel is always a Jew; they could live any part of the world. A Barbadian leaves here and goes to Germany, he's a Barbadian. I am a Cuban of Barbadian descent that was brought to Barbados, and Barbados accepted me. And I would like to think that I made a contribution. But I am a Cuban; that's who I am and will always be until the day I die.

Gilbert Rowe's interview was recorded on 5 February 2018 at his property "Sandalwood Estate" in Hothersal, St Michael.

CHAPTER 9

GRACIELA KING

Hometown: Guantánamo City, Guantánamo
Barbados connection: Father
Occupation: Spanish teacher
Arrival year: 1973

I REMEMBER SO MANY THINGS ABOUT GROWING UP in Guantánamo. I was born in Guantánamo on the first of January 1958. I was always a studious person, so going to school was a lot of fun for me, because I always wanted to do my best. I was the Spanish monitor in my Spanish class, and that allowed me to teach the class, and I used to read the news from *Granma*, the diary of what was happening with Fidel every day. I had liked reading and was always happy to read. So I enjoyed going to school.

Apart from that, I remember that being home in the neighbourhood, we used to play a lot. A group of us, we used to make a circle and play all sorts of games. A guy used to pass selling *biscocho*, or *maní*, so we used to look forward to that. My mother used to allow us to come out after school and play around five o'clock, and by seven o'clock or eight o'clock, we had to get ready to go in our bed. It was my brother, two sisters and myself.

Also, when I was a little bit older, I used to go out with my sisters on weekends. We used to go to the park. We used to go all around the park, all around the park, and we used to meet this body and the ... every weekend we used to meet the same people, but we used to look forward to that. So things like that, I can't forget.

My mother was Cuban; she was born in Cuba. Her name was Francisca Salinas Torres. She was a very loving mother. I was very close to my mother. Almost everywhere she went, I used to go. Every week, we used to go to visit the family. So we used to go by my aunt, then after we leave my aunt's house we used to go by my uncle. Sometimes we would leave my grandmother's house and go by my aunt. We used to go from house to house like that.

When it was *carnaval* time, that was a special time. My father used to make sure that he would take us, and he used to buy all sorts of things for us. We used to be all over the place. But then, they used to have these two guys; one we used to call Negro Fino and the other one we used to call him Bobito. And there was another guy whose name I can't remember, but he wasn't as popular. They used to have *paseos*. Let me tell you, when they used to have rehearsals and you had *congas* coming out, everybody used to come out at night and everybody behind them. ¡La conga!, and so on. My mother didn't let me out because I was still small, but I would never forget this evening ... we used to go to lessons at these two ladies who lived not too far from us at the corner ... and one of those ladies had loved the *conga*. Let me tell you, that evening I said, "I am not staying." I left the house with her and we gone behind *la conga*, and it was wonderful!

Another thing is, not too far from where I used to live, there in El Tres on the corner, the guys used to get together every weekend and they used to be beating drums and everything. And I love the drums, it's one of my favourite instruments. So I come along with that beat, that kind of African beat. That's what I love more about Cuba.

My father was Barbadian. His name was Nathaniel Niles. He told me he was about twenty-one when he left here to go to Cuba, and he was born in 1900. He told me that Barbados looked a lot like Cuba, and that it was a British colony and so on, but that was all I heard. He didn't used to talk a lot, but I believe that he started cutting cane, but maybe for a very short time. His brother had taught him carpentry before he left here. So then he went to work doing carpentry, and then fairly early he worked at the US naval base as a carpenter. He worked there for about thirty years, and that's where he retired from. He came back to Barbados in 1969. They wouldn't have paid his pension if he remained in Cuba.

My mother, my sister Ydania and I came in 1973. My sister and brother Taida and Pedro, were in their twenties and they remained in Cuba. My brother Emilio too. We left Cuba and went to Mexico. We spent three days in Mexico City. There were other Barbadians . . . other people . . . that left around the same time as us, that were connected to these islands. It was an experience. They spoke English among themselves. Then we went to Jamaica, and then to Barbados. We spent only hours in Jamaica; we got there around midday and then we left in the evening around six o'clock.

My father was at the airport to meet us, together with a couple of friends. He was so happy because he spent those years without us. And he used to cry all the time, he missed us, and he wanted my mother to come. He had already purchased a house there in Kensington New Road. That's where we settled down.

Coming to Barbados was hard. At first, I was happy because I was leaving Cuba. But then after, when I got here, and I could not speak a word of English, and I didn't know anybody, I wanted to go back to Cuba. I used to cry, I wanted

Figure 9.2. Graciela (*right*) with other members of the Niles family. *From left to right*: sister Ydania, mother, Francisca, and father, Nathaniel. She is holding her nephew Onel. Courtesy of Graciela King.

to go back to Cuba. But I couldn't go back. My parents would not have let me go to live with my brother and sister. So it was very hard at first. I was brokenhearted when I first got here.

Apart from not speaking the language, I think that another thing was that when I got here, Barbados was not developed at all. I couldn't believe what I saw when I got here because I saw men walking barefoot. I mean in Cuba, although things were difficult and so on, I never saw anybody walking without shoes. I saw men pulling this thing like a cart, and the women, they were wearing these big dresses, carrying these things on their heads. I didn't expect that, because in Cuba when I lived there, everything was so modern to me. All of that had me very, very sad. I was a bit disappointed.

But then I said, "I have no choice; I have to learn to speak the language." And I tried to adapt myself. My father got us enrolled at Springer Memorial [Secondary School]. There were a couple of teachers there who spoke Spanish – Spanish teachers. So they were able to help us if we needed any help, or in translating something. But we didn't have a teacher to teach us the language; I had to learn the language by listening and I had to sit in the class like everybody else. When they were doing history . . . my father bought us all the books . . . I had to try to follow. And I had an English-Spanish dictionary, so I used to communicate with the dictionary, word for word. I had to look for the word and tell my friends what I wanted to say. Or if they told me something, they would look in the dictionary and show me what they wanted to tell me. And that's how I used to communicate. If I heard a word often, I would go home and ask my father, "What does that mean?" And he would tell us, "Well, it means this . . .", and so on. That's how I learned the language. That's how I learned to write it to a certain extent, and to read it, because I used to follow up with the reading at school.

I made friends at school. There were a couple of girls who were from Trinidad. When I got to school, the children would not go to the classes. They wanted to hear my sister and me speak Spanish. And that had me so upset, because I said to myself, "They never heard about another language? Why are they getting on like that?" I was so vexed. We used to sit down under a tree to have our break, and the principal had to come and send the children to the class and move them from around us, because they wouldn't leave. My hair was longer than this, and they wanted to know . . . pulling my hair, "This is your hair?" I didn't like that experience. To me, it was a bit annoying. I didn't expect that. But, apart from that, they were nice.

Figure 9.3. Graciela (*left*) with her sister Ydania at a picnic during their early days in Barbados. Courtesy of Graciela King.

As I said, I met the girls from Trinidad. They were very friendly, and some Barbadians too from my class. We used to communicate. There was a girl who used to live not too far from us, and her uncle went to Cuba. So she told us, "My uncle went to Cuba, he speaks Spanish." So then I went by her house once or twice to meet her uncle, and we used to be kind of close.

After Springer Memorial, soon after that, I started to work. I didn't do many CXC [Caribbean Examinations Council] subjects; I did Spanish. I worked first of all at a place that was called India House, next to Cave Shepherd [department store]. And after that, I went to Holiday Inn and worked at the front desk. Then the name was changed to Grand Barbados. Then I left Grand Barbados. I was tired working shift, and I had my children by then. I said, "I don't want to work shift all the time." And they paid me out. I started to work then at BNB [Barbados National Bank]. I worked there for three months. But I had applied to the Ministry of Education and while I was at the bank, they called me and said they wanted me to come and work in the schools.

At first I was at four schools in Christ Church – St Christopher, Vauxhall, Christ Church Girls and then St Matthias, which is now Arthur Smith Primary. Right now, I am between St Mary's Primary and Wesley Hall Primary. I love working with the primary school children. They make me laugh a lot. The majority of them want to learn the language. Because I make sure that they participate often, they look forward to be part of the class and to do the

Spanish. I let them sometimes come to the class and ask questions, and they like that. They like to be in charge, so I allow them to be in charge many times. I like teaching the Spanish.

I went back to Cuba only once. That's when you and I went together; your mother and mine were on that trip too. That was in 1989. That first visit was really wonderful. I was so happy to be back, I almost cried. I was so happy to be back in that environment, and with my family and the people and the culture. It was wonderful! I can't forget that experience, it was really nice. Living in Cuba, I didn't get to go many places. But by going back, I spent a very short time in Havana, and I was able to visit different places with the tour and see other places. So that's why I really enjoyed it. When I went back and we went to Guantánamo, it was *carnaval* time. So we went out with my sister and so on. And in Paseo, we had a lot of drinks and so on. It was nice. I really hope that I can have that experience again soon.

Your mother and mine used to talk all the time; they went back to Cuba together since that first trip. I'm now trying to get myself organized to go back. Because having the children, I decided that I didn't want to travel at that time. It was more difficult. But now that it is better, it is easier, I'm making arrangements and I hope that this year I can go back. My children Alina and Kynan, and John [King] my husband, they would like to go. They would love to go. Kynan asks me, "Mummy, why didn't you let me be born in Cuba?" He loves Cuba, although he has never been to Cuba. They've heard so much about Cuba. I would tell them about Cuba, my mother and so on. So he is really looking forward to going now.

My father died in 1992, and my mother in 2002. I still have a sister in Guantánamo, and a brother, Emilio. My sister in Cuba is Taida. My brother Pedro passed away. I was born after Pedro. Taida and I communicate often. And one of my mother's brothers – one of my uncles – we talk often. He's been here a couple of times, so we still communicate. My nieces and nephew, we still keep in touch.

My sister that is here, Ydania, her English is not like mine. Although I don't consider mine to be the best. But she didn't do so well at school. She doesn't speak English as fluently as me. But I think that she kind of adapted faster. She's younger than me and she had her children before me. She was able to communicate, not the best, but very well in her broken English. I think that she is very comfortable. I find that she is happy to be here. She has five children and five grandchildren. She has never been back to Cuba since she came. So I would have to find out if she considers herself Cuban or Barbadian. I would not be surprised if she said Barbadian.

I still feel that I'm Cuban. I know that I've lived here longer, but I consider myself Cuban. So I still try to follow up and do a lot of things as a Cuban. I still make *el macho* . . . *puerco asado* . . . and everything like a Cuban. I knew in Cuba that at some stage, we had to learn another language. But to be able now to speak both English and Spanish, to this level, I am very proud about that. I am proud that I can speak two languages.

Let me tell you the truth, I don't always feel accepted in Barbados, not all the time. I find that people still discriminate. If they hear that you speak with an accent, that makes a difference. They still don't consider you a Barbadian. I am a Barbadian by descent, but not everybody welcomes you as a Barbadian. Sometimes I can see the difference and I don't feel happy about it, but there's nothing I can do about it. I think that they feel because you were not born here, you don't know what's going on. You're not smart enough or something like that. That is the feeling I get sometimes from people. So sometimes I have to let people know in a smart way that I have been living here for a long time, don't mind I was born in Cuba. And my father was a Barbadian. I have to make that clear to them sometimes.

On 12 January 2018, Graciela King's interview was recorded at her home in Crystal Heights, St James.

CHAPTER 10

ISABEL DEANE

Hometown: Guantánamo City, Guantánamo
Barbados connection: Husband
Occupation: Banker
Arrival year: 1975

MY DAD WAS FROM ST LUCIA AND NOT Barbados. His name was Charles Enrique (Henry) Willie, known to all Cubans as Enrique and to his fellow West Indians as Henry. He migrated to Cuba in 1927. He was twenty-five years old at that time and worked in the sugar cane industry.

Then he went over to work at the US naval base in Guantánamo, where he was a carpenter for over thirty-five years. In those days, the people working on the US naval base lived mostly in Guantánamo vicinity and commuted to and from the base every day by bus or boat, departing from the port of Boquerón (a small fishing village half an hour's ride from Guantánamo).

He met my mother there – Eunice Dolores Adlum. She was born in Cuba of Jamaican parents. They were married in 1948. My mom worked from home as a seamstress, she even made my wedding dress in 1975. She had seven girls and then one boy to complete the family – Carmen, Delia, Lilvina, then me, Norma, Dolores, Deisy, and my brother, Juaquin.

I remember that Guantánamo was a little town, not very developed, with around 120,000 inhabitants. It didn't have a lot of buildings and stores, just little shops, but a very warm community and family around us. I only knew my mother's father. All the other grandparents had passed away.

Figure 10.2. Isabel's parents, Eunice and Charles Willie. Courtesy of Isabel Deane.

Growing up, we skipped, played house with dolls, and I remember living very close to a river, which was a recreation venue with other children in the neighbourhood. We played baseball and we did lots of skipping games. I attended the primary school José Maria Mendive and the secondary school Regino Boti. In Cuba, we didn't study English, and my dad hardly spoke to us in English. My mother didn't know any English either. Then during the summer vacation, we had to go into the fields to complete field work in a programme known as *De cara al campo*. We had to spend a few days away from home to pick tomatoes, coffee, cucumbers or any other fruits and vegetables, instead of going to church.

As life started to get harder with the communist system, my father said he was told that if he remained in Cuba, he would receive his naval base pension from Washington in pesos, and there was no proper exchange at the time. That urged my dad even more to leave Cuba for his birthplace, St Lucia, with six of us. Carmen and Delia, who were married, remained with their spouses.

My father tended not to speak much about St Lucia, so we didn't even know about our family in St Lucia. I know he had left two sisters and a son we met when we went to live in St Lucia in 1969. But he never spoke about his parents.

Figure 10.3. The Willie family. Back row (*left to right*): daughters Norma, Delores, Lilvina, Isabel. Front row (*left to right*): daughter Deisy, patriarch, Charles Enrique (Henry) Willie, matriarch, Eunice, and son, Juaquin. Courtesy of Isabel Deane.

Leaving was very traumatic and a bittersweet occasion for us, because we were leaving friends and family that we grew up with, and at the same time it was the first time we were going on an aircraft, which was very exciting for us. I was only nineteen when I left Cuba, and the others were younger than me, except Lilvina. So it was exciting to leave. And that was the first time that we went to Havana. We went from Havana to the Cayman Islands, then to Jamaica, and from there to St Lucia.

Arriving in St Lucia was like going to another world, because we didn't expect to see certain things that we were accustomed to. The excitement was the plane, but when we got to St Lucia, Hewanorra Airport, it was very deserted, lots of animals around it. They didn't have a lot of cars or buses in those days, so it was really traumatic commuting on foot. We drove from Vieux Fort in the south to the capital Castries in the north. My father had a friend, Sam; he and his wife used to live in Cuba too. They waited for us and took us to Castries and into their home until we found a house to rent.

When we got to St Lucia, we could not speak English at all, but we were forced to learn. When my dad inquired about schooling, he was told that we were too old to attend secondary school, and without any background of English it would have been very difficult. So we attended private lessons. Only Deisy and Juaquin were enrolled at school. We had to learn the language because when people were speaking to us we didn't understand and they laughed at us. We girls used to wear stockings, and they would tease us saying that we were wearing false legs.

I started to work in a retail store as a sales clerk. Then a new bank called Chase Manhattan Bank was coming to St Lucia, and I applied there. The general manager was from Puerto Rico and he spoke Spanish. My interview was done in Spanish. I worked in the bank from 1972 until 1975, when I came to

Figure 10.4. Isabel and her husband Brian sharing a happy moment at home.

Barbados to live with my husband. I met my husband, Brian Courtenay Deane, in St Lucia in 1973.

His parents were Barbadians living in St Lucia. We both are Methodists and his mom also. We got married in 1975 here in Barbados at Bethel Methodist Church. His father is now deceased, but his mother is still alive. She's eighty-nine years old.

To me it was exciting because I used to come to Barbados on holiday before and it was much more advanced than St Lucia. I always said that if I went to live anywhere else it would be in Barbados. I liked the pace of life, the buildings, education, et cetera. I was at home for a couple of months but then my sister-in-law was able to get me a job at the same attorney's office where she worked as a typist. I also did typing and filing. Then the attorney was closing his office because he was going up for election. I told him that I had experience in banking and he had a contact in banking whom he referred me to. I went for the interview and passed, and then joined the bank in 1977, while I was pregnant with my first child.

I worked at Canadian Imperial Bank of Commerce. Then it became First-Caribbean International Bank. And then the name was changed to CIBC First-Caribbean. I worked there for thirty-six years. I started as a teller and worked in different areas. I went to the corporate department as a loans officer, disbursing large loans and dealing with security documents. I left with a wealth of knowledge.

It was a little difficult because my English was not that good, but by doing courses and so on I managed to progress. You tend to learn by listening to people, and I give kudos to my husband. He really, really helped me a lot.

Knowing Spanish has been an advantage for me. I actually did a lot of translation for the bank, free of charge. I was the translator for the entire bank, dealing with customers and documents. One day when a customer learned from one of my colleagues that I was born in Cuba, he said he thought that Cuban people were more clear-skinned people. I said, "That's ignorance." Before, people here thought that the people in Cuba were living in huts and eating from the garbage dump. But now people are more educated and they understand that is not so.

Now I'm retired since 2013 and enjoying life. In the first year I missed work. At the beginning, I was like a fish out of water, but now I'm busier than ever, doing line dancing, enjoying the camaraderie with the group and the activities that we do. I'm also involved in the church [Hawthorn Methodist Church], assisting with the communion and visiting the shut-ins with the minister. I also do a great deal of gardening at home.

Brian and I have two children – Aisha Lois, born in 1977 – and then a son – Aaron Nicholas, born in 1978. Right now they are so far away from us. Aisha married a young man from Zambia and they have a daughter named Everly. We've been there twice to visit them. And Aaron is married to an Ethiopian Canadian and residing in Ottawa, Canada.

At the beginning, the Cuban community here in Barbados was close, but I find that a lot of people have come in now that you don't even know them. Sometimes they have activities and you don't even know. You only hear that they had something. We're not that close anymore.

I've never returned to Cuba. I don't know why. Every year we're planning to go, but we don't get there. So people are saying to me, "How come you've been to Africa twice but you've never been back to Cuba?" I say, "Cuba is just there, but Africa is so far away." We're all planning to meet in Cuba in 2019. Keeping our fingers crossed. We kept in contact with our sisters in Cuba regularly 'til they died. Whenever there is someone I know going to Cuba, I take the opportunity to send money to my family. Delia has a daughter who still lives in Guantánamo, and she has a daughter of her own. I also have some cousins in Havana.

Of course I consider myself a Barbadian, after living here for the past forty-two years. Even when travelling, I miss Barbados. When I go anywhere, after a little while I say, "It's time to go home."

This interview with Isabel Deane was conducted at her home in Frere Pilgrim, Christ Church on 8 November 2017.

CHAPTER 11

COLBERT BELGRAVE

Hometown: Baraguá, Ciego de Ávila
Barbados connection: Father
Occupation: Music teacher and organist
Arrival year: 1979

MY FATHER, CLEOPHAS BELGRAVE, LEFT HERE WHEN HE was about seventeen/eighteen years old. He spent about two years in Cuba, and then he came back, and went back the following year. Because, as you would understand, life was very difficult here at that point in time. It was either cutting cane . . . well there wasn't anything else to be done.

He went to Cuba. There he met my mother, Monica Gill, and they got married in 1938. My mother was born in Panama but her father was Barbadian and her mother was Jamaican. Her father originated from Water Street in Christ Church. The place where my parents ended up being was Central Baraguá.

I was born in Baraguá, on the 11th of October, 1950. I remember going to the Adventist school. There we had a teacher who was also an Adventist, by the

Figure 11.2. Young Colbert (*centre*) at school with teachers and other members of his class in Central Baraguá. Courtesy of Colbert Belgrave.

name of Ruby Skyers. And from there then we went on to secondary school, and then on to college.

But growing up in Baraguá was always beautiful. Because I grew up in Bajan Town, which – as you know – was where most Bajans, and West Indians on a whole, lived. So we had a lot of customs and things that are done here in Barbados that when I came here to Barbados I was not a stranger to. For example, like now coming on to Christmas season, you would have a lot of sorrel and a lot of black cake.

Growing up there was an experience because in my mind I never thought I would travel to Barbados. My father always said he wanted to come to Barbados, but we as children – my brother Eddy and I – felt that was a joke. And today I realize that it's a reality.

My father always used to praise Barbados. He would always say it was difficult, it was hard, but Barbados was the loveliest island in the Caribbean. I used to ask him, "But Daddy, if it was so lovely, why did you come to Cuba?" So he would say, "Well things were hard at that time, but I want to go back there. I want to rest my bones there, and I want you and Eddy to be there with me."

At that point in time, growing up in Cuba, we had this law that when you reach a certain age, you could not leave the island. You had to go to military service. I was born being an asthmatic, and my father knew that and he said that he never wanted me to go through the military service. So what he did, which was very tactful and helpful, he made sure that by the time I was fifteen years old, I had a British passport. So that would have meant that I could not go to military service. But you still had to do the theory part at university or college. And then quickly after, I got me a Barbadian passport.

I came to Barbados with my mother in 1979. My brother had come with my father in 1973. Seeing that my brother was going to complete his fifteen years shortly, my father did not want the military service to catch up with him. So what he did, he brought along my brother first. So my brother lived here two years, and then my aunt Melba Reece, my mother's sister ... she's dead now ... sent for him in the United States. He's there up to now, in Kansas City.

So when I landed here in Barbados, I landed with my Cuban passport, my British passport and my Barbadian passport. But I didn't know any better, because my Cuban passport had the visa for the entry into Barbados. So I took out my Cuban passport and I showed it to the immigration officer. He was very annoyed. He said, "I don't understand that thing. You ain't no Bajan. Your mother, yes. Your mother can stay, but I don't understand your situation. I might have to deport you back." I said to him ... I was so angry ... "Look, if you're going to deport me, do it before Cubana leaves, because the plane is leaving shortly." My mother was saying, "Colbert, don't argue. We just left Cuba. Look your father is up there waiting. Don't say those things." I said, "But Mum, he's saying that he is going to deport me, and this is the passport that Cuba stamp saying that I can leave Cuba and I have permission to enter Barbados."

He asked me, "So who's waiting for you?" I said, "Look my father." He said, "I give you permission to go out there and call your father." I said, "No, you call him." So my father was upstairs. At that time they didn't have it all sealed off like how it is now. And my father came in. As soon as my father came in, my father said, "Colbert, where is your Bajan passport?" I said, "I have them all here. I have the Cuban, the Bajan and the British passport." So as soon as I said that, the immigration officer changed his attitude completely. "Oh no, no", he said. "You have no problem. Come let me see. You are fit to go. Can I have your telephone number here?" I told him, "Ask my father; I don't know the telephone number here." So my father gave him and a few days later he called, and he came down and visited us in St Peter. Because we were staying in St Peter at that time. We are very good friends now, Clarence Harewood.

So it's a history of mixed feelings because leaving Cuba to come to Barbados, never travelled out of Cuba in my whole life, that was quite painful. I missed Cuba those first months and years. I cried all the time, and that used to get my father annoyed. Because he said, "I struggled to get you all here, and now you come to Barbados, you are not happy here." I said, "Well Daddy, I just miss my friends. I just can't get adjusted here. I wish I could go back tomorrow."

It was an adjustment. One, yes, I spoke a little bit of English. Not as well as I can now, but I defended myself. The language was a bit of a barrier. And especially when the folks spoke Bajan dialect! That threw me away totally. I could not understand one thing. But it took a while to get more or less readjusted, to meet friends. Thank God I met quite a number of friends here who have been very supportive. And then the church family too. That made a great difference to me. At the end, today, I feel happy being here in Barbados. I feel happy to have been able to achieve the things that I have achieved in life here. Because it wasn't easy, but with hard work, you persevere to get things done.

I didn't go to school here. I did some courses with my music, with the organ. Because I never played the organ in Cuba, it was the piano. Then when I started teaching at Lodge School in 1983, I had to go to Erdiston [Teachers' Training College] for some training for certain things regarding the same music stuff.

My first job was at Lodge School. I really enjoyed teaching there. The students were witty, but they were mannerly. Today I am happy because they are now big grown-up men and women. They see you and they show you the respect. I really enjoyed teaching at Lodge School. From Lodge, I went to St Lucy Secondary School. That was a transition that totally transformed me from night to day, because I really had to work a bit harder. The children there were a bit slower and you had to explain things over and over. But in the end when they saw that you were persistent with them, and showed them that you care, then they would come around. They were kind too in the end.

Coming from Lodge School was an adjustment. Let's look at the journey. I was living here in West Terrace. Although they say that no place is far in Barbados. But coming from St John to St Lucy, from one extreme of the island to another, you say, "Well, wow!" That's something that you have to get accustomed to now. With time, I got there. I spent ten years at St Lucy Secondary. I was teaching part-time, three days a week. So I would leave from here, and go down a track down the bottom of the hill here. It wasn't with steps as there are now, so sometimes you would fall down and you get back up. And you go down those hilly tracks 'til you get to Jordan's Supermarket, and that's where I would get my bus that would go to St Lucy.

So it wasn't easy. I tell people that yes, I have a car, and today I can get around easier. But in those days, you didn't have a car, so you had to do a bit of walking and a little bit of riding on the bus. Like how we say in Cuba, "*Un poco con San Fernando*" [A little with San Fernando], San Fernando meaning the two legs that you have. The rest, you wait for the bus.

From St Lucy, I then came over to West Terrace Primary School in 1997. But there was familiar to me, because before I started teaching here, I used to go and help them for graduation or any other special occasions that they had. Because I have a very dear friend of mine, Yvonne Jordan, and she would come for me and take me to West Terrace to practise the children. So I knew West Terrace before I went there to teach, so it was an easy transition. I knew partly all the teachers who were there and they knew me. So it wasn't difficult really to get things done there. And I enjoyed my nearly twenty years there at West Terrace. The children are nice, and you see them grow up and become young men and women and that they have achieved something in life. I retired from the teaching service in the last school term and I'm trying to enjoy it to the fullest.

One of the things that I'm proud of is the fact that, with God's help, I've been able to buy this house that we're in. Because when we came from Cuba, we came without practically anything. And that was one of the things that my father said to me. He would say, "Colbert, I don't want to die leaving you here renting nobody's home. I want you to get your own home, and that you will be able to pay for it and enjoy it. And if you don't want to live here in Barbados, don't sell it. Rent it out, but when the year come, you can come back and spend some time here in Barbados. But don't you ever sell your house." So that's one of the things I'm really happy about, that God has helped me to really achieve that as one of the major things I wanted to achieve in life.

I am happy for the achievements, that God has allowed me to get the things that I have been able to achieve. And also I want to thank the government of Barbados for allowing me to be here and to be able to work here in Barbados and to be able to achieve the things that I have achieved here.

In terms of my career, when I went to Lodge School, something I think of is my very first Speech Day. I was new to the school and they informed me that they were going to have this Speech Day and they wanted several things done with the choir and myself. I said, "Okay." But then I spoke with some of the other teachers and I said to myself, "Okay, I don't want that this choir go up there and just perform for a Speech Day." Because they told me that it's something big and they're going to have the parents and the folks from the

Ministry [of Education]. "I want to get these children looking different." They asked, "How different?" I said, "Well, I want them to wear blazers over their uniforms." They said, "Mr Belgrave, that will take some money." I said, "Yes. I would understand. What I'm going to do is, I'm going to get a letter written to all the parents, and I'm going to speak to Mr Abed – because I knew him personally – to see if he can give us some kind of discount on the material."

And don't doubt me, it was Speech Day time, the guests arriving and the choir ready, and the blazers were not there as yet. I was panicking! And about five/ten minutes before the programme began, this van turned up with all these blazers. That time I had to rush and get the children and try on the blazers to see which fit who. But eventually, everybody had their blazers. This was something that I wanted done, and I got it done.

Then I went to St Lucy Secondary. Obviously because of the slower process of the children learning, this education officer, Radcliffe Hinkson – he's Adventist too – said to me, "I want you to do the impossible with these children, but you must show them off for me on Speech Day." There again, I said, "Well I'm not going to get blazers, but I have to work with these children hard enough and make sure that I teach them the words to these songs. I'm not giving them to go home with it, because I know the situation. I'm going to teach them the words and teach them these two songs. And they must learn these words for me."

The three days [a week] I go down there, I told the headteacher, "Look, I cannot teach any other class. I have to make sure that I have the choir in here so that they learn these words. He said, "No problem Mr Belgrave. If you can get them to learn the words, that's all I want." I really went through horrors to get them to learn the words. But they did learn the words. And the day of the Speech Day, again they made me proud. They sang; nobody fumbled or mumbled. And at the end, coming off the stage they said, "Mr Belgrave, did we do well?" I said, "Yes, you did well." So that was another achievement in my teaching.

Coming to West Terrace, about the second year I was there, I told them that I wanted to have this music festival. And I was bringing some other invited guests, but performers that would perform with the children. I wanted the choir to be the main highlight. So they told me, "No problem." I spoke to NCF [National Cultural Foundation] to bring the stage. They set up the stage. And there was a teacher there, Mrs Prescod . . . she's now retired. Her husband is a pastor, and he said he could get us a tent. But this tent was a big tent, because they use it when the Adventists having crusades. The tent came the evening, and I'm wondering now how we're going to get up this tent. He came, and between himself, his wife, and another teacher who is still there, Mrs Blackman, and myself, we decide to put up this tent. And we put up the tent. I had never pitched a tent in my life, so you can imagine. At that time I was playing the organ at St Lucy's Parish Church, and it was a Thursday night and we had rehearsals. After we done get the tent up, you know the tent fell back down again. Well there we are, struggling to put back up the tent, and when we finished it was nearly eight o'clock. From there I left straight. I didn't even come home, I didn't shower, nothing. I went straight to St Lucy to practise.

The following day was Friday. When we got to the school, the tent was still standing. I said, "Good! Praise the Lord. At least we did something good because the tent did not fall down again." The press was there that day, the children performed well, and I was kind of pleased. I was even more pleased that the tent did not fall down. So those are things that I look at, that I have really felt happy about, that I was able to do here in Barbados to help the nation's children, and to really see them do something good.

Apart from playing the organ for the Seventh-day Adventist church, of which I am a member, I started playing for the Anglican church at St Andrew's Parish Church for Father [Edward] Gatherer.[1] That was in 1995. I had never been to St Andrew before, so I didn't know how to get there. Someone explained to me that I should take the bus in Eagle Hall, and that would take me to St Andrew, going up hills and valleys. I'm thinking, "What time am I going to get there?" The first day playing, it was raining and I got there late. Service began at eight o'clock, I got there around eight thirty. I apologized to the priest. He said, "No problem." So I kept working there.

And I remember one day, a lady who used to work . . . she was a loans officer at Barclays Bank. One day she came to me and said, "Mr Belgrave, how you get up here every Sunday? Very seldom you're late and you're

Figure 11.3. Colbert playing the organ at church in Barbados. Courtesy of Colbert Belgrave.

here for eight o'clock service." I said, "Well, I leave home early. I leave home at six o'clock, and I take the bus in Eagle Hall at XY time, and I get up here. She said, "You don't need a car?" I said, "Yes, I would really love a car, but I can't afford a car now. And with my salary, working two and a half, three days . . ." She said, "I'm going to think about it, and I'm going to give you a call, because you need to get some kind of transportation to get up here." Eventually she got it all sorted out, and I got my little red car. So I was going to St Andrew much easier. I could leave here around seven, quarter past seven, and get up there in time for worship. I played there until the year 1999, when I went on to play at St Lucy's Parish Church.

Well that was a little more responsibility, more work, but I enjoyed playing at St Lucy's Parish Church. I played there from 1999 to 2004. And I went on to St Cyprian's. I played there for a year, and from there, I am at Holy Trinity now playing. I enjoy it, but it's a bit challenging sometimes.

I've been back to Cuba several times to visit. I can't count the years, because there've been so many times that I've been back. But I'm sure I went back this year. Because due to my health challenges now, I was in Cuba this year in the month of August. I spent a whole month in Cuba. I'm always excited when I go back to Cuba, because of family. But also I have a host of friends that we grow up together, so there's always this joy going back home. Regardless of how difficult things can be sometimes, and are in Cuba, I'm extremely happy. From the time that I know that I am going to Cuba, I have the ticket, I am excited. By the time I get on the plane, and touching down in Havana, I get more emotional. Cubans are very emotional. It's only that sometimes when I get into Cuba that, like your mother used to say, Sharon, you wonder, "¿Que va a pasar ahora?", "What's going to happen now, when I get to Customs?" Because I'm taking in so many things. This last time it worked out quite well; there were no questions. Everything went off quite well. I'm always happy going back to Cuba.

It's only about the past three or four years that I realized that I have relatives by my father's side in Cuba. I did not know. I thought they all had died. But there I met some cousins, and when we checked back everything . . . the history, they're Belgraves also. And my father's uncle, which is my great uncle, used to live in a place called Central Delicias in Oriente. And they are from there too, but they're living in Havana now. So we all link back up now again. So I can say, yes, I have quite a number of cousins in Cuba still from my father's side. I maintain contact with them. And now with the help of technology we can communicate via the WhatsApp and Messenger, and whatnot. I communicate with them quite often. Up to this morning a very close friend of mine sent me an email. We are in constant contact. I try in whatever way possible to keep in touch.

My brother who lives in the United States always laughs at me, because he says that I am still very Cubanized, *muy cubano*, while he is very much American. He's never been back to Cuba, and it's over forty years that he left. He wants to go back now. Every year he wants to go, and he can't decide yet. He says now that when he goes, he has to go with me. He's not going there alone. And I tell him, "Nothing is going to happen to you." But the idea is that I always felt that I should be of help in some way to them, those Cuban friends and relatives. Because when I was there, they were very close to me, and I think it's a way of giving back something to them. I try to assist in whatever way possible.

I'm a Cuban Barbadian. Barbados is home because I plan to live here. I have a home here, thank God for that. But as I always tell my friends here in Barbados, and my friends in Cuba as well, that I will always be there with them and for them. I love my Cuba, and whatever I can do, I will always be there. But I know that I have roots here in Barbados. My father was Barbadian, and my grandparents too. So I am proud to be a Barbadian, a Cuban Barbadian.

The interview with Colbert Belgrave was done on 6 December 2017 at his home in West Terrace, St James. Colbert made his final visit to Cuba in August/September 2018. He died in Barbados on 4 November 2018.

CHAPTER 12

MARIA THOMAS FERRIER

Hometown: Guantánamo City, Guantánamo
Barbados connection: Father
Occupation: Accountant
Arrival year: 1994

MY FATHER, GERALD ETHELBERT THOMAS, LEFT BARBADOS TO go to Cuba at twenty-one years old, with two of his brothers – Everton Aaron Christopher and Leonard, who died some years later. My father was born 17 December 1899, in Grave Yard, St Lucy, Barbados.

He met my mother, Romualda Ferrier Hechavarria, in Santiago de Cuba in 1930. They married six months later and she remained a housewife. From that marriage, they had nine children – Sylvia Dora, José Francisco, Alicia Esperanza, Gerald, Maria Guillermina, Roberto, Francisco Alonso, Maria Rosenda and Adriano Thomas Ferrier. The older siblings were born in Santiago de Cuba, the younger ones were born in Guantánamo. I was born 17 March 1949, in Guantánamo.

I remember when my father's friends used to come to visit our house, they used to talk in English. Among their friends was Nathaniel Niles, Mr Carl, Mr Henry, Mr Earl Alonso "Panama" Greaves. I remember none of us understood a word of English. We learned through my mother the story of how she met my father. We heard this story many times that my father was from Barbados where the native language was English. She spoke of the many times my father tried to teach her English. My mother would happily recall how strange the words sounded, and how with each attempt to repeat the words she would break down in fits of laughter.

As I recall, there were regular gatherings of friends and family at major celebrations, especially at Easter, Christmas Eve, Old Year's Night, New Year's. From my father's side, the only family I knew were my two uncles. My mother always said to us that my father had more family but they lived in Barbados, including his mother, Elvira Thomas. After he was in Cuba for some years, he received the letter with the sad news that his mother had died.

My father worked in the construction field as a foreman in Guantánamo Bay. My parents used to wake up early, around five o'clock each morning, from Monday to Saturday. Everybody had to wake up early too, helping my mother to prepare breakfast. He would leave for work at six o'clock and come back in the evening around six o'clock. Everybody would be waiting eagerly for my father to come from work on Fridays. Fridays because it was payday, and my father had the custom to give his children pocket money. For us children, that was a princely sum of money. With fifteen and twenty-five cents we lived like lords and ladies, feasting on all manner of sweets, gums and sweet biscuits.

I recall my father was a man of few words. He only engaged us in conversation when he needed to fix something around the house. He would seek the help of everyone. We would handle a chair or a table, saw, nail and hammer. My father never told us any stories about Barbados. During the Revolution, no one could go out and we could not go to school. When everything was normalized I was twelve or thirteen years old. That is when I entered Rafael Oregon Secondary School. After three years, I went to the Nguyen Van Troi Language School to learn English. Then I started working as a secretary at a law firm.

Marriage soon came, and with that my first child. I named her Maritza. My father used to enjoy talking and playing with her. My daughter was three years old and my father was retired. One day he told my daughter, "I am not going to see you anymore." As if Maritza knew what was going on. Later that year, my father came to Barbados, leaving us with my mother. After I moved to Havana, I worked in the day and studied at night. During the day, I worked for a taxi company in San Augustín and went to the university at night for five and a half years. I pursued a bachelor's degree in economic management. In Suchel perfume and soap factory, I worked as head of the accounting department. At Super Centre "Sears", Province Market and Variety Company, I worked as a principal accountant.

My father used to call my mother and tell her it was time for her to move to Barbados and keep his company. In 1978, my mother came to be reunited with my father in Barbados. In January 1989, my father went to Havana to go to the doctor, because he was not feeling well. We found out that he had prostate cancer. He spent about six months in Havana, and after he got the treatment at the Cira Garcia Hospital, he came back to Barbados. Two months later, my brother Adriano came to Barbados on an extended stay, helping with the care of our father.

In 1990, we had the sad news that my father had died. Roberto, Alicia Esperanza and I flew to Barbados for our father's funeral. My mother organized our flight with the Cuban consul in Barbados. They organized everything, and we only had to pick up the Cubana Airlines tickets at the office in La Rampa in Havana. The plane came direct from Cuba to Barbados. We spent a month here. Accompanying us back to Cuba was Hubert Dowridge, who had appointed himself our host while we were in Barbados. He arranged tours across the countryside, visiting places of interest. Mr Dowridge introduced us to fine dining at local restaurants.

After that, feeling somewhat lonely, my mother asked which of her children would like to spend three months with her. So my sister Alicia Esperanza and I came back to Barbados in 1992 for three months. That is when I met the rest of my father's family from St Lucy – Judy Hinds, Oriel Thomas, Sharon Thomas, Anthony Thomas, Patrick Davies, Carmen Austin, Ivan Phillips, Clotel Jordan, John Jordan, James Thomas, and my last surviving uncle, Joe Jordan, who later died in 1998. Among those whom we met on this trip was Rufus Hoyte, himself an early pioneer of that first migration to Cuba. I fondly remember him for the great support he offered my widowed mother. There was also Stephen Bryan, who helped me to secure my first job in Barbados at the Bridgetown Fisheries Complex.

There were several second-generation Cubans who had relocated to Barbados. These included Gloria Nelson, Colbert Belgrave, and Graciela and Ydania Niles. They played an outstanding role assisting my mother with the language barrier. Although my mother lived twenty-five years in Barbados, she had never learned to speak English. Among my mother's support was my uncle Everton Thomas, who lived nearby in Fairfield Main Road, Black Rock, St Michael. He asked my sister and me if we would like to live in Barbados. My sister said that she had her family in Cuba. I told my uncle, "I need to talk with my husband; I cannot answer right now." Also to be considered were my two daughters, Maritza and Niurka. He said "Okay. Take your time, and you can answer after you decide."

The next year – that was in 1993 – my mother went back to Cuba and she gave me the message, "Your uncle ask if you have the answer." I said, "Okay, tell my uncle I spoke with my husband and he said, 'No problem', but that I cannot leave my last daughter behind." Because she was nineteen years old. So I told her, "Tell my uncle that if I go there, I have to bring my daughter. And he will tell me what to do."

When she came back, she talked to my uncle, and he said, "No problem. I will organize for bringing her. You can bring your daughter." I said, "Okay." I told him that I had to wait until my daughter reached twenty years old. The next year, 1994, I started to organize everything, until I got through in June. I told him, "I am ready." He send the money for the tickets for my daughter and me. I came here – the date I'll never forget – 25 June 1994. That's when I came to live in Barbados, until now. Twenty-four years.

Everything was strange for me. I was not accustomed to being so far from all my family. I came here with my last daughter, Niurka, but the first one was still in Cuba with my husband. When I missed the country of my birth and my family, I would console myself with the idea, "If I don't feel comfortable here, I will go back to Cuba." Happily enough, my older daughter, Maritza, who had remained in Cuba joined us in 1995. The year after, 1996, my husband, Juan Matos Campo, came to Barbados, reuniting the entire family.

My good fortune continued. Someone from Guatemala was looking for a babysitter to take care of their little girl named Isabella. I accepted the assignment for two months. It was soon discovered that I was a qualified and experienced accountant. This led to a job offer working with the Guatemalan embassy, until the embassy closed in 1998. Six months before the embassy closed, I got a new job with Fomento y Cubiertas in 1997. Fomento y Cubiertas was a company based in Spain that had been awarded the contract to construct the South Coast sewerage system. I welcomed the opportunity to work at home for the Guatemalan embassy, while attending to the affairs of Fomento y Cubiertas, until I retired from the office in 2016.

A great source of pride is a blessing of a house bought for me by my uncle, and that's an important thing, because that is the basis for me starting my life here. I got the blessing from him. The last words he told me before he died were, "I would like God to keep blessing you." At that time, I wanted to take him to the hospital. I said "Uncle, come, put on your pyjamas. I want to take you to the hospital." He said "No, no, no. I already died. The only thing I want is for God to help you." I had to say, "Yes I would like that, really God bless me."

He bought me a house in Fairfield Main Road, Black Rock, St Michael, in

July 1996. He told me that he didn't want to die and leave me like that. I was renting an apartment in Belleville. The owner intended to sell it three months later, so I began my search for alternative accommodation. I talked with my uncle about what was happening and he told me, "I don't want to see that I die and people put you in the road because you don't have the money to pay rent. I will buy a house for you." He told me he was worried every day about finding a house for me. My uncle only told me after everything happened; he didn't tell me before. He would only ask me, "How you doing?", "You okay?", "You happy?" He didn't tell me anything, but he was worried about that.

So he started talking to people about houses for sale around him, because he wanted me to take care of him, and my mother. So the day he found somebody to talk to him about the house, he talked to me. Because I used to go to my uncle's house every Saturday and help his wife Phyllis and my mother. I was working at the Guatemalan embassy from Monday to Friday, and Saturday, I would go to my mother's house and help her. Then go to my uncle's house and help my uncle and his wife – cooking, washing clothes and pressing. All of those things my two daughters helped me with. After I'm done late in the evening, my uncle's wife's brother would take me home. I was living in Belleville at that time. Until he got me this house. That was July. I said, "Look Uncle, I got the key." He took the key and held it to the sky and said, "God, I can die now."

Everything was good, July, August, September. At the end of September, his wife got sick. She used to suffer from diabetes. He had to take her to the hospital. She went into the hospital in September. Every day I travel from my house and slept in my uncle house. I left my children home. I would go there, cook for him, do everything around the house. I was working at the embassy. That was '96. The embassy let me do the accounts at my uncle's house, because they knew my situation. Every evening we went with him, to see his wife at the clinic.

From October, he started getting sick too, and I arranged to take him to the same clinic. The two of them were put in the same room. That was at the end of November. They died the twenty-sixth of November 1996 and were buried the fourth of December. They died the same day; she died first. The nurse called me at home and said, "Phyllis passed away." I went there and waited until the rest of the family got to the clinic. I heard when the doctor told the nurse, "Mr Thomas is okay. Today, put him to walk a little bit." But my uncle's wife's sister came with me to the room, and she started asking the nurse questions. Both were in the same room, so he heard everything. He had a heart attack. The nurse said, "Go out of the room." And I started seeing all the nurses... running. "He died."

Maybe he heard all of that conversation and he died. She died maybe around six o'clock and he died around nine o'clock in the morning. They were buried together too. The fourth of December 1996. All of this happen so quickly. Then I continued to take care of my mother, until she died in 2003.

In the beginning, every year I would go back to Cuba, and then I would stay away for a little while – three or four years. Then go back again every year, until I retired. After retirement, I can't go because everything is so expensive. I still have family in Cuba. I have three siblings presently resident in Cuba. They are Alicia Esperanza, Maria Guillermina and Francisco Alonso, who is currently there receiving medical treatment. Two other surviving siblings: Roberto lives in Venezuela, while Adriano lives in the Dominican Republic. My siblings who have pre-deceased me are Gerald (1965), José Francisco (1988) and Sylvia Dora (2016).

I have my family with me – my husband, my two daughters, and my five grandchildren. I have three grandsons – Nicholas Holder, Tyrell Dyall and Marcus Otway – and two granddaughters – Nathania and Thalia Dyall.

I would say life has not been bad for me here. I feel proud that I am a Barbadian. I have all the rights of Barbadians, nothing different. I like Barbados, but not more than the place I was born. I consider myself half-Cuban and half-Barbadian.

The interview with Maria Thomas was recorded at her home in Fairfield, St Michael, on 8 April 2018.

CHAPTER 13

YOLANDA NELSON SPRINGER

Hometown: Baraguá, Ciego de Ávila
Barbados connection: Mother and father
Occupation: Spanish teacher
Arrival year: 1994

I WAS BORN IN BARAGUÁ, THE TENTH OF April 1956. I am the youngest out of eight brothers and sisters; we were six girls and two boys. There was a gap between them and me. In birth order, it is Elliot (we call him Birdie); Franklin (we call him Joe Louis); Ernestina (we call her Marva; my father gave her that nickname); Olivia (we call her Beba); Adela (we call her Nena); Gloria (we used to call her Vie; she passed away); Julia; and then me. Well Julia is so fortunate that she never got a nickname.

My father had an eldest son before he went to Cuba, who was born here in

Barbados. His son migrated to Trinidad, married and has children and grandchildren that live there now. His name was Norman Young; he passed away in February 2006. I forgot to mention that my mother had a daughter after Gloria, or before – I'm not too sure – but she died. Her name was Zenaida.

I grew up with Julia, and my peers who were my age, and they were also West Indian descendants. My best friend, her name is Elma, but we call her Suzy. She was an Elcock, Parris Elcock, a Barbadian descendant. And we grew together like sisters. We went to school together, and we only separated when I went away to study overseas. Some of the other Barbadian descendants that I grew up and went to school with are Erica Brewster; Lourdes Grant (she has passed away); Charles Scantlebury; Roberto Lashley (we used to call him Robbie); Gilbert Rowe who is living here now; Suzy's brother, Ernesto Parris (we used to call him Nesty). He has passed away. Alfred Carty, he's living right now in New York, and we correspond a lot on Facebook; Eddy Belgrave, Colbert's brother. He's living now in Kansas City. We were together in a class. The primary school was called Mariana Grajales, the name of a lady who was a national hero. Our classroom was mixed with Cuban children.

In Baraguá, we grew up in a town they used to call Bajan Town. There were a lot of West Indians living there. They had people from all the islands – from Trinidad, Jamaica, Grenada, St Vincent, Antigua, Barbados. I think the majority were from Barbados. I remember the sugar factory; that was one of the main things that we had there in Baraguá.

I saw most of the tradition that I'm seeing here after I came to live here – the great cake that they used to bake around Christmas time, pone and sweetbread, the sorrel, pudding and souse. The First of August; it's a tradition and they still celebrate it now. Also I remember the church harvest. We had a Christian Mission church, the Salvation Army, the Episcopal church, the [Seventh-day] Adventists. We used to go all those churches during harvest and we had to recite. I remember also, at the Salvation Army, a lady we used to call Captain; she was from [British] Guiana. I remember her very good. And we used to go on evenings, twice or three days a week, and she used to show us how to knit and sew; to do hemming and certain things.

I remember Miss Clarke; a lady – she was from Barbados – and she used to teach us English. Because at that time, my mother was preparing to come back to Barbados to live, so she wanted us to learn the language. Miss Clarke was tough; she used to lash a lot. If you come without your homework, it was punishment. I remember her clearly.

I really had a short time with my father, because I was six when he died. He used to work with the American people, and after that he used to work at the port. What I remember is that he was a carpenter. He had to get up early, early on mornings, because he had to take a small train we used to call the *chispa*. It would take him to the port, because the sea was far away. It was a thirty-minute ride on that train. He used to work as a carpenter there at the port, where they used to ship the sugar from the sugar factory.

I remember him being the master of the lodge. And a lot of people used to come to the house from different parts of Cuba, especially from Guantánamo. They used to have these big parties. Some of them used to stay at the house. The house always used to be full of people, and they used to stay at different West Indian houses too. The same thing happened with the church when they had their conventions. They used to come in, and some people used to stay at my house.

My mother never worked, she was a housewife. But she used to look after a lot of people. I remember her looking after every single old person that was from Barbados. They have their children, but you know how it is. They never married, and they used to live in a place we called the *pabellon*, like some barracks. I remember, as a little girl, having to take food for them in this canteen that you used to stack one on top of the other. My mother used to cook the food for them, and she would send it. Even when they were sick, she had a bedroom at the back where she used to bring them and take care of them until they got better. Then they would go back home. I was pretty young, but I remember talk from the others that one even died at our house, sitting down on a step to come into the kitchen, waiting for her to give him some breakfast. And they say when she went to touch him, he was already dead.

In Baraguá growing up, we used to go mostly to the Christian Mission. That was the one that my mother belonged to. But we had to visit all, it was a must. On Sundays, we used to go there on mornings. And then on evenings we had to go to the Salvation Army and to the Episcopal church. When it was Christmas, we would go to one in the night, midnight mass, and then we go to the others the Christmas Day, because we had then to recite.

My mother left Barbados pretty young; she was taken by her parents. What she remembered about Barbados were the traditions that she kept – the sorrel and great cake at Christmas. It was something that the Cuban people never had, and through that same tradition, the Cuban people start to do the same thing. Even nowadays at Christmas, they have sorrel and cake. Well, even though they don't have all the ingredients to get it done like we would do it here, they would try to do it. So now that is one of their traditions also.

She used to give us a lot of stories about Barbados, and we had this vague idea of what Barbados used to look like. But when she left, it wasn't nothing like how it is now. Because apparently it didn't have no electricity, according to what she used to say. Because I remember when she was coming back to Barbados, and we were coming with her, Mr Elcock used to say to us, "You're going to that potato country?" We used to cry a lot because we said, "We're not going anywhere that don't have no electricity."

Most of her stories used to be about Panama though. She used to talk a lot about Panama because she was taken from here to Panama. And then when the work finished in Panama, my grandmother and my grandfather went then to Cuba. She used to tell us that once when they were cutting the trees for the wood, in order to build the canal, she was taking the food for her father one day. And she sat on one of the trees that was cut, because she was not allowed to go any further because it was dangerous. They used to put dynamite, so it was dangerous. When she sat there, she felt like something sliding and moving, and when she got up, it was a serpent. I will never forget that story. She said she was really lucky that it did not bite her. One of the men then came running and chopped it and killed it.

In Baraguá, the highest education was secondary school. After that, we had to go to other cities in order to continue further education. So I went to Santa Clara, a province that was called Las Villas at that time. Then after they did the new administrative divisions, it became Villa Clara. I went there and studied early childhood education for four years. So I got a degree in early childhood education. When I finished, I was awarded a scholarship to study in the Soviet Union, as it was at that time. So I had to do one year in Havana at the Faculty of Language to learn Russian, in order to go over there. And then I went to Leningrad, which is now called St Petersburg, to attend the Alexander Ivanovich Herzen University for four years. I went there in July 1978. I specialized in pedagogy and psychology for pre-schoolers, and was conferred the title of professor of pedagogy and psychology for pre-schoolers (early childhood education) and was granted the scientific grade of master of arts in pedagogy.

It was a nice experience being in the Soviet Union. It was a wonderful experience that I'm still remembering because it taught me so many things. Being away from your country at that age, I had to mature. I was twenty-two. Because you have to look after yourself, and also you have to study. And it was intense,

Figure 13.2. Yolanda (*second from left*) with other foreign university classmates in the Soviet Union. Courtesy of Yolanda Nelson Springer.

being in a different language; in a cold, cold, cold country; a different culture completely. It was a learning and valuable experience.

I went back to Cuba in 1982. After a period of study, you had to give back the government two years of your time, because they paid for your study. So I was sent to work in the same province where I was born, Ciego de Ávila, at the Josué País Pedagogical School for the Training of Teachers. It's similar to Erdiston Teachers' Training College here. I taught in the Faculty of Early Childhood Education for two years. And after that, I went to Havana. And while I was in Havana, I worked at a special education school for children with behavioural problems and learning difficulties. I spent one year there. That was in the province of Havana, in a place called Caimito. Then, after that, I got a transfer to Havana City, to a municipality called Regla. That's where I met my ex-husband, Jacinto Ramírez. There was a port there where he used to work as a mechanic on the ships.

Then there was an opening to return to the school where I'd worked before, Salvador Allende Pedagogical School for the Training of Teachers, in the city of Havana. You had to go and do a test, and have an interview in order to get the post. So I went and worked for a semester, and when I did the test, I got the post. So I taught pedagogy and methodologies there until I left Cuba in 1994.

I decided to leave Cuba because there were too many challenges. I already had a son, Josué. Life had become really difficult; economically it was really, really challenging. I wanted a better future for my son. I already had a Barbados passport, because my mother, before she died, was planning to come back to Barbados to live here with Gloria, Julia and me. The others were married and had their children. She died in 1967. I was eleven years old when she died.

She could not travel with us because we were Cuban citizens, and at that time you could only travel to another country if you were leaving to go and live there. In order to do that, you were required to have a passport from that country that allowed you to live there. She had to get our papers in order to apply for Barbados passports and wait on the government to give us permission to leave the country. During that process, she had surgery for kidney stones, and she died during surgery as a result of internal haemorrhage.

I was only eleven, but Gloria was at an age where she could have come on her own. So Gloria came. When Julia and I were at an age that we could travel, the older siblings asked if we wanted to come. We did not know anybody here. My sisters, Marva, Beba and Nena, and my two brothers were the ones looking after us. So where were we going to go? Plus, they did not want us to leave either, because we did not know our family here. The exception was my brother Elliot, who wanted us to come, and he was really upset about our decision to stay.

While on a visit to Cuba, Gloria saw how things were. And she saw how *I* was, because it was taking a toll on me. I lived really far from where I was working, and most of the time I had to leave my son with my other sister Adela. Because I had to get up too early on mornings in order to get to my work. It was like opposite sides of the city. Then I had to take a ferry, then two buses in order to get to work. So it would be too early to leave him at the day care. It was really stressful, and life became really stressful in Cuba at that time. It was a real crisis, 1993–1994. It was a period when people started leaving en masse, on rafts and anything they could find. I left Cuba the seventh of September 1994.

Gloria had been to Cuba that same year, or the year before. I can't remember exactly when it was. She said, "You have your passport?" I said, "Yes." My brother Elliot, he used to work at the British embassy and he always make sure that we had our papers in order. So Gloria said, "You can come to Barbados." Before, you weren't allowed to travel, but at that time you could travel. She said, "If I send for you, would you come?" I tell her, "Yes." She said, "Well you can come and live here. You should be able to get a job, you're qualified." My family did not hesitate about it. So I didn't have to do anything, just come to Barbados.

The passport needed to be renewed, and she did it. My husband agreed for me to come, because at that time the situation wasn't good, and we were looking to leave in order to get a better life. He joined me in Barbados in 1997.

I left my son with my sister Beba. Oh, you can imagine! But I knew that I was leaving him in more than good hands. Because when he was born, she took care of him also, she and my other sister, Marva, the eldest girl. When I was pregnant with him, I went up to the country to Baraguá because I was really ill, and I had to be on bed rest and in hospital. So they took care of me. After he was born, when my maternity leave had finished, I had to go back to work in Havana. And I had no day care to put him in there, because you had to go on a waiting list until you were called. So I had no other choice but to go back to Havana and leave him there with them; if not, I would have lost my job.

At the beginning, Beba took her holidays. Then after, Marva took her holidays, and then Julia took her holidays in order to look after him. So when all the holidays had finished, and they had to go back out to work, we found a lady that lived right there in the neighbourhood and we used to pay her to look after him during the day. He even used to call her Mami Ana. Then afterwards, we got through with a day care in Havana and he went to Havana to live with us. When I left to come to Barbados, I left him in Baraguá with Beba again.

I had a tough time bringing my son, because as a child he could not travel. Cuba would not allow him to come until Barbados Immigration gave me a paper saying that he was allowed to come and live here. Immigration here was telling me, "He's your son; bring him. We'll give him a permit to go to school until the papers are ready." But Cuba was saying, "No." I needed something legal that said he is allowed to live in Barbados. At that time, the policy in Cuba was that children under eighteen years could not travel. Eventually I got him here in 1999. He came in August 1999.

Oh! Can you imagine how I felt? After so long, and fighting so much in order to get him here? Because he went through a lot. So everything was coming true. I was giving God thanks that I finally had him here with me, because I couldn't go back. At that time, once you left Cuba, you couldn't go back. Now things have changed. Sometimes I would be thinking that he would have to grow up without me. I couldn't bear that idea at all. Beba used to send pictures of him with anyone that was coming to Barbados. But God is good and merciful, and he managed to join me here when he was eight years old.

I do not regret coming to Barbados. At the beginning it was difficult because coming and leaving your friends, getting to know new people, making a new life is not easy. I missed my sisters, because they were like my mother to me. And trying for people to understand you and you to understand them, having a new job that does not have anything to do with what you're accustomed to do and trained to do. Because I started teaching Spanish here. At the beginning when I came, I used to work at the port with a cousin who had a store, until I was finally able to get into the education system. My main focus was that "I need to bring my son; I need to bring my husband". So I needed to find an income that would allow me to do that, and to go on my own. Because up to that time I was relying on my sister Gloria. That's why I miss her so much, because she was really, really ... I don't know how to praise her ... good to me. Because if it was not for her, I would not have gotten through. She really did help me.

After a while, God put me in a good place because when he placed me at Sharon Primary School, he knew what he was doing. When I got there, they received me as one of their own. Most of them knew my great aunt and knew Gloria from living in the neighbourhood there in Jackson. And it so happened that I went to teach at a school connected to the church where my father was baptized – Sharon Moravian Church. When I walked in there everybody was asking, "Are you Gloria's sister?" or, "She is Gloria?" So all the parents came to me and I was embraced. And even now, most of my good, good friends are from Sharon Primary School.

One of the things I accomplished was writing a series of four textbooks. I

Figure 13.3. Yolanda (*fourth from left at the back*) surrounded by some of her students in the Primary Spanish Programme at Sharon Primary School.

feel really proud about that. They are Spanish textbooks, the series *Dime* for the Caribbean secondary schools. The editor is Dr Jeannette Allsopp. I wrote it along with Malva Lewis and Erskine Padmore. I really enjoyed it while we were writing it, and I am thankful to Dr Allsopp for inviting me to join them. I hope to write another one for children.

In August 2008, the Ministry of Foreign Affairs sent me to Chile to do a course at the Universidad Metropolitana de Ciencias de la Educación [Metropolitan University of Education Sciences] to improve the teaching of Spanish as a second language in the English-speaking Caribbean. It was a good experience. I went there for five weeks. It was really useful because I acquired a certificate there. I had been using my skills as a teacher and Spanish as my first language in order to deliver the Spanish classes. So when I went there, it was just putting everything together – the techniques, the procedures. I kept all the papers they gave me and I've been using them and they are really helpful. There were fifteen of us from different Caribbean islands. It was a good experience meeting people from Trinidad, Dominica, Bahamas, Grenada, all the Caribbean islands. So it was a really rich experience.

I maintain contact with all my friends and my family in Cuba. At the beginning it was real difficult calling to Cuba, and expensive! Communication in Cuba is not as it is here in Barbados, but now it has gotten better, because now we can make contact through email. They're allowed to have cell phones now, even though they have to go to a WiFi point. But communication is better. We always, always keep in touch.

I have nieces in Trinidad, and I go there often. I travelled to Venezuela, Jamaica. I have a friend who studied with me in Russia, she lives in Jamaica – Aracelys.

I'm both Barbadian and Cuban. I am Cuban, I have it in my soul. And I'm Barbadian, I have it in my blood. So I am both. Right now I feel that I am a Barbadian, and I don't think I would be able to go back and live in Cuba. I feel really happy and excited when I go back to visit, especially when the time is coming up. Because I'm going to meet my friends, my family, especially the little ones who were born after I left, and see Cuba again. But after a while, I miss my house and my home. When I'm leaving Cuba I'm sad, but when I get here, I say, "Oh, I am back home again."

Yolanda Nelson's interview was done on 26 November 2017 at her home in Clapham, St Michael.

CHAPTER 14

JOSUÉ RAMÍREZ NELSON

Hometown: Baraguá, Ciego de Ávila
Barbados connection: Grandmother and grandfather
Occupation: Student
Arrival year: 1999

I WAS BORN IN BARAGUÁ, CIEGO DE ÁVILA, 16 August 1991. I was raised there and in Havana. But as far as I'm concerned, Baraguá is my home. That's where I come from. I'm a country boy at heart.

I did not remember my mother, Yolanda, while I was growing up, because my mother left when I was very young and came to Barbados. I remember my father. I was old enough to remember him leaving for Barbados. So I was raised by my aunts. And they spoke about Barbados. It felt like this kind of mythological place, that you'd never been there. And my mother was this legend that

I only heard through the phone, and I only saw her in pictures. I didn't have many memories of her.

But everything I heard of Barbados was kind of like that view we have in Cuba of "overseas". Where it is like this land of opportunity where you can just do anything there. Everything that you can't find here, you'd get over there. I guess we kind of had this idea that people in Barbados were rich. We kind of knew that they were better off. It just felt like a great place to be, someplace that I would have wanted to be.

I remember I was a big troublemaker. I was a country boy out with my friends. I was barely home. We used to just go out and play a lot of sports. Sometimes we would just be up to no good. You know, we'd be just living it up in the streets. Everybody knew my name. You knew everybody. We were a very close-knit community. I was very close with my cousins and my aunts. Because, you know, they were the only family I knew. I called my aunt Mum. My cousins were like my sisters and my brothers.

Some days I ate lunch at my friends' house, and their parents were more than glad to feed me. As far as I knew, I was their son. The same courtesy was extended to my friends. They would stay over, and as far as my aunts were concerned, they were their children. It's a very close community. As far as I'm concerned, I have three moms. There's Mami Beba, there's Mami Ana who used to take care of me when Mami Beba had to go out of town or I needed someone to babysit me, and my mother, Yolanda.

In Cuba, our favourite pastime at night after the news would be to watch soap operas. So sometimes when our parents would be watching soap operas, the kids would be outside playing games in the street. We played baseball. I was very big into baseball. I remember that I was very good at baseball, which is the sport of Cuba. And we had a stadium that I would go to all the time. I would watch baseball games there. And we would play tag, and Red Light, Green Light, 1-2-3. We played a lot of physical, contact games. This is at night, when sometimes the power would go off. We would just be out under the tree in the park talking. And sometimes, if the power went off, everybody would just be outside.

When my mother said that I was coming to her in Barbados, I wasn't happy. That was in 1999. I was very sad, because I knew everybody in Baraguá; I felt so close to everyone. I felt like I was maybe going to visit; I didn't figure that I was going to be staying. So I remember the last day of school, the kids in my class gave me a farewell party. Everybody said, "Come back. Don't forget us when you're over there in *La Yuma*," as we call it. I was very sad. I was saying, "I'm coming back. I'm coming back, I'm not staying."

We first had to get a car to go to Ciego. Once we got there, we go into the metrobus to go to Havana. We spent maybe four days in Havana before we left. While we were there, I saw my cousin Arabeisy . . . she's nineteen now . . . but she was still a little toddler back then. My brother Julier came to visit me. I hadn't seen him because I lived in Baraguá. My grandmother lived in Guantánamo, and Julier lived in Havana. That last week was the first time that we connected. He's my half-brother from my father's side. It was a long time that we hadn't met, and when I first found out about him we spent a lot of time together. During those last four days he would come over to visit me, and I was very happy to have a brother there to talk to and to look up to.

And I remember that at the airport, I cried. I bawled, because I didn't want to leave. "Sure, you're coming back", my aunt told me. Her name is Olivia, but I call her Mami Beba. She raised me when my mother came to Barbados. "You're just going to visit", she told me. She was obviously lying to me. I was not happy at all. Despite Barbados being a place that I would have wanted to be at, the reality of leaving everyone that I knew and not coming back, that scared me.

From there we went to Jamaica, and that's the first time I went to Jamaica. That was my first time on a plane. Before that, I had only seen about planes that crashed. I had also heard about the Cubana plane [which was blown up shortly after leaving Barbados in 1976]. So that coloured the way I saw planes. You were just going to die on a plane. It was probably not the healthiest way to view planes, but through all these movies and news reports, that's what I thought. I was just holding my aunt's hand and asking, "You sure it's not going to crash?" She told me, "No. Just fall asleep. That makes the ride easier." And it did.

We arrived in Jamaica and stayed overnight at a friend of my mom's, Aracelys. I asked her a few questions about my mother because she was my mother's friend. I know my mom used to send me toys and stuff, but I just knew her from over the phone. I had not seen my mom since she left.

When we landed in Barbados, everybody on the plane was whooping and applauding. They were just happy. That didn't happen when we were going to Jamaica. It didn't happen when we stopped in other places. But for some reason when we reached Barbados, everybody was just happy. When I approached my mother, she was crying because she was very happy to see me. I was trying to tell her, "It's okay. It's okay. I'm here now." My aunt Gloria was there. I had seen her before because she had come over to Cuba a couple times. And I met my cousin Osvaldo, her son, who I had seen in pictures. I was very happy to be with him and to have someone to play with. I was seven, going on eight years old.

When I came, the only English I knew was "yes" and "no". My first day in Barbados, I went out to play with the children in the neighbourhood. We were playing kickball. It was just confusing because I couldn't understand anyone. It's a weird feeling where someone is speaking and you just hear words. You just hear sounds, but nothing makes sense. It's very intimidating. It can get annoying and frustrating too. I knew no English, so that was something that was a big challenge for me.

The first time that I went to lessons, I was taking English classes. But I wasn't retaining it very well because I wasn't paying attention. I was still a child. I was a very hyperactive person. So sitting down in a class in a one-on-one and you're being taught like, this word, that word, it didn't work with me. I did not pay attention in classes at all.

And then when it was time to go into school, it kind of hurt me, because I did not understand English. So I used to get into a lot of fights. Because, you know, some kids would bump me, and you can't say, "Excuse me. I'm sorry." They would think you probably did that on purpose. Or you were just in their way. And I would just end up fighting. The teachers . . . I couldn't understand the teachers. There was a teacher that I got lashes from, because I think that she was giving me some order. To this day I don't know what she was telling me. But she was telling me something and I obviously did not understand it. She figured that I was not complying, and I got lashes because of that. So my mother was brought to the school, and told, "Your son is misbehaving." She explained that I really didn't understand the language.

So when it came to learning, it was my mom's friend, who I call Auntie Juliette. She helped teach me English. It was her and my mom. So every day after school, I would go to her because she was an elementary school teacher. She would start off giving me some lessons, and then she would come home with me, and both her and my mom would give me lessons. As they kept teaching me, I would then go to school and I found that I was understanding things that they were saying.

I remember the big thing was that I had my first apple. I had never had an apple before. I had only seen apples watching foreign movies. I had seen people eat apples, and I always wondered what they tasted like. So the first time I had an apple, I was amazed. I was like, "This is wonderful!" I think I ate three the first night. My mom was like, "Hey, you can't keep eating them like that." And

Figure 14.2. Josué (*second from right*) after his arrival in Barbados. He was being entertained at the home of the Marshalls with other members of his family. Left to right: Delcina Marshall, his aunt Olivia, Sharon Marshall, aunt Adela, mother, Yolanda, and father, Jacinto Ramírez Marino.

I remember that there was a TV where you could just watch cartoons all day. Childish things like that. Cartoon Network, that was on all the time. And I also picked up English by watching the cartoons, because when they would speak, I would mimic what they said. I perfected my pronunciation in that way. It was a lot of information. It was a little overwhelming.

My earliest memory was when my dad took me to Bridgetown. He also got me an apple there too. I remember going into the ZRs [minibuses]. That was completely different. I had been living in the countryside. If you wanted to get to Ciego [de Ávila] or Havana, you go in a bus, like a metrobus. And you are there for maybe four hours or six hours. You might have to overnight to get where you want to go, because Cuba is a big place. And you go into this cramped ZR, and the music is blaring, you're moving very fast, people are just obstructing you, everybody is packed together. It was wild! I didn't know what to make of it back then, but I know that was very confusing. My dad was like, "You have to move quick with these ZRs. You have to come out quick, go back in quick, right?" I was like, "Huh?!" I would get up, the conductor would open the door and everybody would go back out, to just shuffle back into the seats to make room. And people would be squeezing you together. And you'd be like, "But what are you doing? There's no room." Everybody had to fit. My first ZR drive was uncomfortable. It was very overwhelming being here at first.

This is home now. I relate to so many things here now, like being a part of the culture. I still feel like a bit of an outsider at some points though. I would get into a conversation with some Barbadians and they would say things from their youth that make no sense to me. I experience it through their experiences, but I still very much feel like I'm a foreigner. But I feel very comfortable here. I have the audacity to feel like I'm Bajan. I've been here for so long now, I've made so many connections with people, that I can't imagine not living here.

But I'm definitely Cuban. I have a podcast that I do. I became very much into nerd culture. So in the podcast I use the moniker the Rubik's Cuban. It's like a play on Rubik's cube. I would never, ever deny my Cuban heritage. I make sure to let everybody know that I'm Cuban.

As I said, Baraguá is a community. When I go back to Cuba, that is still a thing that is there. Everybody looks out for each other. You know every neighbour by name, you know everything that is going on with them. Here in Barbados, I guess that depends on what kind of person you are, you may know your neighbours more closely. But you're not as close.

There're maybe two of our neighbours here that I know intimately. And one that I know to the point that they would ask me to babysit for their child. But over there, you knew everyone, no one was a stranger. So I like that aspect when you go back. I like that people always remember you. And I like the inventiveness and resourcefulness of Cubans.

Because life here has been made to accommodate you, there's a market for everything. If your heater is broken, there's someone that will come and help you fix it. If your fan is broken, you can get it fixed. You can get anything here that you're lacking. But in Cuba, you don't have as much resources and you have to improvise. If you don't have running water, you have to find a way to bathe with buckets. If you don't have a solar heater, you have to find a way to make the water hot. So I like the resourcefulness of my people when it comes to not having enough. When you lack, you have to make up for it. I find that we are always making up. And I think that if we have one edge, we would go so far.

I remember initially it was terrible because I could only communicate with my friends through letters. Or every now and then we were able to make an overseas call. If one of them was at my aunt's house, we would talk. But I felt out of contact with a few of my friends. But the best thing is that when I go back, it's like we've never been apart. We always catch up, and we're always great. We're always cool together; there's not that awkward moment that we're so far apart that we don't have too much in common. I like that we still stay in contact. My closest friend (we call him Pinpi), every time I go back, he's the first person I see. For the whole time that I'm back in Cuba, he always takes me around. So I like that we're that tight.

There's another one of our friends. I've kind of forgotten the names, but I know them by nicknames. Everybody had a nickname; mine was Pocholo, after a character in the television cartoon *Pocholo y su pandilla* [Pocholo and His Gang]. This might not be appropriate, but we call him *El Gordo* [fat man]. He has a cane juice stand. As my mother would say, we have a family history of diabetes, so she always tries to make me regulate my sugar intake. But every time I go there, and I meet Gordo, he completely fills me with cane juice. He gives me free servings of cane juice, once, twice or three times. I remember once when I was leaving, before I left I said I just got to meet everybody and tell them I've got to go. It was probably thirty minutes left before the car took us back to Havana, and I went to visit him at his stand. He just had me there for thirty minutes and we were talking and he said "Take one man." I was getting ready to give him the money and he was, "No, no, no. Your money is no good here. Just have this." He was giving me three, four, five servings. I was like, "Listen man. If I take any more, I'm going to go into diabetic shock right here. So I'm going to have to leave."

But I like that I'm still close to my friends. Now that they have the internet, I meet some of them on Facebook. But they're not able to log in as much. Sometimes they would send a message and I'm not near my cell phone, so I can't respond. But when I respond, they're already off the internet and I don't hear from them until the next week. So that kind of gets in the way of the communication.

My family is always close. We are always in contact. No matter how far apart, we're always close. My mother calls all the time. Almost every week she calls. I get in contact with them through Facebook as well. My cousins are on Facebook. Back in Cuba, I have my brother, Julier, and a nephew. My brother has a newborn son. I have most of my cousins, my aunts and my paternal grandmother. They're the ones I'm always in contact with when I go back there. Top of the list.

It's been interesting living in Barbados. It was different, and I think adapting to the differences was something that took some time for me. The way of life here was much faster. People weren't as close as they were back in Cuba. So I think for me it was a bit harder to make friends, especially when I was in school. Because I was just like "the foreign person". The first friends I made were Andwele and Alchino, two friends of mine that I'm friends with them to this day. We were like the three musketeers. Everything we experienced together. We had this shared love of nerd stuff like superheroes and card games and video games. These were the people who introduced me to that world. I knew about Teenage Mutant Ninja Turtles and I used to watch cartoons on Saturdays. But these guys saw it all the time. I loved spending time with them. They were really great friends. Really good people. I didn't connect with other people as well as I connected with them. I guess the gap in culture too. They're not the typical Bajan, so that's probably why I connected with them. Not that there's anything bad about Bajans, right? But it was that they weren't as tied into the culture as other people were. So it was easier for me to mesh with that group.

I was very different from the other students when I went to secondary school. Everybody was into calypso. Everybody was into soca music, into dub. I was just not really into that, I knew nothing about that stuff. That wasn't my interest. I guess I was more of an outcast as things went on in secondary school. I had to kind of leave aside my hyperactive self to be more studious and more disciplined in school.

Ever since my mother was first called about me misbehaving, I tried to curb that. I guess in Cuba it's a little different. In Cuba, it's more rowdy. You're more active without supervision. Teachers weren't as strict on you about fighting and stuff like that. They would probably say, "Oh Lord. He's fighting again. Stop. Stop. Get away. Alright, talk it out." It wasn't as disciplined as it was here. I think that made me buckle down. I was a little bit more disciplined. I became a little more quiet. I think I became a little more anxious since I was here. I think it was the act of punishment. You do get lashes here. You get punished for doing something. I guess I did not internalize that in a good way. So it made me a little more afraid to make mistakes in school. So that would make me more anxious. And that expanded into me being afraid to make mistakes in social interactions. So I became a little more shy, more withdrawn. I was more into my books, and I used to get teased because of that. I was the guy who used to read at lunchtime. I didn't talk to many people. So I didn't have a lot of friends. I had my comic books, my video games, stuff that I would just draw into.

I feel like if I was in Cuba I would have been a different person. I would be more outgoing. I would be more outspoken. That's just a few of the ways that I changed living here. I have no regrets about that. I think for some people, growing up can be rough. It's not something that I hold any grudges against or have any resentment towards. I just feel that I had a different journey, and I came out of that in my own way.

I'm six feet three inches. I was a very shy person, and shyness and height don't go well together. As a shy person, I try to dress very low key. I don't wear bright colours. I try to keep myself in a way that I can blend in with other people. But then I have this height. Someone will always pick me out in a crowd. So it kind of went against me, because I was so noticeable. I told someone recently that I didn't know how much of a privilege it was to be tall. I had this height privilege and I didn't know how to access it. But I think that after I went to BCC [Barbados Community College] to study mass communication, and people started to comment more on my height, and the girls started to pay more attention to me because I was tall, I kind of realized, "Hey, I have height privilege. So let me access it."

I feel like my biggest accomplishment is still to come. You could say maybe that I excelled in school. I wanted to make sure I wasn't that guy who ... I wanted to perform well in school. I was always good at English. I remember when we first had a spelling test and I got 97 per cent. The teacher was like, "How did this foreign guy, now learning English, beat all of you all in a spelling test?" This was strange.

I did very well in the Common Entrance exams. I made it to the St Michael School. I had a lot of tutors to help me get past the language barrier. I read a lot of books too, Harry Potter books which helped me with my vocabulary and my English. I think that my mother was a little worried about me in CXCs [Caribbean Examinations Council exams]. But I did very well in CXCs. I did my Spanish CXC exam in third form. I left school having passed all my CXC subjects – English, maths, literature, chemistry, biology, information technology, and Caribbean history. I aced them all.

I wanted to do law at first, basically because someone told me that I was very argumentative, and I always have a retort for something. And they said, "You would make a good lawyer." I thought, "That would work." But when I went to apply at BCC, the guy who was accepting the applications went for lunch and he never came back. And that was the last day. So I tried to hand in my application at the principal's office, but I don't think that ever made it to the Law Department because I was not accepted.

But it was a good thing that I had mass communication as a backup. That was my mother's influence, because she told me, "You should try that." I didn't know what it was about, but she told me, "You would be good for this." And she pushed me for it, and I did it. And then when I looked at what mass communication was about, I was very glad that that was what I chose. Because the media studies, as a person so much into nerd culture who spends so much time processing information about films . . . I know more things about films that most people probably won't care to know . . . a lot of useless information in mind. That was a place where this useless information became useful doing media studies and so on. I absolutely fell in love with it.

Maybe I'm hard on myself, but I feel that my biggest accomplishment is yet to come. I definitely have been interested in media studies. My main thing was being able to go to CBC [Caribbean Broadcasting Corporation] and work. As an intern, they allowed me to do three radio programmes just about music. I produced it myself, I came up with a concept on my own, and then I aired them online. I presented them on my own. I would say that was an accomplishment. Because this was a point when I felt I knew what I wanted to do. I have hopes for the future, working in media and reading the news someday.

I would love to go back to Cuba. My relationship with Cuba . . . I think most people who have been foreigners feel this way . . . in some ways you are part of an identity, part of a culture. But because you're so far away from it for so long, there are some ways that you're estranged from it.

I'm in Barbados and I'm not really Barbadian, because there are so many parts of the culture that I'm estranged from. So in a way you feel like you don't belong. But I always feel connection to Cuba. I felt that connection more as I got older. I realized that there were things about Cuba that I didn't know, and I would then go back and do more research. Like research on the Orisha culture. It's good to know about that, about the music. About Celia Cruz and the stuff that she was talking about. I learned more about the race relations in Cuba, and the politics of it. What it was like when Castro took over. More information about Antonio Maceo. The history of it; I've been more curious about it, now that I'm getting older and I realize that there are gaps in information that I don't know. As I read that, I feel more connected.

That is my country. I definitely want to go back. I'd like to go back at least once a year. As far as living, I'm not sure that I will go back to live. But I'm waiting for that change in the society, in the political aspect, so that I can go back to my country. A country that is going to be thriving and developed.

I very much love my country. I would definitely encourage people to go and visit and just get a look at what it's like. The tourist perspective and the resident perspective are two very different things. If you go to Cuba, try to have some more conversations with the people who live there to know what it's like. I definitely have heard very rosy depictions of Cuba from people who visit. And that's fine, because it is a beautiful place. But there's more to it than just the visual perspective, just from looking at it as a consumer. It is a beautiful country, but it is a country that definitely needs to develop. If at any point, we get just one edge, a chance to develop like any other country does, I think Cuba will be much better. And the people will be much better. I love my people, I love my country. I'm always for them.

As for feeling Cuban, in some ways, yes, in some ways, no. As I said, I'm still so different that when I go back, I notice the gaps. I'm a Cuban who can't salsa dance very well. That's always something that gets people confused. They say, "You should go to Latin dancing. You're Cuban. You should know how to do that." I may step on your toes. I won't sweep you off your feet. I feel in some ways that I don't belong.

My main thing when I went back in 2006 was the slang. Being a young boy in Cuba, there's some slang that you're familiar with. But slang is kind of like how you communicate with your peers. It is kind of like how Shakespeare spoke to his people, in a certain way. Slang is like how we speak to our people in our own way. Same way we have our Bajan dialect. The thing is that Bajan dialect changes. Some old-time sayings that you have, you wouldn't say that now. It was the same way in Cuba. So when I went back to Cuba, there was all this new slang that I was so confused about. And I was still using this old slang. People would be like, "Where you from? No one says that anymore." For example, a coin was *un fula*, and when you felt that something was really great it was *escapade*. Those are examples of the way that I was so disconnected from the culture. And when you go to a party, the way I danced was very different. Everybody was into salsa dancing.

But I don't feel any less Cuban when I go back. I still feel that rush in my spirit, that excitement. Like I'm back home.

This interview with Josué Ramírez was recorded at his home in Clapham, St Michael on 7 November 2017.

CHAPTER 15

THE YEARWOODS

Hometown: Manatí, Las Tunas
Barbados connection: Father
Occupation: Florencia (*left*), Spanish teacher
Arrival year: 2000
Occupation: Juana, Spanish teacher
Arrival year: 2000
Occupation: Ernesto, cleaner
Arrival year: 2003

JUANA "JENNY" YEARWOOD

ALL OF US ARE FROM CENTRAL ARGELIA LIBRE, that was known in the past as Central Manatí. I was born in Chaparra, but only remained there a week. That was in 1951, the fifth of August 1951.

151

For up to twenty-something years I lived in Manatí. I had my friends, I had my upbringing. In those times we didn't have internet, so we used to play with the neighbours, run, do all types of things.

My father was Vivian Israel Yearwood Smith. At first, my father used to work in the *central*, in the sugar factory. He also used to work teaching English for people who were able to pay. But then, when the Revolution came, he started working in the secondary school as a secretary and as an English teacher. He enjoyed that. Everybody remembers him as *Maestro*, Teacher, *Maestro* Vivian. Everybody really loved him. We admire him and appreciate everything he did for us. He worked thirty-five years with the Ministry of Education and received a national order. Anything you put in Facebook talking about him, all the children that he taught for a lot of years will respond and say, "Yes, my Teacher. Vivian the teacher" and so.

My mother was Winifred Hendrickson Providence. She was born in Cuba, but her parents were West Indians. My grandfather was from Nevis and my grandmother was from Antigua. It was a whole Caribbean family. We knew about dumplings and all those nice things from the West Indians. I didn't learn about them here in Barbados; I knew them there, baking and doing all type of nice things. When things were hard, they always had something to provide for us.

They were married on the eighteenth of December 1949. My mum didn't work then; she worked in the house and raised the children and so on. She used to sew a lot. Everyone is going to say that their parents were lovely. But we enjoyed being children and being raised by them.

Eventually my mother moved to Havana and then from Havana she moved to Santa Cruz del Norte. My father and my mother never divorced, but they were separated for some time and my mother made a new life for herself. My mother

Figure 15.2. Young Juana (*seated*) with her parents and brother Felipe in Cuba. Courtesy of Juana Yearwood.

worked in a dairy farm that she used to clean. Imagine, that is very hard work. From there, she retired because her [blood] pressure started going up. In the end my brother Ernesto, who was studying different places, went with his mother. My sister Florencia was small. She had Florencia and a daughter that passed away, Irma. Another son, Felipe, he died too. My mother had the opportunity to come to Barbados in 2006 to meet our family. She stayed for four months.

My father, he never lived by himself. He always used to have somebody in his company. Irma would go to stay with him. And at the end, I got married, and then had children. So I told Daddy, "Look Daddy, the whole family is in Santa Cruz. The best thing would be for everyone to be in Santa Cruz. I have an apartment in Hershey and I would like to invite you to stay there. Leave everything, sell everything. You will be comfortable." We were so happy to have Daddy close to us. But he was sick. He had some problems with his kidneys. He got worse and worse, and he passed away.

I decided to come to Barbados looking for a better life because the situation in Cuba, everybody knows how it was. I was thinking of my children, Alexander and Jenny, of their future. The [Cuban] government provide a lot of good things for children, to go to school and study free, free health care and all that. But the situation with food and so was difficult, and I decided to take that step.

I came to Barbados in January 2000. From 2000 to now, things have changed in Barbados. When I first came, it was strange. I didn't speak a lot of English. Moving from a city to the countryside was something different. My life turned different completely.

I came to the land and the house where my father was born. This is in Harrises, St Lucy. The house is still there. And my aunt, his sister, her name is Ethel O'Neale. They used to call her Itha. She was a teacher for a lot of years, and she was a principal. She really was the person that help us, to pay our tickets and do everything to bring us here.

We started a life in a new country, met our family that we never saw before, our cousins and so on. It was like a revolution, things that are happening new for you. It was like something strange. But I always remember that there was where my grandfather and grandmother grew up, and my father and his family. That was an experience for us. We never imagined that we would come here to Barbados. I never, never imagined that. It was a new life for us, being an immigrant, to get accustomed to the culture. Because we have a Spanish culture, it's different.

When I came to Barbados, I remember I met a lady from St Lucia and she asked me, "Jenny, what would you like to do here?" I said, "I would like to do any work that I'm able to do." And she went and spoke with Mr Clarke in Alleynedale to see if I could get a job there. This is a farm. My first job here was collecting eggs. I went and worked, collecting eggs, washing eggs, cleaning the area, feeding. It's something I never did before. But I wanted to make money to help my family in Cuba. And I said, "This is my first step, and I'm going to start and I'm going to try." I worked there for about two years with him. I worked almost all my life in Cuba in accounting, in an office dealing with salaries. So this was something new for me, which I didn't know how to do, and I did it. That's the way God was helping me, one way or the other, and I accepted it.

After that, I went and worked at the Animal Flower Cave, in a small shop which a lady had there selling souvenirs and so on. She gave me a job selling there. I did it too. Then I went to work at the restaurant at the Cave. And I was there for about two years, up to one day when the Ministry [of Education] called for Spanish facilitators. I went to the interview and I was successful. I joined the Primary Spanish Programme in 2002. I teach at Deacon's Primary, Westbury and Grazettes.

I was never frightened for work. Because when my father went to Cuba, he went and cut cane for twenty cents a day, because things in Barbados were very bad. You had no job, nothing. Everybody started looking for something to do. I say if he went and cut cane, why I can't go and work in a farm collecting eggs?

It's something strange that happened because he went to Cuba and in the end he finished in a school. Some years ago I was thinking, "My father went to Cuba and in the end he helped in the society with what he knew – English. Then we came to Barbados and in the end we're going to end in a school doing the same work – helping people in the community with Spanish." And then I say, "That is so strange. And who did it? We that follow the same immigrant that went to Cuba, and then his children came to Barbados and end in the same situation." It's like God makes plans that we don't know.

Barbados is like my second land, my second country. Now when I go to Cuba, I want to come to Barbados. When I'm in Barbados, I would like to go to Cuba. People ask me, "Where are you from?"

You came from a person that emigrated to a country, Cuba. And you never think about moving from there. You live all your life and you surprised to see that you're in a next country. Sometimes I ask myself, "But what am I doing here?" But then I say, "You're in Barbados."

FLORENCIA YEARWOOD

I was born on the ninth of August 1962 in Manatí.

I came to Barbados on the twenty-eighth of April 2000. Coming to Barbados was wonderful. Because I remember that something came to my mind, and I said, "I want to do something different." And my aunt, my mother's sister, she lives in America and she went to Cuba. We have the same name, Florencia. She said, "I will take you to America." At that time, I was looking around, and I said, "I want to go to any place. I will go to America." But you know God always has a plan for us. I sent a letter to my aunt and my aunt said, "In God's time, everything will work out. You be quiet and wait." I was waiting, waiting, and I tried to go to America. I got forms to send to the programme that they call it *biombo* in Cuba, the US [diversity] visa lottery. I submitted like three forms.

But one day, something told me, "Go to your sister's house and ask her if she has any letter from Barbados, from my aunt here in Barbados." Because a long time ago I heard that my aunt sent a letter to my father. And I went to my sister's house a few times, you know? And I asked her to give me the letter and the address. But she said, "I have to look and see where it is." One day I went, and I know that she had a suitcase, a little suitcase, and the letter was there with a lot of papers from my father. Her husband told her, "Jenny, give her the

Figure 15.3. Florencia on her wedding day. Courtesy of Florencia Yearwood.

address." And that day she went and gave me the address. I said, "I have to send a letter to my family in Barbados, to my aunt Itha." I said, "Oh, I don't know how to write in English." Then I said, "Ah, I know." Because I was working in a day care, and the secondary school is below. And I called one of the English teachers and she wrote a letter for me. And I was waiting, waiting, waiting, waiting. A whole year passed.

Then one day I went to a cultural activity with the children, to sing. And I saw my mother in the door of the place where we went to sing with the children, to perform. And she had a letter in her hand. I started smiling and she was smiling too. When I finished, she said, "The letter come from Barbados!" And she opened that letter and we went to my sister to read the letter. My aunt said that she was so happy to hear from us.

In my letter I talked about the economic situation in Cuba. Because I went to university, I had a good salary. But I didn't have the money when my son Yanier was to graduate to buy his clothes to go to the graduation. And the family here understood. In a few months, they went to Cuba. They saw our situation. Where are they supposed to sleep? One of my friends gave me a mattress. I put two beds in one bedroom, and they slept over there. They were so happy over there. My aunt was walking around the place, happy. Because she has the same face like my father. At first when we saw her, it was like seeing a female that was my father. The same, the same thing. They had a wonderful time over there, eating the food we buy for them. They brought fish from Barbados – flying fish and dolphin. And we ate a lot with them. And she said, "I will invite all of you to go to Barbados. If you like Barbados, you can stay in Barbados."

Jenny came before me because the [Cuban] Immigration stopped me because they said that professionals could not leave Cuba. But God always has his plan and his time. I said, "No problem." After that, I said I would go to see the minister of education in my place. And I went. He said, "Okay, I will call the province." He called the province, and the province said, "Okay, send her with a letter." And you know that I came fast to Barbados. I was so happy when I came to Barbados. Happy, happy, happy, happy. And I tried to learn English by myself, but I didn't get success. But I said, "No matter. I am here."

One of the persons I met here, he is a teacher. He invited me to go to Alma Parris School in Speightstown to cook. I told my sister, "We're going to cook over there." We went to that activity and I met another person that he knew, a Venezuelan who has a workshop. And I went over there to paint. When I went to school, I remember that we had a subject called drawing. So I said, "I think

I have this ability." She told me, "If you can paint these little chattel houses, I will pay you sixty-five cents for each one." Every week my salary was twenty-five dollars. But I was jumping. And I started to do more and more with more ability. Then she said, "I will pay you two hundred dollars Barbadian." I would send the money to my son. I left him with my mother in Cuba for three years. I sent money to help the family.

Then I applied to the Ministry of Education in 2001 and I got through. I was so happy when I started working. I teach at Blackman and Gollop Primary, St Giles and Charles F. Broome. But my English, the first time I went to the school, I only said, "I'm coming here to help." The class teacher made the students be silent, and she started applauding.

I feel so familiar in the Barbadian community. I am happy here; I am happy here. I said, "If people have any spirit of life after death, my father was jumping." Because he tried to come to Barbados to bring us to Barbados. He never got through, but we got through. The father didn't reach the land, but the children reached the land, the Promised Land.

The last time I went to Cuba was in 2005. I didn't go when my mother was dying. When I was a little girl, I always asked God not to let me see my mother in the coffin. And when that happened, I was talking with her, the day before. And she told me, "I didn't sleep well last night, and I don't think I will sleep well tonight again." I would always say to her, "Read the Bible, read the Bible." She died, but she is with God. I couldn't go because my passport was expired. God works in strange ways that we don't understand. But he has his plan and he hears you when you ask for something.

ERNESTO YEARWOOD

I was born in Manatí in September 1957.

I studied to become a merchant marine. I worked many years as a merchant marine, many years. Afterwards, I left the merchant marines and went to work in the thermo-electrical field for sixteen years. I was in the role of safety specialist. I was in charge of dealing with all the technical matters, with the breakdowns in the equipment pertaining to the industry.

In 1978, I went to Angola on a technical mission. On the way back, the plane stopped to refuel in Barbados and I said, "This is my father's country. I would like to visit one day."

After a certain time, my sisters were here in Barbados, and I decided to come here. I've been here five years, I came in 2003. The reasons? Everyone knows the reasons: economic. Our parents migrated to better their lives; we migrated for the same reason.

I feel happy to be here because I can help my family, my children above all. I hope that at some time, they can also come to Barbados. I have some difficulty with that because of their age. If they were minors, they could have come with me. But they had finished their studies in Cuba. Every morning I wake up I think of my daughter, Onilet, and of my wife and my friends in Cuba. At the moment my son Israel is here visiting from Cuba. He has to come and go as a visitor. He can't stay, he has to leave and come back. My father used to say that he arrived in Cuba without any documentation from anywhere, but Cuba is my country. I'm Cuban. Well, half-Cuban, half-Barbadian. But he acquired all his documentation and all his work, all his life in Cuba, until he died on the sixth of January 1980. He was seventy-seven years old.

As I told you, I worked for twenty years as a merchant marine and then spent sixteen years at a thermo-electrical plant. These were things that I studied for in Cuba and became a specialist. Here, in Barbados, for all practical purposes, these positions don't exist. Here there are no big merchant ships and there's only one thermo-electrical plant. In Cuba there are around forty thermo-electrical plants. Here, I have nothing else to do but work in a cleaning company. I feel happy that I can help my family. All my co-workers love me and I cooperate wherever possible because of my technical knowledge fixing the equipment. Above all I can also cooperate helping my children.

JUANA "JENNY" YEARWOOD

I want to say something. There are lots of controversies about how the Cubans live, about the things that happened in all those years, the economic situation, the politics and everything. But none of that would have happened to us without us being prepared.

Florencia studied in a teachers' college to become a teacher. And thanks to that, she received her degree in primary education. She didn't have to pay any money for that. The [Cuban] government provided the free opportunity for her to educate herself.

I studied in university and graduated with a degree in economics, and I didn't have to pay anything. I worked during the day in accounting and in the evening I went to a workers' course to study until one in the morning, and at seven in the morning I was in the office again. In one way or another, we were prepared. With the scarcity and the situation in Cuba, people had to prepare themselves and people had to survive. And that has helped us a lot here, to survive. If not by this road, then by another road, but always a good road.

Ernesto studied ship mechanics. He is a man who was at sea for many years from young. So all of this helped to form you, to make you who you are, to be able to confront life. I think that the Cuban migrants will survive wherever they go.

These interviews with the Yearwood siblings were conducted on 5 January 2018 at Florencia's home in Emerald Park, St Philip.

CHAPTER 16

PEDRO HOPE JÚSTIZ

Hometown: Guantánamo City, Guantánamo
Barbados connection: Grandfather and wife
Occupation: French and Spanish teacher
Arrival year: 2000

I WAS BORN THE TWENTY-NINTH OF JUNE 1956, in Guantánamo, Cuba. I was the youngest child. I have a brother, Guillermo, and a sister, Tamara.

The memories that are still with me from Cuba, I should divide in two parts. The first part is seeing my father going to work at the US naval base in Guantánamo and coming back from the base. And then his leaving in the evening to play piano at the Kumora Club. He was also the pianist in an orchestra named *Típica Harmonía*, so there was a time when they had a lot of rehearsals at home with lots of musicians. So I was close to my father. That's why I love music; because I grew up listening to the rehearsals of the orchestra at home and then going to different festivals when I was a student. So this is part of my culture. Apart from that, once my father retired from the base ... he was retired by force in 1966 ... he began teaching Physics and English as a foreign language.

And I heard from my mother that my grandfather was a Barbadian who married my Haitian grandmother Lidier Glemeaud. My grandfather, Edmund Lee Hope, was a tailor. I could not meet him, because he passed away in 1947, eleven years before I was born. But I learned about my father addressing his father, my grandfather, in English and addressing his mother, my grandmother Lidier, in French. And my mother was saying how strict Mr Hope was in terms of education and teaching good manners. This was amazing to know. My father wanted me to be a musician too, so I went to study music at the school of music in Guantánamo. But my passion at that time was, and still is, to learn modern foreign languages, more precisely English and French.

There's a second part of my memories that is very close to my grandmother, Lidier. Being her youngest grandchild, I was very close to her and I wanted to learn English and French. I remember when she said, "*¿Pedrito, tu quieres hablar inglés y francés?*" ["Pedrito, would you like to speak English and French?"]. And I would say, "Yes, yes." "*Oui, oui.*" She was always close to me and trying to teach me something.

There is another thing concerning my memories of growing up in Cuba. In Guantánamo City, with the Cuban side being close to the American naval base, there was a time that some young people and neighbours were trying to reach the naval base to leave the country illegally. It was a lot of confusion. "You heard so and so reached the base?" Or, "So and so died trying to reach the base." Or they were on trial. At that time my brother Guillermo was always trying. He tried three times to reach the naval base, until he managed in 1973. He's still living in America.

The concept of Barbados that I had at that time was precisely when my generation began attending the British West Indian Welfare Centre in Guantánamo. There were different activities for the different countries represented there, and there were some celebrations about Barbados. The Welfare Centre was the place where we could get the atmosphere of the English-speaking Caribbean. I learned that I was a second-generation Barbadian descendant. So I always wanted to be there in the land of my grandfather. That was a dream from a long, long time.

And then in our neighbourhood there were three Barbadians, as far as I remember. There was Adolphus Collymore, who was a Barbadian immigrant. I used to call him Uncle Collymore. He was always telling my father to teach me English, to speak to me in English. And I used to go there. I remember Uncle Collymore, a very dark-skinned man, always with a toothpick in his mouth and his shoes well-polished, with his hat, always well dressed. He used to work at the naval base too.

And it was my dream to come to Barbados. Unlike other Barbadian descendants who live here in Barbados, I could not talk about all these culinary things, because there was a stronger influence of Jamaicans in Guantánamo... the ackee, the dumplings. And there were lots of Haitians. But the few Barbadians who were in Guantánamo, and the few that I managed to meet and their children... the descendants... they talked about Barbados as a place of good manners. In a way, I think my parents tried to raise me in that aspect of good manners. And there were lodges. And I used to see all these ladies dressed in white and speaking in English. So I asked my mother about them and she said, "These are *jamaiquinas* going to the lodge."

When I was in secondary school, I was involved in sports. First, I was in fencing after my father passed away in 1969. And then I moved to judo. But my passion was English. In 1972, I began my study of English at the language school in Guantánamo. I was the monitor while I was learning English at secondary school. I was granted a scholarship to study English as a Foreign Language (EFL) to become a teacher of English. That was a great experience. I spent four years at Warner Moro Institute of Foreign Languages in Santiago [de Cuba]. There it was not only modern languages and modern linguistics, but also culture. So I joined the choir, and because of my deep voice I was a bass.

Figure 16.2. Pedro celebrating his graduation from the Warner Moro Institute of Foreign Languages with his mother Irene Jústiz. Courtesy of Pedro Hope Jústiz.

After my four years of teacher training, I began teaching English at secondary school. Then I had five years more to get my degree, because I was studying and teaching in the Modern Language Department at the same alma mater ... Guantánamo Teacher Training University. I was also dealing with linguistics.

I remember in October 1985, I was on my way to Guyana. Since I had chosen to become a teacher of English as a career, I was given the possibility to go to the University of Guyana for a training course. And there was a stopover here at the airport and I said, "One day, I will come here and see the land of my grandfather." And that dream has come true.

Once I became a teacher, I joined the dance company, Jagüey, and we managed to tour Europe. We participated in a folkloric world festival in 1991. I was a manager of that dance company and a musician. We toured France, Spain and Belgium. And then again in May 1995, we were invited to *la Fête du Travaille* in Pas de Calais, France. I was the group's spokesperson.

It's well known that the economic situation in Cuba was really tough at that time, in the late '80s and early '90s, what we call the Special Period. The East Bloc, the Soviet Union, collapsed and therefore that was reflected in the economy of Cuba. So it was tough. Because of my English and French, I was a member of the group they called English experts that were in charge of supervising the teaching of English in the tourism industry in Cuba. So I found the possibility to move to tourism.

That was a very tough decision in my life because I was a senior lecturer in the university – Guantánamo Teacher Training University. And I switched from that into entertainment, into public relations, into hospitality. It was for almost half of the salary I had been earning, but because of the tips I could earn several times my teacher's salary. That was a way of survival and a way to really help my family, my children. I'm talking about the late '90s. At that time I had Yeneisy, that's my first daughter, and then in 1989, I had my second daughter, Aimara. My mother was very old and sick.

Working at the Guantánamo Hotel was an opportunity for me to get some tips from tourists and also practise my English and French. Many teachers of English moved to tourism to earn more from the tips. But I always said, "One day I will come back to my career, and I will study for my master's." And thank God I did it here in Barbados. I did my master's at the Cave Hill campus, University of the West Indies. I graduated in October 2015 with a master of arts degree in linguistics (applied linguistics) after two years of study.

I love French; I have a passion for French. I also did the DELF (*Diplôme d'études en langue française*) – Intermediate and Advanced, B1 and B2, with the Alliance Française de Bridgetown. And now I'm preparing to pursue my DALF

Figure 16.3. Pedro receiving his MA in linguistics (applied) at the 2015 graduation of the Cave Hill campus of the University of the West Indies. Courtesy of Pedro Hope Jústiz.

(*Diplôme approfondi de langue française*) C1. I hope to do the test either in July or November.

I came to Barbados the twenty-third of December 2000. It is a very loving and lovely and beautiful story. While I was working at Guantánamo Hotel, I met a beautiful lady that I thought at first was from Jamaica. The bartender told me, "Peter . . . that's the way they used to call me there in Cuba . . . there's a lady from Jamaica looking for you." I went there and introduced myself. The lady said, "No sir, I'm not from Jamaica. I'm from Barbados." I said, "My grandfather was from Barbados." And that started a relationship. Time passed and then she invited me to go back to my roots and to see where my grandfather was born. I accepted her invitation. She was the person that changed my life. To take that decision at forty-four years old. I think that I'm blessed to have met that lady, who is now my wife – Dr Sharon Marshall.

I left from Guantánamo to Havana. I had to stay two nights there at a hotel, so that I could get the Jamaican visa at the Jamaican embassy. The flight was Air Jamaica from Havana to Jamaica, and then from Jamaica to Barbados. On arrival in Barbados, I had an experience here at the airport with Immigration. They asked me what I was going to do here in Barbados. I explained that I was invited. At that time the person that invited you had to send a letter of invitation to Cuba, and the person had to state that they would take care of you financially. That you will not work. All these things. I also mentioned that I was going to the jazz festival and they thought I was going to work, so there was some confusion. Fortunately, you were at the airport to meet me, so I was allowed to get out of the airport. There was an issue that they did not stamp my passport, so the next day when we were in town trying to make a duty-free purchase at a store, they realized that my passport was not stamped. So I had to go to the Immigration Department to get that sorted out.

When I came to Barbados, to be honest, I was very impacted by this small island and the level of development, as compared to Guantánamo. You could see the infrastructure. Of course, Barbados was not in the same economic situation as Cuba was when I left. So I had a different perspective. Although in my case, before coming to Barbados I had gone to Guyana, so I had a picture of the Caribbean, although Guyana is in South America. And in 1998, I had a training attachment at Sandals Resorts International, so that also gave me a perspective of Jamaica. I could see that Barbados was very different from the rest of the English-speaking Caribbean.

At first, it was not easy for me to adjust. Because from the sociocultural point of view, in my neighbourhood in Guantánamo it was normal to hear "*Oye Irene*", "Hey, Pedro". It was very noisy, with neighbours talking and calling out to each other, "I need some salt", or this and that. Imagine I'm now in a very nice neighbourhood, very quiet. So with you and your mother having tea, watching the evening news, and going to bed, and after that everything around us was very quiet. Nine o'clock. I remember I went twice and sat in the front porch and I see all the houses in our residential area, everything closed, quiet. Nobody on the street. I said, "Oh my God!" It was totally different to where I come from. I said, "Okay, let's see." And I adjusted to that situation and I did well. Now I love this quietness, I love this residential area where I have been living for seventeen years.

An advantage was, of course, that as a lecturer in English, and with the experience I had from Guyana and from Jamaica, I tried to understand the local English. From the sociolinguistic perspective, I always paid attention to how people codeswitch from standard English to Bajan English and from Bajan English to standard [English]. But I managed to really survive. And then, there is a period when you are an immigrant that you don't have a job. So that process of finding a job is really complicated. And it's really frustrating because you rely on the person . . . in my case you . . . that sponsored me.

It was very frustrating going to interviews this place and the next. "Wait for a call", and I'm still waiting for a call. And all doors closed. 'Til I began working in September 2001 as a teacher of Spanish, thank God. I learned about the Primary Spanish Programme, and I was successful in the interview with the Ministry of Education, based on my experience in Cuba. That was really an experience in my life; from university to a primary school programme. I remember that first Monday that you took me to Christ Church Boys School at seven thirty in the morning. I saw all these kids just playing and making a lot of noise. I was like shocked. You said, "Get out of the car. Get out of the car." I was like, "Oh my God!" But I took that as a positive, and things were good.

Figure 16.4. Pedro conducting a choir from the Christ Church Girls Primary School. Courtesy of Pedro Hope Jústiz.

In the Primary Spanish Programme, I taught at Christ Church Boys, Christ Church Girls and St David's Primary School. That was in 2001. And then in 2002, I saw in the newspaper the advertisement of a permanent post at Garrison Secondary School, as it was called at that time.

I attended the interview at Garrison Secondary School and I was successful. So then I moved from primary to secondary school. I started teaching there at Garrison in 2002 until 2003, when I moved to Harrison College on secondment. I spent two years at Harrison College, from 2003 to 2005, when I returned to Garrison, which is now Graydon Sealy Secondary School. I've been appointed head of the Modern Language Department at Graydon Sealy. It's been four years since I've been appointed, but at first I acted in the position on two different occasions.

I was also a part-time Spanish tutor at the Barbados Language Centre at the Barbados Community College. That was a great experience there because I worked from 2002 to 2012. I worked from 5:00 to 7:00 p.m. in different courses. Also, from 2005 to 2006, I was a part-time tutor of Spanish at the Hospitality Institute. That was a good experience too. The only place that I have not taught Spanish is at UWI [the University of the West Indies]. In those years of teaching Spanish, primary school, secondary school and the Barbados Community College, I always wanted to share my experience as a native speaker of the language with Barbadian teachers of Spanish and have them practise Spanish in a very authentic way.

When you migrate and you leave your family behind . . . part of your family, because now you make a new family . . . you try to ensure their economic maintenance through remittances. Therefore, my two daughters were minors when I left, so through working here I tried to send them some cash. There was no easy way to transfer money to Cuba, as now with Western Union. Before, you had to get somebody travelling to Cuba, or through the bank try to send Canadian dollars or pound sterling, but not US dollars because of the embargo, to get that to my sister and my mother. It is a fact that – like Barbadian migrants who once they were in the UK or Canada or United States, sent remittances to their families as a way of support – you become the financial support of your family. It was not easy in the case of Cuba, because of all the difficulty with the embargo.

I was well known in stores downtown, buying all these female things for my two daughters. After seventeen years here, they are now adults. They became women, mothers. Yeneisy has a daughter, Irene, who is eight years old. She's going to be nine in September this year. And then Aimara, my second daughter . . . she's a medical practitioner in Cuba . . . she has my grandson, Pedro Guillermo, and he is five years old. From my sister, I have a niece and two great-nieces. So the shopping does not stop.

Since 2002, I have been visiting Cuba almost every year to maintain contact with my country of birth and with my family and friends. But I've always had that dream of my children getting out of Cuba to experience vacation. It's not only to migrate, but to have that experience of what is the world outside Cuba. Aimara spent a month in Barbados in 2009. That was fantastic for her; it was the first foreign travel in her life, and getting the experience of driving in her father's car. I never had a car in Cuba; I lived forty-four years in Cuba and never had a car. I didn't even know how to drive. So I got my driver's licence at forty-six. It's never too late.

Then I always wanted to have my granddaughter here. But at that time, the Cuban migration policy did not allow minor children to come to visit, just to migrate. But now the policy has changed. And in 2015, Yeneisy and Irene managed to go to Grand Cayman when you were working there, and they spent a lovely time there with you and me.

When I left Cuba, it was my dream to enjoy a certain quality of life, and I love travelling and visiting different countries. You and I got married in St

Lucia in 2001. My first overseas vacation was in Grenada during Christmas 2003. In 2004, we went to St Vincent, and to St Maarten in 2005. I've been visiting the United States since 2006, Miami, New York, Philadelphia, Las Vegas... I've had the opportunity to enjoy four cruises with you, so far. The first one was from Miami around Cuba to Labadee, Haiti; Ocho Rios, Jamaica; Grand Cayman, Cayman Islands; Cozumel, Mexico; back to Miami in 2006. And 2007, from Barbados, Aruba, Puerto Rico, Dominica, St Lucia and back to Barbados. There was another one from Puerto Rico to St Thomas, US Virgin Islands, to Tortola in the BVI, Antigua, and back to Puerto Rico in 2008. In 2010, we went from Miami to Cozumel, Belize City, Roatan Island in Honduras, Grand Cayman, and back to Miami. So I've been travelling around.

When I go back to Cuba, I feel that I am back to my roots, to my culture, and to my family and friends. It's a mixed feeling you know, of going back to the place where you were born. I'm Cuban. It's not for the material things, but with the life I have in Barbados, sometimes there's a kind of confusion. I enjoy spending time with my family, with my children and friends and neighbours there. But things have changed. Time has passed. I enjoy my stay in Cuba, but I'm always thinking about coming back to Barbados. I'm CuBajan; I'm Cuban, Bajan and Haitian. I'm a Caribbean man.

My great achievement has been to reach age sixty-two; I'm going to be sixty-two in June. I've been able to pursue some of my dreams like travelling and getting in contact with all the cultures. Another great achievement has been to have the quality of life that I always dreamed about since I've been living here, and getting my master's degree. I'm thankful for all the blessings I have here in Barbados.

My grandfather, Edmund Lee Hope, travelled from Barbados to Cuba and he died there. It seems that I'm going to die here in Barbados, or in Haiti. Barbados is my second home. I've told you that when I pass away, you should get my ashes and send them to my family in Cuba.

This interview with Pedro was recorded at our home in Amity Lodge, Christ Church, on 6 February 2018.

CHAPTER 17

PABLO ATWELL

Hometown: Havana City, Havana
Barbados connection: Great-grandfather
Occupation: Hotel executive housekeeper
Arrival year: 2002

MY MOTHER WAS ORIGINALLY FROM HAVANA, BUT MY father was from Baraguá. He migrated to Havana where he met my mother. I was born in Havana, in Vedado, on the thirtieth of May 1971. I have five siblings.

About growing up in Cuba, I remember the link with the family and neighbours and friends, the way how we grow so close knit in terms of the human part. In spite of the challenges which we faced due to the economic situation and so forth, we always kept that human relation. We were very close between the families, friends, neighbours, which made life easier by far than what it was.

I've been to Baraguá many times. I used to spend some of my childhood there during vacation time. That's where we got the first exposure to the Bajan culture and roots. My great-grandfather was from Barbados. I was very young and I don't remember many things, but I remember about some dishes like coucou, souse, the sorrel in December. I also remember the Landship, because they used to do that too. My grandfather, Joseph Atwell, was a very good musician. I played his guitar. He was a very smart man, with a lot of wisdom, very calm. I never saw my grandfather upset. He was a very level person, speaking very low. He never talked loud. My grandmother's name was Isidora Davis; she was caring, and a great cook.

I worked for five years at the British embassy in Havana. At some point in time, I decided that I wanted to experience living in a different place. Barbados was in the picture, but I didn't see how that would be really possible. Because my grandfather wasn't there at that time – he was the only link to the Bajan roots. So that was out of my picture. I really wanted to go to the Bahamas because of the proximity to Cuba. But it so happened that during my work at the British embassy, I met a Barbadian, and we established a close relationship, and he asked me if I wanted to come to Barbados, so I accepted.

I came to Barbados on the twenty-seventh of April 2002. It wasn't easy leaving Cuba, I must say. It wasn't easy, because of the differences in cultures. It is a totally different culture here to the one I was leaving behind. Different language, plus when I came what I was hearing on the road, it wasn't English. It was the dialect. And my knowledge of English wasn't less bad than it is right now. I wasn't sure that I wasn't in China, because I couldn't understand a word that anybody was saying. I literally couldn't understand anything.

Then I had to learn to blend into the Barbadian culture and get to understand certain things that I misunderstood otherwise. So I got to understand why certain things were like that. I adjusted and welcomed the change. It wasn't easy dealing with the language at first. Then because of the fact that I wasn't from here, I faced certain challenges. Not all the sectors of the population are open to migration from the country that I come from. Even though the Cuban diaspora here is pretty small, I faced some challenges dealing with some persons.

I actually got to meet a good branch of my family here. One time I was working in Christ Church and somebody called me over the intercom. They called me by my last name. So a gentleman was passing and asked the security guard who was that person with that name. He said, "Some Cuban guy who is here." So that gentleman wait until I finished work, and when I was walking he told me to get in his car. I said, "No, I don't know who you are." But when I looked at him, I saw my grandfather's face, very similar. He told me that his family went to Cuba years ago, but they lost contact. He invited me to his house and it so happened I found out that he was my cousin. His name was Cyrus Atwell. He passed away last year, or year before. I developed a very close relationship with his wife and children. At the funeral, I met a large branch of the family from St Lucy. That was a good experience.

After a few months, I left the island and returned to Cuba. Subsequently I travelled to Grenada, where I got married to a Barbadian. We have two girls; one of them is biologically mine. The opportunity presented itself to work in Grenada, so I took it. It was good. Initially it was as a supervisor at a workshop because it required mechanical engineering skills, which is my profession. Then I got the opportunity to work in the hotel industry and I grabbed it. I was the executive housekeeper at a hotel in Grenada. I learned from it, and I continued working in the hospitality industry.

So from there, I came back to Barbados and worked as assistant executive housekeeper at the Hilton Barbados Resort, where I spent ten years. Then the position of executive housekeeper opened up here at the Radisson Aquatica Resort. Right now, I am the executive housekeeper. I am responsible for maintaining the brand standard in terms of cleanliness and the standards in the

Figure 17.2. Pablo on the job at the Radisson Aquatica Resort, Barbados.

rooms, plus keeping inventories, payroll for the staff, doing the weekly rosters. I'm the head of department, so I'm responsible for anything that the department entails.

If things were as they are right now, I don't know if I would have adjusted so easy. Then it was easier to live here. Right now the economy is a bit contracted. Actually, I don't know if I would have stayed here.

I'm one hundred percent Cuban. I try to go to Cuba as often as I can. Most of my family is in Cuba, so I try to go there as often as the financial constraints allow me. I feel very good when I go back. I feel good about the fact that I can see the family and friends. I don't feel so good with the fact that I see that the country is going backwards, because I don't see an improvement in the standard of living, as far as the people are concerned. And the infrastructure of the country seems to be doing the same. So sometimes it's kind of shocking to me when I . . . They say you shouldn't make comparisons, but when I make the comparison – because I'm living here – and I see what a small, little island with 277,000 people has done to keep a certain standard of living for the majority of the people. It might be tough now, but people still have a certain comfortable way of living.

And Barbados doesn't have the natural resources that we have in Cuba, and the level of professionalism in science and medicine that we have over there, or the volume of tourism that we have over there. And when I see the standard of living here, compared to the standard of living there, that's what makes me feel bad. What makes me feel bad also are the friends that I left, family members, that they have a high educational level, and the condition that they actually live in is not matching one with the other. So I congratulate the people of Barbados for what they have achieved throughout the years. Because I say they don't have the resources and

Figure 17.3. Pablo received his diploma in tourism management at the 2017 BIMAP graduation. Courtesy of Pablo Atwell.

they have been able to create these conditions for the majority of the people. My concern is why we, with more resources, cannot achieve that. That's what makes me feel bad.

The Cuban community here is not very wide, and there are not many things that I get involved in. Beside work and my studies, I don't have time for much else. My life is very dynamic. I have continued my studies. I just finished a diploma in tourism management at BIMAP [the Barbados Institute of Management and Productivity].

I thank God for everything that I have achieved. I have been able to improve my career and use of the English language. I have been able to travel to places that I wasn't able to go before – Grenada, Trinidad, Jamaica, the United States, Panama. I don't regret what I have done.

Pablo Atwell's interview was conducted at his workplace, Radisson Aquatica Resort, Carlisle Bay, St Michael, on 2 February 2018.

CHAPTER 18

ROBERTO TROTMAN BROWN

Hometown: Buena Vista, Las Tunas
Barbados connection: Father
Occupation: Spanish teacher
Arrival year: 2002

MY GRANDMOTHER WAS FROM MONTSERRAT. HER NAME WAS Maria Lynch. Her husband was Samuel Brown and he was from Montserrat. They went to Cuba when my grandmother was pregnant and had their first daughter there. That was my mother, Sara. My father was Bajan, Adolph Trotman. He came from a place in St Philip close to St Catherine's School. When I came here, I was hoping to find relatives of his, but it's not easy.

I was born in Las Tunas, the twenty-seventh of November 1959. It was a very small neighbourhood called Buena Vista. I grew up there with a lot of Barbadians, Jamaicans and Haitians also. We were ten brothers and sisters – five girls and five boys. I'm the last one of them.

I grew up with people older than I am. So I had to go to the store frequently. Everyone would say, "Go to the shop." "Bring me one pound of pork." "Bring me a pound and a half of sugar." When I come back, I had to go back again. Sometimes I would get vexed with them, you know? I would get punished about that. It was very strict discipline that I see in my house, that I never saw in the neighbourhood. Our discipline was quite different from the rest in the street where I was living. So my friends would laugh at me, seeing the way how we conducted ourselves, you know? We were not allowed to go inside the friends' houses. I could not even go, although I was twelve/thirteen years, to turn on the TV, or to interfere in my parents' conversation.

One of the things that caught my attention when I reached here was the side door that I see in most of the houses in Barbados. And growing up I used to say to myself, "Why my house has that door there?" Because the other houses in Buena Vista were different from mine. But that was the door we had to use to enter and leave, because we could not use the front door. And a lot of things like that that I remember with a little emotion, because I don't have my parents with me anymore. I still respect the way that I was brought up; that gave me a lot. Because when I look back, I see that the rest of my friends haven't reached as far as I have. It gave me a bit of respect, and I have to give thanks for what they gave me.

I had to go to school daily, even if I didn't have all the stuff to go. Sometimes I had shirt and short pants, but I didn't have the shoes. When I had the shoes, I had a tear in my shirt, and they had to sew it. That was a hard time, because it was at the beginning of the Revolution. So there weren't a lot of things in the shop. Even then I could not say I cannot go because I don't have shoes. I had to go. My parents only had to speak one word, that was enough for you to do what they were directing you to do. Sometimes they would make sweets with nuts and sugar and mix it and sell it. And bake flour with coconut... they call it *coquito quemado* in Cuba... and package it. With that money, we grew up. There were a lot of us.

In Buena Vista, there was another gentleman from Barbados, Alan Davis, living in the house in front of ours. There was a Joseph Scantlebury from Barbados living in my house also. So there were a lot of Bajans there. He used to talk a lot about the war, how he went to other countries to fight and then he came back to Barbados. And then a group of them leave Barbados for Cuba in 1921. When they reached into Puerto Padre, they kept walking a lot until they reached to Vásquez. That's one of the small towns between Las Tunas and

Puerto Padre. A lot of people with Barbadian ancestry live there – I think the Goddards, Nelson's family and I think Elizabeth's family. That place they call it Pito Cuatro. There's another place they call Babiney, and the other place is Mesa Cinco. That's where my father and my family settled.

My father travelled to Cuba with his father, George. His mother, Adriana Branch, stayed in Barbados. The job my father did was cutting canes in Manatí, Rincón de Manatí. That's another place where a lot of Barbadians, Jamaicans and Haitians were living. When you go to that city, you will see that ninety-five per cent of the people are black people. He also cut cane in Chaparra. There are a lot of Bajans living there too – Griffith, Chapman, Boyce.

He wasn't a person who spoke a lot. I didn't get a lot of words from him. He said Barbados was a beautiful place with great beaches, but few job opportunities. He said that there was a lot of cane here, but people were not as well paid as in Cuba. They couldn't manage to have a house and raise a family, and live. So that was the reason people left. He never came back to Barbados.

When I was small, he was in the cane field doing his job. Then when he came home, he would put up the hammock... that's the first time I saw that ... and sleep in that. He was a very quiet, decent gentleman. He was very well respected among the Barbadians. A lot of people went to the house to meet with him, even people from Matanzas, Baraguá. He was very qualified in English and gave lessons. I can tell you he used to teach a lot of people coming from the United States, some born in Cuba. They called him to assist in teaching classes. He was qualified to read and write and express himself. Better than me. I can never reach the way he expressed himself when he wanted to. Most of the family can interact and speak in English with anyone. I started teaching over there.

As I told you, I'm satisfied with the way I grew up and the respect they showed me to direct to people and to receive. I remember my childhood with happiness now, although I wasn't so happy then with the strict rules. I think the first time I turned on the TV, I was twenty years old, and had a girlfriend. I couldn't go to the fridge to open the fridge as I would have liked to. Sometimes I would say, "I want food." I would hear, "You have to wait. You have to wait." Even then, when they shared the food... because in Cuba, the small one gets the best... but when my mother share the food, I get the chicken neck. I would ask, "When you going to change that?" She would say, "That will always be your part. That's what I have for you. You will see, you will thank me when you get bigger." After a while, I laughed a little too. So sometimes I would ask her to give me mine first. Because maybe by running around in the street, I was getting hungry sooner than the rest. Sometimes when she look at me, maybe she realize that I'm really hungry, she would take a spoon and share a little bit of food. Sometimes I get some lashes with the same large spoon that she used to share the food.

It was not strange to me to see the cou-cou here. But we didn't call it cou-cou, we called it *harina*. They would make that, but not like you do it here. It was with a bit of salt. They would put some parts of the pork inside, and it was more dense. And for poor people with a little corn flour, it would become a big meal. We ate a lot of that, with milk or alone. We would have that more than three times during the week, night and day.

I am very contented when I look back, to see how far I reached. The opportunity I had to come to Barbados; I could never imagine that I could be here at this time. I studied in Havana, and by living and working in Havana, it came into my mind that I should come and give my effort here. Which place better than my father's land to come and to teach? Because I was teaching English in Cuba and doing a lot of translation.

When I was preparing to come, I went to see Elliot Nelson, Yolanda's brother. He's quite a popular person, you know? And he was the one I took my father's birth certificate to. That's the first time I spoke to you, Sharon. Maybe you don't remember, but you were in Havana and Nelson had said, "There is this person coming, and she's very qualified. You have to come, and you have to wear nice clothes." I think that was '99. I spoke to you by phone, and you told me, "I have to go to Santa Cruz. And tomorrow, I have to leave early to go to Guantánamo." I was speaking to you from the Los Pinos neighbourhood in Havana.

I came to Barbados in 2002. Before I came, I had made some connections. I also met Pablo Atwell. But as I told you, I was speaking a lot with Nelson. He would tell me about groups coming from Barbados. I met Colbert [Belgrave] in one of those groups. I met Wendy Griffith-Watson [former chief education officer] over there. I met Lana Simmons-Rowe. I met Grantley Smith and Melba Smith before I came here. I met Laurie Blackman, she works at the Central Bank now. All those people. I said privately to Wendy that I was teaching in Cuba, and that my father was Bajan, and that I would like to come. So to me, I was thinking of that. First of all, to visit my father's land. I was not expecting any amount of money, because I never asked in Cuba how much I would get. Maybe that is something wrong, but I never did it.

When I came, I went a lot to the Ministry [of Education], but the first job I got was with Jeannette Allsopp in 2002 at the Caribbean Multilingual Research

Centre. She is a very qualified lady, able to speak French, Spanish and English. We finished a translation of about ten magazines for the United Nations. I did the Spanish in that translation. That was my first great job here. I think that is my great achievement here.

When I did that, I didn't have a laptop. I didn't even have a good house to live in. I did that in my own handwriting. And when I finished the first one, I wasn't sure that it was good. So I said to myself, "Let me go and talk to the lady." When I see that she started to read, she start to smile. I asked, "It's good?" She said, "It's a great job. That's a very, very great job. Try to finish what you have, and then come back. Because I have some that have been submitted already that I want you to revise." Up to now, I have a letter from her that I guard like my life. Because when I went to her a whole year afterwards and asked her for a letter of recommendation, I would never have believed that she would write in that way. I did that work not only with her, I was teaching small children throughout the Caribbean. Because the Multilingual was reaching all the region.

My English was better than now, because you lose things when you are not active. And I was teaching Spanish too. When I got to do a seminar with her, she was fixing my English, and when I was ready, she told me, "You're ready to go." So I got to teach some stuff in English too.

When that finished, I was looking for a job to do. I went to a man who had a small hotel in Silver Sands and I told him that I knew how to paint. But my mummy and father, they never sent us to paint and stuff like that; they sent us to school. So after a while, the man realized that I am not so qualified in the painting. When he came back, I wasn't so far in the wall that I was painting, so I told him, "It's better that you finish with me, because I give you double work." He said, "No, something bring you here. I will teach you. I will show you how to do the job, but I know you know more than what you're doing here. When I see you, I don't believe that you are a general worker."

So working at this place, I met a Spanish lady who told me that there was a job opportunity at the university [University of the West Indies, Cave Hill Campus]. When I called the university, they called me back and I started to teach at the university. That is another great achievement here. I have a good letter from them. I worked with them only one year. I went to Cuba with the blood pressure and stuff, and I reached here late. But that I enjoyed a lot, teaching grammar in Spanish. All of those university graduates from that time teaching Spanish today in Barbados passed through my hands and they learned the advanced Spanish from me – Andrew Lokey, Andre Burke, Tonya Brathwaite,

Gemma Skeete, Laura Ann Franklin, Christopher Bowen, Sharifa Yearwood, Tashena Hinds, Anna Grannum, Laura Nicholls, Andrea Millar, Keith Corbin, all of them.

Sometimes when I park in one of the car parks that we have here in Barbados and I see them and they give thanks, that means a lot to me. I walk more strongly when they say, "Teacher. *Señor, gracias, gracias.*" Thanks, you know? They appreciate what you did for them. It's like I have my breakfast already when they say that.

After I came back from Cuba, I joined the Primary Spanish Programme. I went to Wendy, and we remembered how we met. I told her that I would like to join the Spanish Programme. It was a very stressful job, but I enjoyed it a lot because of the attention the children were paying to the Spanish. Barbados is a very multicultural country, although people don't realize it. You have people here from Venezuela, Colombia, Argentina, Cuba . . . There are a lot of people that make the place multicultural. I enjoyed the small children, because when you get them, they know nothing about Spanish. But when you give the work, they get quite excited about it. And that made me work harder. I made my living by my skill working with them.

At that time I had a group in Hindsbury [Primary School] that . . . in my humble opinion . . . was one of the best in the entire country. Even the lady Malva Lewis, one of the education officers from the ministry, she was saying that. I taught these infant children to speak Spanish, all female. I can even remember their names, because they were so nice – Melanie, Debrika. They were speaking Spanish so fast that I was surprised myself. But my style of teaching, by having taught in Cuba I had the practice. In my way, I started to put discipline in them.

I would tell them the reason why they were in that classroom. I told them the same thing that I was told when I was their age, and sometimes they opened their eyes wide. I remember one of the last years in one class four, I said, "You, you will be the prime minister. You will be the minister of finance. You will be the minister of education. Don't feel that [Owen] Arthur will be there forever. Don't feel [David] Thompson will be there all his life. I know you can do the job. Don't feel the same people you see in the bank will be managing the bank. They have to retire. So Barbados is expecting you to be there. The only thing is, you have to be ready to be there."

I used to make jokes in the class with the not-so-qualified students, telling them, "I will see this one as a guard in some bank, and when they see you as a prime minister, the only words they can say are, 'I was at primary school with him'. So if I tell you that I can see you as a guard, you have to study hard. You have to do your best."

I told them, "When I reach sixty-five, you will be the persons in great jobs that I taught here." I'm not far in my believing, and my thinking. Because I was having a problem with my Cave Shepherd [department store] card, and I saw a pretty girl coming close to me and she said she couldn't understand my accent and would go to find the manager, the person in charge. And when the manager came, she said, "Maybe you don't remember me, but you taught me from Infants to Class Four." When I looked at her face, I told her which room and the last class that I taught her, and her class teacher. She said, "You have a good memory." I said, "Yes, you were fat; you used to do this and that; you used to sit in this place. I'm very happy to see you here."

So, as I was telling you, I'm not far in my thinking of what I was telling them that I would see them in great jobs here. I see some of my students who have reached that level. I see Andrew Lokey has a choir here in Barbados, and I see how people show a lot of respect for St Leonard's School and to him.

When I look back on the different jobs that I have done in Cuba and here, I feel contented and proud about them. By living here, I taught more than forty thousand students – children and youngsters. Because I had four schools, including the university.

I never taught the students saying, "Let me make the time." I want for them to learn. The main reason when I leave the class is for someone to say, "Teacher. ¡Hola! ¡Hola!", "¿Como estas?", "Buenos días." I would feel nice when I reached the school and someone would call me, "Señor, Señor." Because I work for that. I don't work to get money. I work to teach. They pay me money to do that, but the reason is to teach.

When I go back to Cuba, I feel at home. That is the little difference that I can see between both countries. Because there we treat all the Barbadians like the Cuban people. When my father was walking the main road, all the people in the neighbourhood would call out to him, "Dada." Because that was the way we called him before I even realized what Dada meant. They showed a lot of respect to him in the shop, in the bank. Because when I was ten/twelve years, he was old already.

But here, sometimes once the people pick up that you are not Bajan born, the treatment is different. And sometimes that hurts me a little. One time I said, "Look the prime minister wasn't born here and look how far he reached."

I told them, "[David] Thompson wasn't born here." I was teaching Thompson's daughter, Osa, from Infants. She started at Erdiston before she went to George Lamming [Primary School]. And he would call me on the phone. Before he came to power, we were speaking a lot, because she made him call me. And her mummy, Mara, would call me too. At that time I was living in the same compound where his guard was living, Robert Jordan.

I used to tell him [Thompson] how I felt about living here. How sometimes you're in the line at the supermarket and the cashier wants to give attention to the person behind you. And when you speak, they say, "Your English is not so good. I can't understand what you're saying." It's a different treatment altogether. In that part, I see the difference. I'm not saying all, just the way *some* people treat us. If you went to Cuba now, people may treat foreign visitors nicer than their own. So when I go to Cuba, I know I'm going home.

Even when you reach the airport here, and show them that you live here, they are not satisfied. Sometimes you show them the Barbados passport and everything, and they ask, "Where are you going to stay?" I say, "I'm going home, sir." "What are you coming to do here?" "I'm teaching here. I live here." A lot of questions, and they see your face more than once. So that still will make you sometimes not take the land as yours, although it gave work to all of us, the best. Because if I didn't get here, I would never get to know this country, and other countries. If we have the ID, you have to believe that we come from a Bajan. Sometimes I've even heard the words, "No Bajan." Those things hurt you a little, you know?

I'm in the process of retiring and it's taking so long. I'm being treated like no Bajan would be. It's like four years waiting for that gratuity. Send me to this place, send me to the other. So many places. Those are some of the things that make you see the place with other eyes. Other than that, the country is very beautiful, very safe. It's nice! You can walk here at any time.

Barbados gave me a lot of opportunities, to know people, to pass through Jamaica, to know Trinidad, to go to the United States faster than my friends from Cuba. Living in Cuba, I could never imagine that I would be in the United States, or even Trinidad and Jamaica. I had the opportunity to teach small children, which I never did in Cuba. I highly appreciate what I got from Barbados. Here I get a bit more money to help myself and my family, to carry back to the family. In Cuba, I have three sisters and four brothers, and they have a lot of children. I go often to visit them.

As I told you, I feel that that's my land. Barbados is also my land. The only

Figure 18.2. Roberto and Pedro enjoying the spirit of the Christmas season in Barbados.

thing is for the people to accept that we take it as ours. It's not the land, the land is already there, you understand? I was so excited that I wrote two songs. There is "Proud to Be a Bajan". I sang it on TV, I sang it all over the school. I didn't struggle to write that song; that song came to me directly. That is the feeling I had when I wrote the song. I'm a musician also.

One of them, "My Land", I sang with an orchestra at the Embassy of Barbados in Cuba, for [Ambassador] Donna Forde, and I sang that song too for the minister of culture and sports, [Stephen] Lashley. I have that recorded too:

> You are in my dreams, you are in my heart
> And no matter how far we are, we'll never forget you
> Because you are my life, you see me grow from a child
> Barbados, you are my land, you are my people.

That's part of the song.

I love the place. I would like to be here all my life. But we need to get more feeling from the people, to see that people love you. I feel sometimes that Barbadian people feel that foreigners come to take what belongs to them, but that's not so. We don't come here to do anything wrong. We come here for the best. We don't need too much, just a little.

This interview with Roberto Trotman was recorded at my home in Amity Lodge, Christ Church, on 20 December 2017.

CONCLUSION

AS STATED AT THE OUTSET, A MAJOR OBJECTIVE of this research was to learn primarily through these oral histories how those who moved from Cuba to Barbados experienced departure, migration and settlement.

For them, the decision to leave was prompted in large part by a desire to escape difficult economic circumstances in Cuba, an ultimatum regarding the receipt of pension from the United States after service at the US naval base in Guantánamo, as well as a yearning to experience the birthplace of their Barbadian forebears and to take advantage of opportunities for advancement. Beyond examining the push-pull factors which influenced the individual and family decisions to migrate, the testimonies clearly depict the transnational nature of the migrants' subsequent existence.

Their means of migration was determined by the historical period in which they travelled, the modes of transportation available during that time and financial assistance from relatives already in Barbados. Settlement in their new country was facilitated by a system of family support and was influenced by the level of acceptance with which they were received by the citizens of their adopted homeland.

CONCEPT OF BARBADOS

Concepts of the ancestral homeland varied from "a paradise place" and a "land of opportunity" to a "potato country". When Frank Philo's mother brought her children to Barbados in 1937, he and his siblings were sad to leave their friends. He says, "But we were very happy to be coming back to Barbados, because Cuba was getting hard, and we're going to a paradise place now."

When the Rowe family left Cuba in 1970, Gilbert recalls that it was not a sad moment for them because "we were coming to this place named Barbados, which would have offered you, in those days, an opportunity to become whatever you could be". Nelson Goddard's father seemed to entertain a similar notion. He recognized the intellect and talent which his son possessed and declared that "we have to take him to Barbados and see if he makes something of himself".

Gilbert's contemporary and neighbour in Baraguá, Colbert Belgrave, reveals that his own father often praised Barbados, describing it as "the loveliest island in the Caribbean". Colbert would question his father about why he left if it was so lovely and he would explain that things were hard at that time but that he wanted to go back and rest his bones there. Roberto's father had told him, "Barbados was a beautiful place with great beaches, but few job opportunities."

Another Baraguá native, Josué Ramírez Nelson, who came twenty years after Colbert, comments, "everything I heard of Barbados was kind of like that view we have in Cuba of 'overseas'. Where it is like this land of opportunity where you can just do anything there. Everything that you can't find here, you'd get over there." This idea of Barbados was a significant improvement on the one which Josué's mother, Yolanda, and her siblings had when his maternal grandmother was attempting to return in 1967. A neighbour from Barbados, Mr Elcock, had dismissed it then as a "potato country", prompting tears from Yolanda and her sisters and the declaration that they did not want to go to a place which had no electricity.

Departure for Barbados would offer the migrants an opportunity to compare their preconceived notions of the country with the reality of what they encountered on arrival.

DEPARTURE

Ofelia Nicholls's mother made the decision to leave Cuba because "she said it was getting too hard". In the 1930s when the Nicholls family left, travel by sea was the only means of transportation, as was the case for Frank Philo, who left the following year. Of the 1936 journey, Nicholls states, "We came on a cargo boat. It was awful." The family waited in Dominica to get a passenger vessel to continue the voyage. Philo, who first came as "a baby in arms" in 1927, has no real recollection of that journey. However, when his mother returned for good ten years later, he recalls that they left from Santiago de Cuba and "we came over on a cargo boat and stopped in Guadeloupe and Martinique . . . and St Lucia . . . and then Barbados".

For those who came much later, air travel links via other countries had been established. Isabel Deane felt a sense of excitement when she and her family left for St Lucia in 1969. "Leaving was very traumatic and a bittersweet occasion for us", she recalls, "because we were leaving friends and family that we grew up with, and at the same time it was the first time we were going on an aircraft, which was very exciting for us." Their route was via the Cayman Islands and Jamaica. Her father had been prompted to leave Cuba for his country of origin "as life started to get harder with the Communist system". He had been told that if he remained in Cuba, he would receive his naval base pension from Washington in pesos, and there was not a favourable exchange rate at the time.

When the Goddard and Rowe families left in 1970, their journey to Barbados was by way of Mexico and Jamaica. The Goddards were being repatriated by the Barbados government, so arrangements had been made to facilitate them along the way. Gilbert Rowe recalls that, despite the regret of leaving friends behind, it was exciting to leave the isolated rural place which had been his home for thirteen years. "I don't know what was more interesting," he says, "travelling overseas, or that first ride from Baraguá into Havana." Graciela King's itinerary in 1973 was also from Cuba to Mexico, then to Jamaica and on to Barbados. On 3 October 1973, Cuba's national airline, Cubana de Aviación, inaugurated direct flights between Havana and Bridgetown. This is how Colbert Belgrave and his mother travelled to Barbados in 1979.

In 1999, Josué left his familiar environment in Baraguá as an eight-year-old to join his mother in Barbados. The first stage of the journey involved travelling by bus to Havana, where he spent some days reconnecting with other family members who lived in different parts of Cuba. On the day of departure, he remembers that "at the airport, I cried. I bawled because I didn't want to leave." There was another source of anxiety connected with Josué's first plane trip: the impact which news of the 1976 Cubana bombing off Barbados had left on his young mind. He and his aunt who accompanied him would overnight in Jamaica before he was reunited with his mother in Barbados.

MIGRATION

"My first impression when I came to Barbados was shock," says Gilbert Rowe. This was in reaction to the fact that there were "some children who would be most unkind to you". Strong family support helped him and his siblings to cope with their new environment. The school experience for Graciela King was not one where she and her sister Ydania were subjected to xenophobia or hostility, but curiosity. She remembers, "I got to school, the children would not go to the classes. They wanted to hear my sister and me speak Spanish." The children also pulled her hair to see if it was real.

Graciela was less than impressed with her father's birthplace when she arrived from Guantánamo in 1973. She recalls: "When I got here, Barbados was not developed at all. I couldn't believe what I saw when I got here because I saw men walking barefoot. I mean, in Cuba, although things were difficult and so on, I never saw anybody walking without shoes." However, when her fellow *guantánamero* Pedro Hope Jústiz arrived in 2000, the island's fortunes appear to have improved with the passage of time. Pedro states, "When I came to Barbados, to be honest, I was very impacted by this small island and the level of development, as compared to Guantánamo."

Pablo Atwell too had a favourable impression of Barbados after he arrived in 2002. He says, "I see what a small, little island with 277,000 people has done to keep a certain standard of living for the majority of the people." He contrasts this with his views on Cuba. "I don't feel so good with the fact that I see that the country is going backwards", he comments, "because I don't see an improvement in the standard of living, as far as the people are concerned. And the infrastructure of the country seems to be doing the same."

Kinship and family networks were important factors in facilitating the migration to Barbados. For example, Florencia Yearwood wrote to her Aunt Itha, who brought her to Barbados. Maria Thomas's Uncle Everton was the one who sent for her and her daughter. Yolanda Nelson Springer's sister Gloria invited her to move to Barbados and hosted her until she could afford to go on her own. Many of the migrants report that relatives were at the airport to meet them and to help them get settled.

The Rowes travelled together as a nuclear family, but family separation was a significant aspect of the migration process for most of the others. In 1973, Colbert Belgrave's father, Cleophas, left Colbert and his mother behind in order to bring his other son Eddy to Barbados before he reached the age for compulsory military service in Cuba. Colbert and his mother, Monica, would join them in 1979. Nelson Goddard came with his father, Ethelbert, in 1970. Nelson's mother, Beatrice, remained behind in Cuba with three boys and two girls. It would be a year or two before his mother and sister, Evelyn, came to join them. Two siblings remain in Cuba and one has migrated to the United States.

Graciela King's father, Nathaniel Niles, returned home to Barbados in 1969 following his retirement from the US naval base after thirty years of service. He did so because he would not have been able to receive his pension from the base if he remained in Cuba. This economic decision meant that he would be leaving without his wife and children. Graciela, her mother, Francisca, and sister Ydania came in 1973, while the older siblings remained in Cuba. Maria Thomas migrated with her younger daughter, Niurka, in 1993. Her older daughter, Maritza, remained in Cuba and joined them in 1995. The following year, the entire family was reunited when her husband, Juan Matos Campo, came to Barbados.

Yolanda Nelson left her husband, Jacinto, and son, Josué, behind in 1994. She was able to send for Jacinto in 1997 and for Josué two years later. The Yearwoods, too, experienced this separation. Florencia came initially without her son, Yanier. "I left him with my mother in Cuba for three years", she recounts. Ernesto's wife and children remain resident in Cuba.

Finding paying work was critical to the migrants in order to gain financial independence, establish themselves in the new country and send remittances to the people they had left behind or bring them to Barbados. Before Juana and Florencia Yearwood were eventually employed as facilitators in the Primary Spanish Programme, they found work wherever they could. Juana explains, "My first job here was collecting eggs. I went and worked, collecting eggs, washing eggs, cleaning the area, feeding. It's something I never did before. But I wanted to make money to help my family in Cuba." Juana adds, "I worked almost all my life in Cuba in accounting, in an office dealing with salaries. So this was something new for me, which I didn't know how to do, and I did it."

Her sister, Florencia, who had been a kindergarten teacher in Cuba after completing university, started her working life in Barbados cooking at a school and painting replica chattel houses at a workshop. From her meagre earnings, she immediately began trying to support those whom she had left behind. She says, "I would send the money to my son . . . I sent money to help the family." Their brother, Ernesto, had acquired specialist skills during his working life. As he explains, "I worked for twenty years as a merchant marine, and then spent sixteen years at a thermo-electrical plant. These were things that I studied for in Cuba and became a specialist." However, he was unable to put these skills to work in Barbados. Ernesto was undeterred by this. "Here, I have nothing else to do but work in a cleaning company," he states. This work enables him to fulfil his main objective in migrating. He says, "I feel happy that I can help my family."

After a first job at the Bridgetown Fisheries Complex, Maria Thomas's career took a different direction when she accepted an assignment with someone from Guatemala who was looking for a babysitter. She recalls, "I accepted the assignment for two months. It was soon discovered that I was a qualified and experienced accountant. This led to a job offer working with the Guatemalan embassy, until the embassy closed in 1998. Six months before the embassy closed, I got a new job with Fomento y Cubiertas in 1997."

Pedro knows well that "there is a period when you are an immigrant that you don't have a job. So that process of finding a job is really complicated." With years of professional experience as a senior lecturer at the Guantánamo Teacher Training University, Pedro initially found work teaching at the primary level in the Primary Spanish Programme. He would eventually move on to the secondary level and the Barbados Community College. He remarks: "The only place that I have not taught Spanish is at UWI."

Roberto Trotman had worked as a teacher and translator in Cuba and, after arriving in 2002, was fortunate to get an assignment assisting with the translation of about ten magazines for the United Nations. "When I did that, I didn't have a laptop. I didn't even have a good house to live in", he remembers. "I did that in my own handwriting." After that project ended, Roberto took on a painting job at a small hotel in Silver Sands, even though he had no particular skill in this area. However, a chance encounter there led to a teaching assignment at the university. This was followed by employment in the Primary Spanish Programme.

Yolanda came to Barbados with qualifications in pedagogy and psychology for pre-schoolers and had been granted the scientific grade of master of arts in pedagogy. She started her working life in Barbados assisting a cousin who had a store at the Bridgetown Port before she was employed in the Primary Spanish Programme.

Juana Yearwood credits their experiences in Cuba with providing the migrants with the skills to cope and their determination to gain a foothold in Barbadian society. She is firm in the view that, "with the scarcity and the situation in Cuba, people had to prepare themselves and people had to survive. And that has helped us a lot here, to survive."

SETTLEMENT

In "Reclaiming Place: The Architecture of Home, Family and Migration", Heather Horst examines how Jamaicans who migrated to the United Kingdom in the 1950s and 1960s and returned home to retire many years later design and use their homes "to attain the dream and realities of return".[1] She posits that "home is not just a place, but also becomes a site for imagining several key relationships in returnees' lives that are ultimately fundamental to the act of reclaiming place" and notes:

> Whether the construction of a home is motivated by status in the homeland, the recognition of an alternative status system for migrants who may be marginalized in the country and communities of migration, or a desire to embed themselves in the land and kinship systems of their birth, it is clear that homes are undeniably one of the key ways that migrants attempt to claim and reclaim their place in the world.[2]

Some of the Barbadian descendants in Cuba who migrated to Barbados came as young children with their parents, others who came as adults were not returnees themselves but proxies for their parents and grandparents who were unable to return. Florencia Yearwood explains that her father, Vivian, had been unsuccessful in his attempts to return to Barbados with his family. "He never got through, but we got through", she states. "The father didn't reach the land, but the children reached the land, the Promised Land." Her brother Ernesto had seen this promised land, albeit from afar, during a 1978 airport refuelling stop when he was on his way back from a technical mission in Angola. "I said, 'This is my father's country. I would like to visit one day'," he remembers. Pedro Hope also had a glimpse of the country on his way to Guyana in 1985. He recalls, "There was a stopover here at the airport and I said, 'One day, I will come here and see the land of my grandfather.' And that dream has come true."

For many of the descendants who moved from Cuba, the attainment of a "home" was just as cherished a goal as it was for the Jamaican returnees. Colbert Belgrave lists the acquisition of his own home as one of the major accomplishments which he was able to achieve as a result of his relocation to Barbados. It was a step which his father had urged him to take:

> One of the things that I'm proud of is the fact that, with God's help, I've been able to buy this house that we're in. Because when we came from Cuba, we came without practically anything. And that was one of the things that my father said to me. He would say, "Colbert, I don't want to die leaving you here renting nobody's home. I want you to get your own home and that you will be able to pay for it and enjoy it. And if you don't want to live here in Barbados, don't sell it. Rent it out, but when the year come, you can come back and spend some time here in Barbados. But don't you ever sell your house."

For Maria Thomas, it was the intervention of her uncle Everton which enabled her to acquire her own house in Barbados. Like the biblical character, Simeon, her uncle felt that he could depart in peace once the purchase of a house for Maria had been accomplished:

> A great source of pride is a blessing of a house bought for me by my uncle, and that's an important thing, because that is the basis for me starting my life here. I got the blessing from him. The last words he told me before he died were, "I would like God to keep blessing you." At that time, I wanted to take him to the hospital. I said "Uncle, come, put on your pajamas. I want to take you to the hospital." He said "No, no, no. I already died. The only thing I want is for God to help you."

When they first arrived, Nelson Goddard and his relatives stayed with an uncle for a few months, but home ownership was always the goal. "We had a house that my uncle bought for my father in Bank Hall," he explains. "When the folks moved out of the house, we went there. Then I bought Bank Hall from my uncle. I still own it now. My oldest son, Orlando, lives there. He also built his own house in Sunbury Tenantry." Nelson also built a home for his family in St Philip. He says of his migration to Barbados, "I like it here. I feel comfortable here, I work here. I make my living here. I built my house here."

For Juana Yearwood, it was important to state that "I came to the land and the house where my father was born. This is in Harrises, St Lucy. The house is still there." Departure from Cuba for Gilbert Rowe and his family was marked by the arrival of a messenger on a motorcycle. The messenger brought news that the family had been given permission to leave the country by the Cuban authorities. The Rowe family's home was immediately sealed and became the property of the government. They were dispossessed. Over time, Gilbert has been able to purchase residential and investment properties, but two houses in Barbados which hold much significance for him are the places where his family stayed after their arrival in Barbados and the home which they later rented:

> We spent a few nights in Union Road, and then Aunt Leotta had arranged for us to rent this house in Congo Road. And it's still there. I make it a habit to make sure that I show my son the house where we spent the first night, and the house that we lived in in Congo Road, because you must know your history. And you must be proud of your history, because that's what propels you.

For him, these houses were perhaps symbolic of reclaiming place, and the antidote to the loss of the house in Cuba of which his family had been dispossessed. Acquiring a house then was as important an act of reclaiming their place in the world for some of the migrants to Barbados as it was for the Jamaican returnees. However, the acquisition of a physical home proved to be no guarantee that the migrants would feel "at home" in Barbados.

Nelson Goddard has been settled in Barbados for half a century. He says, "I feel like a Barbadian, although the Barbadians don't accept me as a Bajan." Nelson adds, "There are a lot of opportunities that I lost, and I know that I did not get them because I'm not Barbadian." In business situations he was told that he would not be successful, and one man vowed that he would ensure that Nelson "would not get anywhere". Gilbert Rowe's success with the jazz festival attracted the envy of some. He recalls, "I remember sitting at this establishment, and somebody ... I would think that they didn't know it was me ... but looking back now, I think they knew it was me. I heard, 'Who Gilbert think he is? We tried doing this and we couldn't get it done.'"

Roberto Trotman laments, "Sometimes once the people pick up that you are not Bajan born, the treatment is different. And sometimes that hurts me a little." Pablo Atwell agrees that "not all the sectors of the population are open to migration from the country that I come from. Even though the Cuban diaspora here is pretty small, I faced some challenges dealing with some persons." Despite the many years that Graciela King has been living in Barbados, she says, "I don't always feel accepted in Barbados, not all the time. I find that people still discriminate. If they hear that you speak with an accent, that makes a difference. They still don't consider you a Barbadian. I am a Barbadian by descent, but not everybody welcomes you as a Barbadian."

CUBAJANS

All migrants tend to exhibit varying degrees of ambivalence about their countries of origin and the societies which host them.

Peggy Levitt and Nadya Jaworsky posit that "migration has never been a one-way process of assimilation" but rather one in which migrants "to varying degrees, are simultaneously embedded in the multiple sites and layers of the transnational social fields they live in". In support of their argument regarding the transnational nature of migration, Levitt and Jaworsky assert that "most scholars now recognize that many contemporary migrants and their predecessors maintained a variety of ties to their home countries while they became incorporated into the countries where they settled".[3] In addition, Elizabeth

Thomas-Hope argues that to view migration simply in terms of pushes and pulls and as a displacement of the household from a negative to a more positive location is inaccurate. She suggests that it is not a passive response to exogenous forces and ought to be understood instead as a transnational set of interactions and linkages associated with the movement of people, ideas, money and goods.[4]

"I highly appreciate what I got from Barbados," Roberto Trotman says. "Here I get a bit more money to help myself and my family, to carry back to the family. In Cuba, I have three sisters and four brothers, and they have a lot of children. I go often to visit them." He notes a difference between how he is treated in Barbados and how he is received in Cuba, "So when I go to Cuba, I know I'm going home." Pedro Hope states, "When you migrate and you leave your family behind . . . part of your family, because now you make a new family . . . you try to ensure their economic maintenance through remittances. Therefore, my two daughters were minors when I left, so through working here I tried to send them some cash." Pedro's annual visits to Cuba were preceded by shopping sprees. He says, "I was well known in stores downtown, buying all these female things for my two daughters. After seventeen years here, they are now adults. They became women, mothers."

Gilbert Rowe is proud of the fact that "I kept my word to my mother who told me, 'Don't forget the family in Cuba.' I've got an uncle and cousins there. I've kept my word to my mother, that I look after Tio and the family. I still do. That means a lot to me." Frank Philo has also kept his strong family ties in Cuba and has returned frequently. He says, "I've been back to Cuba nine times. I love going back. I have my brother over there, Sammy. I think he's eighty-four. I have a niece, Sammy's daughter, Janet. Since I've been travelling to Cuba, I brought three of them over here to see what it is like." Only two of the sixteen interview subjects have never returned to Cuba – Ofelia Nicholls and Isabel Deane.

Brettell and Hollifield refer to the fact that migrants experience "simultaneous membership in two societies".[5] This holds true for those who came to Barbados from Cuba but, for some of them, that membership can be viewed as more tenuous in one society than the other.

Josué Ramírez Nelson considers Barbados home, stating that he can relate to many things in his adopted homeland now. However, he adds, "I still feel like a bit of an outsider at some points though. I would get into a conversation with some Barbadians and they would say things from their youth that make no sense to me. I experience it through their experiences, but I still very much feel like I'm a foreigner." As for Cuba, his absence from the island meant that he was not current with the local lingo. "So when I went back to Cuba", he explains, "there was all this new slang that I was so confused about. And I was still using this old slang. People would be like, 'Where you from? No one says that anymore'."

Nelson Goddard remarks, "Now when I go back, it reminds me of my childhood days. There's something that when you go back you feel – how can I put it? – the ambience. It's different. I feel at home, yes. But still certain things make me not feel at home."

As noted previously, Azicri comments that after the 1959 revolution, it was an urgent priority for the new government to enlist the population in the works of the revolution, thus creating a close identification between the leaders and the masses. In examining what this meant for the West Indian descendants, Andrea Queeley argues, "Links to family and institutions in the English-speaking Caribbean, which suggested an identity not exclusively Cuban, were frowned upon by a state whose agenda it was to consolidate their revolution in part through cultural unification and homogenization."[6]

Dr Aleida Best Rivero is one Barbadian descendant who became part of the political apparatus. When the first elections for the National Assembly of People's Power were held in 1976, she was elected as a delegate and served for twenty-five years. She also served two terms as a member of Parliament from 1998 to 2008 and was part of the provincial direction of the Committees for the Defense of the Revolution. Her father, Joseph Nathaniel Best, was born in Belleplaine, St Andrew, on 1 July 1901. He migrated to Cuba in 1921, settling initially in Puerto Padre and then in Manatí. Mr Best later moved to Las Tunas, where he remained until his death in 1978. In addition to her political involvement, Aleida also became assistant professor and president of the chair of Caribbean studies at Las Tunas University.

In my view, some Barbadians and their descendants managed to embrace whatever benefits the revolution brought them while still holding dear their familial and ancestral links. For example, Juana Yearwood points proudly to some of the signature achievements of the revolution, stating, "the government provide a lot of good things for children, to go to school and study free, free health care and all that". She asserts that "there are lots of controversies about how the Cubans live, about the things that happened in all those years, the economic situation, the politics and everything. But none of that would have happened to us without us being prepared." For her own family, she lists the fact that the Cuban government provided her sister, Florencia, the free opportunity to earn a degree in primary education and that she herself graduated with a degree in economics without having to pay anything. However, Juana explains that "the situation with food and so was difficult, and I decided to take that step" to reconnect with her roots in Barbados.

Colbert Belgrave's father had sought to shield his sons from one aspect of the revolutionary government – compulsory military service. He brought his older son Eddy to Barbados before he reached the eligible age. He also secured a British passport for Colbert so that Colbert arrived in Barbados with three passports – Barbadian, British and Cuban – and risked being rejected at the point of entry for being "no Bajan".

Through their experiences of migration and settlement, the migrants have exercised options to hold fast to traditional concepts of nationality or to construct new ways of self-identifying. "I'm one hundred per cent Cuban," declares Pablo. Gilbert asserts, "I am a Cuban of Barbadian descent that was brought to Barbados, and Barbados accepted me . . . But I am a Cuban; that's who I am and will always be until the day I die." Graciela says, "I still feel that I'm Cuban.

Figure C.1. Some members of the CuBajan community at the funeral service for Colbert Belgrave on 17 December 2018. Seated (*left to right*): Pedro Hope Jústiz, Elizabeth Griffith, Isabel Deane, Juana Yearwood, Yolanda Nelson Springer and Frank Philo. Standing (*left to right*): Jacinto Ramírez Marino, Evelyn Goddard, Hilda Rollock, Aida Greaves and Graciela King.

I know that I've lived here longer, but I consider myself Cuban." Her fellow *guantánamera* Isabel feels differently. She says, "I consider myself a Barbadian, after living here for the past forty-two years."

After leaving Cuba more than eighty years ago, Frank Philo feels "more Barbadian than Cuban, but I love Cuba so much". Colbert states, "My father was Barbadian, and my grandparents too. So I am proud to be a Barbadian, a Cuban Barbadian." Maria has forged a hybrid identity, saying, "I consider myself half-Cuban and half-Barbadian." Ernesto Yearwood also describes himself as being "half-Cuban, half-Barbadian", while Pedro embraces all aspects of his ancestry, declaring, "I'm CuBajan: I'm Cuban, Bajan and Haitian. I'm a Caribbean man." Yolanda claims both heritages: "I'm both Barbadian and Cuban. I am Cuban, I have it in my soul. And I'm Barbadian, I have it in my blood."

Although there are naturally differences and variations in the histories of each individual migrant, there are a number of commonalities. It is my hope that this work clearly demonstrates that, in general, migrants tend to be extraordinary individuals who are driven by a high degree of self-motivation, adaptability, determination and perseverance. This is certainly true of the CuBajans in Barbados.

NOTES

PREFACE

1. The word "CuBajans" in the title is a reference to Cuban Barbadians, or Cubans of Barbadian descent. It is comparable to other terms signifying double nationality identification, such as Bajan Yankees and Bajan Brits.

INTRODUCTION

1. This is the colloquial term for Barbadians. Bajan is the dialect spoken in Barbados, and the word Bajan is also an adjectival reference to aspects of the island's culture.
2. A reference to the umbilical cord. The boast by Barbadians that "my navel string buried here" signifies that they were born in Barbados.
3. Melissa Wickham, "Digging into Roots", *Sunday Sun*, 16 April 2006, 12A.
4. *Sunday Sun*, 16 April 2006.
5. Donna Sealy, "Cubans Looking up Roots", *Weekend Nation*, 13 April 2006, 24A.
6. Ibid.
7. Caroline B. Brettell and James F. Hollifield, *Migration Theory: Talking across Disciplines* (New York: Routledge, 2015), 5.
8. Ibid., 11.
9. Peggy Agard, interview by the author, Christ Church, Barbados, 9 January 2019. All quotes attributed to Agard are taken from this interview.

CHAPTER 1

1. Wayne Smith, *Portrait of Cuba* (Atlanta: Turner, 1991), 55.
2. Ibid., 57.
3. Ibid.
4. Juan Pérez de la Riva, "Cuba and West Indian Migration 1900–1931", *La Republica neocolonial Anuario de Estudios Cubanos* 2 (Havana: Editorial Ciencias Sociales, 1979), 69.
5. "Revolution in Cuba", *Barbados Herald*, 15 August 1931, 2.
6. Smith, *Portrait of Cuba*, 58.

7. Marc C. McLeod, "Undesirable Aliens: Race, Ethnicity, and Nationalism in the Comparison of Haitian and British West Indian Immigrant Workers in Cuba, 1912–1939", *The Free Library* (22 March 1998), https://www.thefreelibrary.com/Undesirable aliens: race, ethnicity, and nationalism in the...-a020574141 (retrieved November 24 2019).
8. Hugh Thomas, *Cuba: The Pursuit of Freedom* (New York: Harper and Row, 1971), 543.
9. Lara Putnam, *Radical Moves: Caribbean Migrants and the Politics of Race in the Jazz Age* (Chapel Hill: University of North Carolina Press, 2013), 109.
10. Ibid.
11. Ibid.
12. Ibid., 109–10.
13. Elaine Pereira Rocha, " 'Another Black like Me': Strategies of Identification in Afrodescendientes in Latin America", in *Another Black like Me: The Construction of Identities and Solidarity in the African Diaspora*, ed. Elaine Pereira Rocha and Nielson Rosa Bezerra (Newcastle upon Tyne: Cambridge Scholars, 2015), 16–17.
14. *Supplement to the Official Gazette* 80, no. 37 (7 May 1945): 250.
15. Ibid.
16. McLeod, "Undesirable Aliens".
17. "Emigration to Cuba", *Barbados Herald*, 17 February 1923, 8.
18. "West Indians Ill-Treated in Cuba", *Barbados Advocate*, 27 October 1924.
19. T.J. Morris, British Chargé d'Affaires, Havana, to Principal Secretary of State, Foreign Office, London, 23 December 1924, FO 277/200, PRO.
20. Ibid.
21. "Cuban Press on Events of the Day", *Havana Post*, 20 August 1924, 4.
22. Robert Vansittart, Foreign Office, to Under-Secretary of State, Colonial Office, 30 January 1925, FO 277/201, PRO.
23. McLeod, "Undesirable Aliens".
24. Sharon Milagro Marshall, *Tell My Mother I Gone to Cuba: Stories of Early Twentieth-Century Migration from Barbados* (Kingston: University of the West Indies Press, 2016), 71.
25. McLeod, "Undesirable Aliens".
26. Marshall, *Tell My Mother*, 134.
27. Ibid., 164.
28. Letter from Thomas Brimelow, British Consul, Havana, to Acting Colonial Secretary, Belize, British Honduras. 2 March 1949. FO277/255/66, PRO.
29. Jorge L. Giovannetti, "The Elusive Organization of 'Identity': Race, Religion, and Empire among Caribbean Migrants in Cuba", *Small Axe*, no. 19 (February 2006): 18.

30. Jorge L. Giovannetti, "Empire beyond the Imperial Domain: British Colonial Encounters in Cuba", *British Academy Review*, no. 12 (January 2009): 24.

CHAPTER 2

1. Bonham Richardson, *Panama Money in Barbados, 1900–1920* (Knoxville: University of Tennessee Press, 1985), 19.
2. Ibid., 26.
3. Ibid., 78.
4. Ibid., 43.
5. *Barbados Blue Book*, 1909 to 1910.
6. G.W. Roberts, "Emigration from the Island of Barbados", *Social and Economic Studies* 4, no. 3 (1955): 245.
7. Ibid.
8. "Cuba Rapidly Returning to Prosperity", *Barbados Herald*, 4 February 1922, 3.
9. "The Webster SS Company – Bi-Monthly Sailings for Cuba", *Barbados Herald*, 21 October 1922, 4.
10. Ibid.
11. "Repatriates from Cuba", *Barbados Herald*, 11 November 1922, 4.
12. "Notes and Comments", *Barbados Herald*, 6 January 1923, 4.
13. "Emigration to Cuba", *Barbados Herald*, 27 February 1923, 4.
14. Ibid.
15. "Emigration to Cuba", *Barbados Herald*, 4 November 1923, 4.
16. Ibid.
17. "Population, Unemployment and Emigration", *Barbados Herald*, 24 January 1925, 4.
18. Ibid.
19. Roberts, "Emigration", 246.
20. Ibid., 250.
21. Ibid.
22. Ibid., 257.
23. Ibid., 262.
24. Ibid., 270.
25. Velma Newton, *The Silver Men: West Indian Labour Migration to Panama, 1850–1914* (Kingston: Institute of Social and Economic Research, University of the West Indies, 1984), 55.
26. *Official Gazette* 73, no. 96 (1 December 1938): 2288.
27. *Official Gazette* 72, no. 85 (24 October 1938): 2004.
28. *Official Gazette* 74, no. 47 (12 June 1939): 1119.
29. *Official Gazette* 77, no. 13 (15 February 1943): 118.

30. *Official Gazette* 78, no. 15 (22 February 1943): 754.
31. *Supplement to Official Gazette* 80, no. 28 (5 April 1945): 34.
32. "Emigration to Cuba", *Barbados Herald*, 17 February 1923, 8.
33. Ibid.
34. *Official Gazette* 71, no. 77 (24 September 1936): 1602.
35. Ibid.
36. Legislative Debates, session 1935–36, vol. 48, 17 November 1936, 230. Subsequent quotes are from this session.
37. House of Assembly Debates, session 1935–36, 17 November 1936, 770.
38. Ibid.
39. Legislative Debates, session 1937–38, vol. 49, 16 February 1937, 27.
40. Legislative Debates, session 1937–38, vol. 49, 15 June 1937, 128.
41. Ibid.
42. Legislative Debates, session 1937–38, vol. 49, 17 August 1937, 162.
44. Ibid.
44. Dreadnought, "Sayings by the Way", *Barbados Advocate*, 27 May 1936, 10.
45. Legislative Debates, session 1935–36, vol. 48, 43.
46. *Extraordinary Official Gazette* (21 January 1936), 1.
47. *Barbados Herald*, 14 March 1936, 8.
48. *Official Gazette* 71, no. 8 (25 January 1936): 163.
49. *Official Gazette* 71, no. 83 (15 October 1936): 1753.
50. Ibid.
51. "Current Items", *Daily Gleaner*, Kingston, Jamaica, 29 November 1932, 2.
52. "Reflections in a Studio", *Barbados Herald*, 30 May 1936, 8.
53. Ibid.
54. Clarence Roberts, interview by the author, St Philip, Barbados, 27 December 2018.
55. *Official Gazette* 71, no. 98 (7 December 1936): 1998.
56. House of Assembly Debates, session 1935–36, 1 December 1936, 810.
57. House of Assembly Debates, session 1935–36, 24 November 1936, 790.
58. Ibid.
59. *Official Gazette* 73, no. 44 (2 June 1938): 956.
60. *Extraordinary Gazette*, 12 December 1936, 1.
61. Ibid.
62. *Official Gazette* 73, no. 48 (16 June 1938): 1065.
63. Ibid., 1060.
64. Ibid., 1126.
65. Legislative Debates, session 1935–36, vol. 48, 1 December 1936, 231.
66. George Gmelch, *Double Passage: The Lives of Caribbean Migrants Abroad and Back Home* (Ann Arbor: University of Michigan Press, 1992), 25.

67. Ibid.
68. Ibid., 26
69. Percy Sinclair Leverick, *Leverick's Directory of Barbados, 1921* (Bridgetown, 1921), 46.
70. Ibid.
71. Ibid., 83.
72. Ibid.
73. Message from His Excellency the Governor to the Legislative Assembly, 10 February 1919, 4.
74. O. Nigel Bolland, *On the March: Labour Rebellion in the British Caribbean, 1934–39* (Kingston: Ian Randle, 1995), 27.
75. David V.C. Browne, *Race, Class, Politics and the Struggle for Empowerment in Barbados, 1914–1937* (Kingston: Ian Randle, 2012), 43.
76. Ibid., 44.
77. Basil Maughan, "Some Aspects of Barbadian Emigration to Cuba, 1919–1935", *Journal of the Barbados Museum and Historical Society* 37, no. 3 (1985): 245.
78. Glenford D. Howe, "De(Re) Constructing Identities: World War I and the Growth of Barbadian/West Indian Nationalism", in *The Empowering Impulse: The Nationalist Tradition of Barbados*, ed. Glenford D. Howe and Don D. Marshall (Kingston: Canoe Press, 2001), 126.
79. David Browne, "Go Bravely Big England; Little England Is Behind You": Barbadian Society and Polity during World War II" (presentation to the History Forum, Department of History, University of the West Indies, Cave Hill, Barbados, 7 February 1997), 10.
80. Ibid.
81. Isabel Fonseca, "This Earth, This Realm, This Little England", *Condé Nast Traveler*, 10 June 2009, 57. "George VI, facing war with Germany in 1940, must have had his courage redoubled on receipt of a cable from the distant colony of Barbados, signed by Grantley Adams, later to become the island's first premier: 'Go on, England,' it cheered. 'Little England is behind you.' This story, which crops up everywhere in the literature of Barbados, has supplied a lasting tag. Little England: a source of unexamined pride for many, a marketing tool for some, and an embarrassment for two generations of Barbadian intellectuals." See also Austin Clarke, *Growing up Stupid under the Union Jack* (1980; reprint, Toronto: Vintage, 1998), 41. "And we heard that our leader, Grantley Adams, sent a cable up to the King, His Britannical Majestical George the Sixth, King of England, Northern Ireland and the British Possessions Beyond the Seas, and told the King, 'Go on, England, Little England is behind you.' And from that day we are known with pride or embarrassment as 'Little England'."

82. House of Assembly Debates, third session 1969–71, 8 December 1970, 2147.
83. *Official Gazette* 75, no. 103 (23 December 1940): 2147.
84. *Official Gazette* 76, no. 5 (16 January 1941): 61.
84. *Official Gazette* 78, no. 16 (25 February 1943): 148.
86. *Official Gazette* 78, no. 18 (4 March 1943): 78.
87. *Supplement to the Official Gazette* 80, no. 51 (25 June 1945): 341.
88. *Official Gazette* 81, no. 5 (1 July 1946): 1003.
89. *Official Gazette* 80, no. 73 (10 September 1945): 819.
90. *Official Gazette* 81, no. 83 (17 October 1946): 868.
91. Ibid.
92. *Official Gazette* 77, no. 40 (20 May 1943): 920.
93. Ibid.
94. Ibid., 922.
95. Ibid.
96. Browne, *Race*, 90.
97. *Barbados Herald*, 7 April 1923, 6.
98. Browne, *Race*, 83.
99. Bolland, *On the March*, 111.
100. David V.C. Browne, "The 1937 Disturbances and Barbadian Nationalism", in *The Empowering Impulse: The Nationalist Tradition of Barbados*, ed. Glenford D. Howe and Don D. Marshall (Kingston: Canoe Press, 2001), 150.
101. Browne, *Race*, 141.
102. Richard Hart, "Labour Rebellions of the 1930s in the British Caribbean Region Colonies" (London: Caribbean Labour Solidarity/Socialist History Society, 2002), https://libcom.org/library/labour-rebellions-1930s-british-caribbean-region-colonies-richard-hart.
103. F.A. Hoyos, *The Quiet Revolutionary* (London: Macmillan, 1984), 49.
104. Ibid.
105. Ibid., 50.
106. The Barbados Volunteer Force was formed in 1902 and was founded as a volunteer unit raised to provide local defence for the island following the withdrawal of the British Garrison. https://www.bdfbarbados.com/the-barbados-regiment/.
107. Browne, "1937 Disturbances", 157.
108. Ofelia Nicholls, interview by the author, St Michael, Barbados, 31 October 2017.
109. Frank Philo, interview by the author, Christ Church, Barbados, 31 October 2017.
110. Barbados Rediffusion Service Limited began operations on 1 February 1951, taking over the assets and liabilities of its predecessor Radio Distribution (Barbados) Limited. Radio Distribution had started on 2 April 1935, but in 1937 "the wired network service extended south as far as Oistins and West to Black Rock". It

therefore would not have been available in country districts like St Philip, even if working class Barbadians had been able to afford the subscription fee. See Gladstone Yearwood and Mike Richards, *Broadcasting in Barbados: The Cultural Impact of the Caribbean Broadcasting Corporation* (Bridgetown: Lighthouse Communications, 1989), 8, 10.
111. Clarence Roberts, interview by the author, St Philip, Barbados, 27 December 2018.
112. Bolland, *On the March*, 112.
113. Mary Chamberlain, *Empire and Nation-Building in the Caribbean: Barbados, 1937–66* (Manchester: Manchester University Press, 2010), 5.
114. Ibid.
115. "The Royal Commission in Barbados", "First Commission Enquiry in Brief", *Daily Gleaner*, 25 January 1939, 19.
116. "Former Administrator of St Vincent Testifies", *Daily Gleaner*, 25 January 1939.
117. "Official Welcome Given Members at Queen's Park", *Daily Gleaner*, 25 January 1939.
118. *Official Gazette* 73, no. 62 (4 August 1938): 1422.
119. *Official Gazette* 74, no. 96 (30 November 1939): 2247.
120. Hoyos, *Quiet Revolutionary*, 51.
121. Sir Frederick Smith and Alan Smith, *Dreaming a Nation* (London: LifeBooks, 2015), 155.
122. Rose Mary Allen, "Cultural Adaption of the First and Second Generation British West Indian Migrants in Curaçao", *Modus Statistisch* (Central Bureau of Statistics, Curaçao) 13, no. 4 (2013): 29.
123. Ibid.
124. Ceri Peach, *The Caribbean in Europe: Contrasting Patterns of Migration and Settlement in Britain, France and the Netherlands* (Coventry: University of Warwick, Centre for Research in Ethnic Relations, 1991).

CHAPTER 3

1. The hurricane which struck Cuba on 9 November 1932 is regarded as the deadliest one in the island's history. It was the only Category 5 Atlantic hurricane ever recorded in November. The town of Santa Cruz del Sur, as well as an extensive portion of central and eastern Cuba, was devastated by the storm surge and rain. It is estimated that more than three thousand people died as a result of the hurricane.
2. The Royal Barbados Police Force had responsibility for immigration services up until 1 June 1980, when civilian control was transferred to the Immigration Department.

3. Grantley Adams International Airport was previously known as Seawell Airport, which was established in 1956. In 1976, the airport was renamed in honour of Sir Grantley Adams, the first premier of Barbados, the first and only prime minister of the West Indies Federation, and a national hero of Barbados.
4. The Curaçaose Petroleum Industrie Maatschappij was later renamed Shell Curaçao N.V. in 1959.

CHAPTER 4

1. "Janet started as a tropical wave located just off Barbados and retained this status until September 21, when within a 12 hour period, it strengthened first to a category 1 and then into a category 2 hurricane. When Janet hit the island, it was a category 3 system packing winds of 120 mph! Janet went on to become the most powerful hurricane of the 1955 season, reaching category 5 status with winds of 175 mph. The storm killed 38 people in Barbados alone, caused 5 million dollars in damage, and left as many as 2000 Barbadians homeless. In fact, the only hurricane hunter plane to be lost in the Atlantic on a reconnaissance mission occurred during Hurricane Janet. On September 26, the pilot lost radio contact at 10:15 PM, before flying into the then category 4 storm. By 11 PM, the US Navy classified the plane as overdue and the crew was officially reported missing. Neither the remains of the plane nor any signs of the crew have ever been found." Barbados Museum and Historical Society, "Today in History – Hurricane Janet", Facebook, 22 September 2014, https://www.facebook.com/barbadosmuseum/posts/10153665807498383?comment_tracking=%7B%22tn%22%3A%22O%22%7D.
2. *Q in the Community* is a regular open-air broadcast programme organized by radio station Q 100.7 FM in Barbados. It is held at different locations across the island, and attracts a more mature crowd, including returned nationals and visitors to the island. In addition to food and drink, they enjoy DJ music, line dancing and karaoke contests.

CHAPTER 5

1. Smith, *Portrait of Cuba*, 74.
2. House of Assembly Debates, session 1959, 18 March 1959, 203.
3. Ibid.
4. Max Azicri, *Cuba: Politics, Economics and Society* (London: Pinter, 1988), 25.
5. Ibid., 52.
6. Ibid., 34.
7. Andrea Jean Queeley, "El Puente: Transnationalism among Cubans of English-

Speaking Caribbean Descent", *Department of Global and Sociocultural Studies* 10 (2011): 14, https://doi.org/10.1080/17528631.2012.629438.
8. Azicri, *Cuba*, 65.
9. House of Assembly Debates, session 1961, 17 March 1961, 398.
10. Ibid.
11. Ibid.
12. Ibid.
13. Ibid.
14. Gilbert Rowe, interview by the author, St Michael, Barbados, 5 February 2018.
15. Colbert Belgrave, interview by the author, St James, Barbados, 6 December 2017.
16. Ibid.
17. Yolanda Nelson Springer, interview by the author, St Michael, Barbados, 26 November 2017.
18. Ibid.
19. Ibid.
20. Florencia Yearwood, interview by the author, St Philip, Barbados, 5 January 2018.
21. Louis A. Pérez Jr, *Cuba: Between Reform and Revolution*, 2nd ed. (New York: Oxford University Press, 1995), 343.
22. "Guantánamo Admiral Rebuts Castro Accusation; Denies Navy Base Sentries Killed Cuban Soldier", *New York Times*, 30 July 1964, 7.
23. Tim Reynolds, "Returning Guantánamo", *Jacobin*, 25 March 2016, https://www.jacobinmag.com/2016/03/guantanamo-gtmo-obama-castro-havana/.
24. Ibid.
25. INRA is the Spanish abbreviation for Instituto Nacional de Reforma Agraria or National Institute of Agrarian Reform. It was created under the agrarian reform law enacted in May 1958. The law's main provisions limited land ownership to 966 acres per individual, while rice, sugar and cattle holdings could be as large as 3,300 acres.
26. Tad Szulc, *Fidel: A Critical Portrait* (New York: William Morrow, 1986), 463.
27. H. Michael Erisman, "The Odyssey of Revolution in Cuba", in *Modern Caribbean Politics*, ed. Anthony Payne and Paul Sutton (Kingston: Ian Randle), 215.
28. Ibid., 216.
29. William M. LeoGrande, "Cuba: The Shape of Things to Come" edited by Susan Kaufman Purcell and David Jochanan Rothkopf, *Cuba: Contours of Change* (Colorado: Lynne Rienner, 2000), 1.
30. Ibid.
31. Fidel Castro, Address at the closing ceremony of the first national meeting of chairpersons of the Credit and Service Cooperatives, International Conference Center, Havana, 3 June 1998, in *On Neoliberal Globalization, the Economic Crisis*

and Other Subjects (New York: Mission of Cuba to the United Nations, 1998), 31.
32. Rachel Kushner, *Telex from Cuba* (New York: Scribner, 2008), 14. "Oriente was where we lived, and it was Cuba's largest, poorest, blackest province. It has the best climate and most fertile land for growing sugarcane. Castro has it all divided up now, I don't know why; Back then the entire eastern half of the island was just one province, Oriente."
33. Carlos Moore, *Castro, the Blacks and Africa* (Berkeley: University of California Press, 1988), 166.
34. Ibid., 296.
35. Ibid.
36. Smith and Smith, *Dreaming a Nation*, 155.
37. Ibid., 160.
38. Azicri, *Cuba*, 226.
39. Szulc, *Fidel*, 637.

CHAPTER 6

1. The Constitution of Barbados, https://www.oas.org/dil/The_Constitution_of_Barbados.pdf.
2. Ibid.
3. House of Assembly Debates, third session of 1969–71, 3 February 1970, 971.
4. Ibid.
5. Ibid., 28 July 1970, 1933.
6. Ibid.
7. Ibid., 1934.
8. Ibid., 1939.
9. The Constitution of Barbados, https://www.oas.org/dil/The_Constitution_of_Barbados.pdf, 10.
10. George Alleyne, "Nationality Law Changes Are Coming", *Barbados Today*, 21 November 2019.
11. *Diplomacy and Development: A Review of the Foreign Policy of Barbados* (Barbados: Ministry of Foreign Affairs, 1987), 4.
12. Ibid., 11.
13. Smith and Smith, *Dreaming a Nation*, 157.
14. Ibid., 157–58.
15. Ibid., 174.
16. *Diplomacy and Development*, 12.
17. Ibid., 94.
18. House of Assembly Debates, third session of 1969–71, 17 March 1970, 1318.

19. Ibid.
20. Ibid.
21. Ibid.
22. Nelson Goddard, interview by the author, St Philip, Barbados, 9 January 2018.
23. Errol Barrow, House of Assembly Debates, third session of 1969–71, 18 March 1970, 43.
24. Ibid.
25. Constance R. Sutton, "Cuban Connections and Presence in Contemporary Barbados" (presentation to a panel on Circum-Caribbean and Latin American Connections: Regional Migrations of Peoples, Ideas, Cultural Practices, and Politics, 106th Annual Meeting of the American Anthropological Association, Washington, DC, 28 November–2 December 2007), 4.

CHAPTER 11

1. The Reverend Canon Edward Gatherer was the oldest stipendiary priest in the worldwide Anglican Communion when he retired at age eighty-nine on 27 March 2011, after serving fifty-five years as the incumbent of St Andrew's Parish Church in Barbados.

CONCLUSION

1. Heather A. Horst, "Reclaiming Place: The Architecture of Home, Family and Migration", *Anthropologica* 53, no. 1 (2011): 29, http://www.jstor.org/stable/41475727.
2. Ibid.
3. Peggy Levitt and B. Nadya Jaworsky, "Transnational Migration Studies: Past Developments and Future Trends." *Annual Review of Sociology* 33 (2007): 130.
4. Elizabeth Thomas-Hope, "Current Trends and Issues in Caribbean Migration" (paper presented at the Group Expert Meeting on Migration, Human Rights and Development in the Caribbean, Port of Spain, Trinidad and Tobago, 14–15 September 2005), 54.
5. Brettell and Hollifield, *Migration Theory*, 5.
6. Queeley, "El Puente", 16.

SELECTED BIBLIOGRAPHY

OFFICIAL DOCUMENTS

Colonial Office correspondence
Constitution of Barbados
House of Assembly Debates
Legislative Council Debates
Official Gazette
2010 Population and Housing Census, vol. 1, Barbados Statistical Service

NEWSPAPERS AND PERIODICALS

Barbados Advocate
Barbados Herald
Barbados Today
Condé Nast Traveler
Daily Gleaner (Jamaica)
Havana Post
New York Times

BOOKS, JOURNALS AND CONFERENCE PROCEEDINGS

Allen, Rose Mary. "Cultural Adaption of the First and Second Generation British West Indian Migrants in Curaçao". *Modus Statistisch* (Central Bureau of Statistics, Curaçao) 13, no. 4 (2013): 29–42.
Azicri, Max. *Cuba: Politics, Economics and Society*. London: Pinter, 1988.
Bain, Mervyn J. *Soviet-Cuban Relations, 1985 to 1991: Changing Perceptions in Moscow and Havana*. Lanham, MD: Lexington Books, 2007.
Blight, James G., Bruce J. Allyn and David A. Welch. *Cuba on the Brink: Castro, the Missile Crisis, and the Soviet Collapse*. Lanham, MD: Rowman and Littlefield, 2002.

Bolland, O. Nigel. *On the March: Labour Rebellion in the British Caribbean, 1934–39,* Kingston: Ian Randle, 1995.

Brettell, Caroline B., and James F. Hollifield, eds. *Migration Theory: Talking across Disciplines.* New York: Routledge, 2015.

Browne, David V.C. " 'Go Bravely Big England; Little England Is Behind You': Barbadian Society and Polity During World War II". Presentation to the History Forum, Faculty of the Humanities, Department of History, University of the West Indies, Cave Hill, Barbados, 7 February 1997.

———. "The 1937 Disturbances and Barbadian Nationalism". *The Empowering Impulse: The Nationalist Tradition of Barbados,* edited by Glenford D. Howe and Don D. Marshall, 149–64. Kingston: Canoe Press, 2001.

———. *Race, Class, Politics and the Struggle for Empowerment in Barbados, 1914–1937,* Kingston: Ian Randle, 2012.

Castro, Fidel. Address at the closing ceremony of the first national meeting of chairpersons of the Credit and Service Cooperatives, International Conference Center, Havana, 3 June 1998. In *On Neoliberal Globalization, the Economic Crisis and Other Subjects,* 13–50. New York: Mission of Cuba to the United Nations, 1998.

Chamberlain, Mary. *Empire and Nation-Building in the Caribbean: Barbados, 1937–66,* Manchester: Manchester University Press, 2010.

Clarke, Austin. *Growing up Stupid under the Union Jack.* 1980. Reprint, Toronto: Vintage, 1998.

Diplomacy and Development: A Review of the Foreign Policy of Barbados, Bridgetown: Ministry of Foreign Affairs, 1987.

Erisman, H. Michael, "The Odyssey of Revolution in Cuba". In *Modern Caribbean Politics,* edited by Anthony Payne and Paul Sutton, 212–37. Kingston: Ian Randle.

Giovannetti, Jorge L. "Empire beyond the Imperial Domain: British Colonial Encounters in Cuba". *British Academy Review,* no. 12 (January 2009): 21–24.

———. "The Elusive Organization of 'Identity': Race, Religion, and Empire among Caribbean Migrants in Cuba". *Small Axe,* no. 19 (February 2006): 1–27.

Gmelch, George. *Double Passage: The Lives of Caribbean Migrants Abroad and Back Home.* Ann Arbor: University of Michigan Press, 1992.

Hart, Richard. "Labour Rebellions of the 1930s in the British Caribbean Region Colonies". London: Caribbean Labour Solidarity/ Socialist History Society, 2002.

Horst, Heather A. "Reclaiming Place: The Architecture of Home, Family and Migration". *Anthropologica* 53, no. 1 (2011): 29–39. http://www.jstor.org/stable/41475727.

Howe, Glenford D. "De(Re) Constructing Identities: World War I and the Growth of Barbadian/West Indian Nationalism". In *The Empowering Impulse: The Nationalist Tradition of Barbados,* edited by Glenford D. Howe and Don D. Marshall, 103–32. Kingston: Canoe Press, 2001.

Hoyos, F.A. *The Quiet Revolutionary*. London: Macmillan, 1984.
Kushner, Rachel. *Telex from Cuba*. New York: Scribner, 2008.
LeoGrande, William M. "Cuba: The Shape of Things to Come". In *Cuba: Contours of Change*, edited by Susan Kaufman Purcell and David Jochanan Rothkopf, 1–12. Colorado: Lynne Rienner, 2000.
Leverick, Percy Sinclair. *Leverick's Directory of Barbados, 1921*. Bridgetown, 1921.
Marshall, Sharon Milagro. *Tell My Mother I Gone to Cuba: Stories of Early Twentieth-Century Migration from Barbados*. Kingston: University of the West Indies Press, 2016.
Maughan, Basil. "Some Aspects of Barbadian Emigration to Cuba, 1919–1935". *Journal of the Barbados Museum and Historical Society* 37, no. 3 (1985): 239–75.
McLeod, Marc C. "Undesirable Aliens: Race, Ethnicity, and Nationalism in the Comparison of Haitian and British West Indian Immigrant Workers in Cuba, 1912–1939". *The Free Library* (22 March 1998). https://www.thefreelibrary.com/Undesirable aliens: race, ethnicity, and nationalism in the...-a020574141.
Moore, Carlos. *Castro, the Blacks and Africa*. Berkeley: University of California Press, 1988.
Newton, Velma. *The Silver Men: West Indian Labour Migration to Panama, 1850–1914*. Kingston: Institute of Social and Economic Research, University of the West Indies, 1984.
Peach, Ceri. *The Caribbean in Europe: Contrasting Patterns of Migration and Settlement in Britain, France and the Netherlands*. Coventry: University of Warwick, Centre for Research in Ethnic Relations, 1991.
Pérez, Louis A. Jr. *Cuba: Between Reform and Revolution*. 2nd ed. New York: Oxford University Press, 1995.
Pérez de la Riva, Juan. "Cuba and West Indian Migration 1900–1931". In *La Republica neocolonial Anuario de Estudios Cubanos 2*, 5–75. Havana: Editorial Ciencias Sociales, 1979.
Putnam, Lara. *Radical Moves: Caribbean Migrants and the Politics of Race in the Jazz Age*. Chapel Hill: University of North Carolina Press, 2013.
Reynolds, Tim. "Returning Guantánamo". *Jacobin*, 25 March 2016. https://www.jacobinmag.com/2016/03/guantanamo-gtmo-obama-castro-havana/.
Roberts, G.W. "Emigration from the Island of Barbados". *Social and Economic Studies* 4, no. 3 (1955): 245–88.
Richardson, Bonham. *Panama Money in Barbados, 1900–1920*. Knoxville: University of Tennessee Press, 1985.
Rocha, Elaine Pereira. "'Another Black like Me': Strategies of Identification in Afrodescendientes in Latin America". In *Another Black like Me: The Construction of Identities and Solidarity in the African Diaspora*, edited by Elaine Pereira Rocha

and Nielson Rosa Bezerra, 1–23. Newcastle upon Tyne: Cambridge Scholars, 2015.
Smith, Sir Frederick, and Alan Smith. *Dreaming a Nation*. London: LifeBooks, 2015.
Smith, Wayne. *Portrait of Cuba*. Atlanta: Turner, 1991.
Sutton, Constance R. "Cuban Connections and Presence in Contemporary Barbados". Presentation to a panel on Circum-Caribbean and Latin American Connections: Regional Migrations of Peoples, Ideas, Cultural Practices, and Politics, at the 106th Annual Meeting of the American Anthropological Association, Washington, DC, 28 November–2 December 2007.
Szulc, Tad. *Fidel: A Critical Portrait*, New York: William Morrow, 1986.
Thomas, Hugh. *Cuba: The Pursuit of Freedom*, New York: Harper and Row, 1971.
Yearwood, Gladstone, and Mike Richards. *Broadcasting in Barbados: The Cultural Impact of the Caribbean Broadcasting Corporation*, Bridgetown: Lighthouse Communications, 1989.

ORAL SOURCES

Agard, Peggy. Interview by the author. Christ Church, Barbados, 9 January 2019.
Atwell, Pablo. Interview by the author. St Michael, Barbados, 2 February 2018.
Belgrave, Colbert. Interview by the author. St James, Barbados, 6 December 2017.
Deane, Isabel. Interview by the author. Christ Church, Barbados, 8 November 2017.
Goddard, Nelson. Interview by the author. St Philip, Barbados, 9 January 2018.
Hope Jústiz, Pedro. Interview by the author. Christ Church, Barbados, 6 February 2018.
King, Graciela. Interview by the author. St James, Barbados, 12 January 2018.
Nelson Springer, Yolanda. Interview by the author. St Michael, Barbados, 26 November 2017.
Nicholls, Ofelia. Interview by the author. St Michael, Barbados, 31 October 2017.
Philo, Frank. Interview by the author. Christ Church, Barbados, 31 October 2017.
Ramírez Nelson, Josué. Interview by the author. St Michael, Barbados, 7 November 2017.
Roberts, Clarence. Interview by the author. St Philip, Barbados, 27 December 2018.
Rowe, Gilbert. Interview by the author. St Michael, Barbados, 5 February 2018.
Thomas Ferrier, Maria. Interview by the author. St Michael, Barbados, 8 April 2018.
Trotman Brown, Roberto. Interview by the author. Christ Church, Barbados, 20 December 2017.
Yearwood, Ernesto. Interview by the author. St Philip, Barbados, 5 January 2018.
Yearwood, Florencia. Interview by the author. St Philip, Barbados, 5 January 2018.
Yearwood, Juana. Interview by the author. St Philip, Barbados, 5 January 2018.

INDEX

Note: *Italic* page numbers refer to figures and tables.

Adams, Grantley, 40, 69; as advocate of emigration, 20
African immigration schemes, review of by Barbados authorities, 26
African liberation struggles, Cuba supported, 76
Afro-Cubans, 13–14, 68
Agard, Peggy, 5
Allen, Rose Mary, 50
Alliance Française de Bridgetown, 163
Allsopp, Jeannette (Caribbean Multilingual Research Centre), 139, 177–78
American-owned sugar mills in Cuba, 9
Anglo-American Association, contributed to repatriation relief, 28
Anglo-Cuban relations, 15–16
Angola, 77; Cuban troops sent to (1975), 76; Ernesto Yearwood travelled to, 157
anti-apartheid measure, Barbados provided landing site for Cuban planes as, 76
Antigua, 152; Bajan Town residents from, 132; Barbados emigration to (1863), 26
Appropriation Bill (1970), relief for Barbadians in Cuba and Old Peoples' Home in Panama, 82–83
Appropriation Bill debate in 1970, discussion of financing for repatriation, 84
Archer, G.S., recruiting agent for Cuban sugar estates, 21, 39
Aruba, Barbadian emigration to, 50
Ashby, Alexander, and contribution to war effort, 37–38
Asociación de Fomento de la Imnigración (Association for the Promotion of Immigration) 1911, 9
Atwell, Pablo, *169, 171, 172,* 169–73, 177; childhood in Cuba, 169–70; comparisons between Barbados and Cuba, 172–73; connected with Barbadian family, 170–71; Cuban community in Barbados, 173; cultural changes, 170; employment in Barbados, 171–72; exposure to Bajan culture, 170; first impressions of Barbados, 186; grandparents, 170; identifies as Cuban, 172, 194; immigrated to Barbados in 2002, 170; migrants not accepted as Bajan, 191; received diploma in tourism management in 2017, 172, 173; travels in the Caribbean, 171
Austin, Harold, nominated as Barbados representative to Coronation celebration in London, 36
Azicri, Max, 68, 69, 77, 193

213

Bajan Town, Baraguá, 95, 117, 132
Baraguá, 52, 63; Pablo Atwell travelled frequently to, 169–70; train track divided Bajan Town and American side of, 95; West Indians in, 17
Baraguá, Ciego de Ávila, hometown of: Colbert Belgrave, 116; Yolanda Nelson Springer, 131; Ofelia Nicholls, 52; Frank Philo, 59; Josué Ramírez Nelson, 140; Gilbert Rowe, 94
Baraguá Sugar Company, 16
Barbadian descendants in Cuba, 5; migration of, 189
Barbadian government: financial relief for Barbadians abroad by (1943–48), 28; inclusiveness measures (1954 and 1958), 49–50; resolutions on repatriation in 1930s, 28, 29–30
Barbadian labourers and emigration, 26; as British subjects, protection of the British flag for, 23–24; assistance in returning home for, 25; in Cuba in 1930s, 29; recruiting of for Cuban sugar industry, 39; transported to Cuba in 1922 and 1923, 22–23; to the United Kingdom (1955–66), 51, 51
Barbadian ruling elite, post-WWI emigration strategy embraced by, 38–39
Barbadians in Cuba, complaints regarding ill-treatment were processed through the British consul, 70
Barbadians: growing political consciousness of, 45–46; invited to London Coronation, 36; migration to the United Kingdom (1955–66), 51; serving in British military (WWII), colonial secretary requested information from relatives on, 40–41
Barbados: agreement with Cuba for airport use in, 76; as "Little England", 36–37; as the Promised Land, 189; Bajan Town residents from, 132; and the British Empire, 31–33; concepts of, 183–84; Coronation celebrations in, 35–36; decline in population, 80–81; described as land of opportunity in Cuba, 141; and emigration to Antigua and St Croix (1863), 26; foreigners in, 98; formal diplomatic relations with Cuba (1972), 81; full self-governance of (1961), 49–50; harsh conditions for return migrants, 83–84; independence achieved (1966), 59; infant mortality rate (1906), 19; migrant labourers in Curaçao oil-refineries from, 50; memorial to the late King George established in, 33–35; mourning of death of King George V by, 32–33; post-independence period, 78–86; provided landing site for Cuban planes as anti-apartheid measure, 76; rebellion (1937), 46–50; supported the empire's war efforts, 37–43
Barbados Advocate, support for British Empire by, 32
Barbados Blue Book and labourers' wages (1909–10), 20
Barbados Community College, 148, 188; Pedro Hope Jústiz as Spanish tutor at, 166
Barbados compared to Cuba, 106
Barbados Democratic League (1924), 45
Barbados government: compensation for 1937 riots provided by, 49; emigration sanctioned by (1863), 26; financial relief for Barbadians abroad by (1943–48), 28; financial relief for

West Indians in Cuba, 13; inclusiveness measures (1954 and 1958), 49–50; legislation deterring emigration (1838 and 1839), 26; position on emigration and repatriation, 25–28; repatriation in 1920s, 28; resolutions on repatriation in 1930s, 28, 29–30; WWII war effort supported by, 38, 39–40

Barbados Herald: news of Cuba in, 10–11; notice of tribute wreath sent by Barbados in tribute to late King George V, 32; a proponent of emigration, 20–21, 22, 23, 24, 25; report on opening of King George V Memorial Park, 33–34; UNIA recruitment through advertisement in, 45

Barbados House of Assembly, legislation restricting emigration enacted by, 26

Barbados Immigration Act (1952), 79

Barbados Independence Act (1966), 78

Barbados Jazz Festival, *100*, 101

Barbados labour movement, 45–46

Barbados migrants to Cuba, first group of in 1919, 21

Barbados Ministry of Foreign Affairs booklet (1987), relations between Barbados and Cuba described by, 81

Barbados Resident Mission in Cuba (2010), 82

Barbados Volunteer Force, called on during Bridgetown riot, 47

Barbados Workers Union, formation of (1941), 49

Barbados Workingmen's Association (WMA), 45–46

Barbados-Cuba bilateral relations, 81–82; Cuban embassy established in Barbados (1994), 82; trade and agricultural exchanges began in 1971, 81

Barrow, Errol: allowed Cuban planes to refuel in Barbados, 76; debate over citizenship for foreign husbands, 80; disapproved of financial assistance given to the UK during WWII, 40; discussion of repatriation of Josephine Maxwell's family, 84–85; ended diplomatic isolation of Cuba, 81; Old Peoples' Home in Panama visited by, 82–83; views on Cuban revolution, 67–68

Batista, Fulgencio, 11; corruption under, 67; emigrants' conditions under, 83; severed ties with Soviet Union, 74

Belgrave, Cleophas (father of Colbert Belgrave), 116, 117–18, 186; returned to Barbados, 71

Belgrave, Colbert, 71, *116*, *117*, *122*, 116–122, 127, 132, 177, 184; achievements in Barbados, 120; adjustment to life in Barbados, 119; arrival in Barbados in 1979, 118; attended Adventist school in Baraguá, 116; Bajan traditions held in Cuba, 117; childhood in Bajan Town, 117; communicates with relatives living in Cuba, 123–24; departure from Cuba, 185; held three passports, 194; identifies as a Cuban Barbadian, 124, 195; importance of family for migration to Barbados, 186; importance of home ownership in Barbados, 189; maternal grandfather was Barbadian 116; maternal grandmother was Jamaican, 116; memories of music festival at West Terrace Primary, 121–22; memories of Speech Day at Lodge School and St Lucy Secondary,

Belgrave, Colbert (*continued*) 120–21; mother, 116, 186; organist for multiple churches in Barbados, 122–23; received car for commuting to St Andrew's Parish Church, 122–23; shielded from compulsory military service in Cuba by father, 194; teaching positions held, 119–20; visited Cuba many times, 123

Belgrave, Eddy (brother of Colbert Belgrave), 71, 117, 118, 124, 194; friend of Yolanda Nelson Springer, 132

Best Rivero, Dr Aleida (Cuban politician of Barbadian descent), 193

Best, Joseph Nathaniel (father of Aleida Best Rivero), 193

biombo programme (US visa lottery), 155

black Cubans, improved socioeconomic conditions resulted from 1959 revolution, 68

black West Indians in Cuba, 13–14

Bolland, O. Nigel, 46

Boquerón (fishing village outside of Guantánamo), 110

Boxill, Neville, debate over citizenship for foreign husbands, 79

Boyce family in Chaparra, Cuba, 176

Braithwaite, C.A., 34

Brancker, J.E.T., dissatisfaction over Barbados celebration of Victory Day, 42

Brazil, Barbadian emigration to, 50

Brettell, Caroline, 5, 192

Bridgetown riots (July 1937), 46–47

Britain, 51; and tensions with Cuba over treatment of migrant Barbadians, 15; Barbadian legislature provided financial support during WWII to, 39; Barbadian migration to, 50; financial interests in Cuba, 15

British Armed Forces, Barbadians served in, during WWI and WWII, 37

British consul at Caracas, reimbursement from Barbadian government for repatriation of Barbadians, 27

British consul in Havana: arrangements for returnees to Barbados made by, 84; concerning cost of repatriation, 30; relief fund for British West Indian migrants provided by, 17–18

British Guiana: Barbadian emigration to, 50; planters in, 25–26; proposal to resettle Barbadians in, 42

British Honduras, proposal to resettle Barbadians in, 42

British Hotel and Restaurant Association, Barbadian labourers recruited by, 51

British Nationality Act (1948), 51

British Rail, Barbadian labourers recruited by, 51; Frank Philo worked for, 62

British West Indian Welfare Centre in Guantánamo, 161

British West Indians: advantages held over Haitian immigrants in Cuba, 16; British consular relief fund for, 17–18; in Cuba during 1940s, 13, 18; migration of in early 1900s, 9; oil-refining industry work, 50–51

Browne, David, 38, 39, 46, 47

Browne, Theophilus A., and wife, repatriation of in 1936, 28

Burnham, Forbes, ended diplomatic isolation of Cuba, 81

Bushe, Governor, concern over unemployment by, 43

Cabezas, Lázaro, first resident Cuban ambassador to Barbados, 82
Canada, Barbadian migration to, 50
Canadian Imperial Bank of Commerce (CIBC First-Caribbean), 114
cane cutting in Cuba, 116
Cape Verde Islands, Cuban planes to Africa refuelled in, 77
Caribbean studies at Las Tunas University, 193
CARICOM and diplomatic relations with Cuba, 81
Carrington Village School, 48, 55
Castro government, social security denied to Barbadians in Cuba by, 84
Castro regime and U.S relations, 72–74
Castro, Fidel, 58, 67–8, 76, 100; and Cuban troops in Africa, 77; declared revolution as "socialist", 72; positive spin on Special Period in Time of Peace, 75; and Soviet Union, 75; 1998 visit to Barbados and unveiling of monument to those killed in Cubana Airways bombing, 81–82
Cayman Islands, 112
Cenotaph War Memorial, Bridgetown, 43
Central Foundry strike (1937), 46
Central Hershey, Cuba, 17
Central Preston, 9
Chandler, J.D., 29
Chaparra Estates Limited (sugar producers), 22
Chaparra, Cuba, 88
Christian Mission Church, 17
Citizens' Contingent Committee (1915), 37
citizenship in Barbados, 78–81; to be made available to descendants of a Barbadian citizen, 80–81; categories of, 78; Cubans of Barbadian descent, 78–79; discrimination against foreign husbands of Barbadians, 79–80; legislation amended for foreign spouses (2000), 80
Colonial Office and requests for protection of migrants, 25
Colorado, Cuba, 95, 96
communist system in Cuba, life under, 111
congas in Cuba, 104
Congress of the Communist Party of Cuba (1975), expansion to fourteen provinces under resolution by, 75
Coronation Celebrations, 35–36
Costa Rica, West Indian community in, 13
Costa Ricans as facilitators in the Primary Spanish Programme, 5–6
cou-cou (coarse cornmeal), 61, 62
Crab Hill, St Lucy, branch of UNIA at, 45
Crawford, Wynter, 13, 41, 42; as advocate of emigration, 20; charges of racial profiling of merchant seamen during WWII by, 44
cricket clubs, West Indian migrants established, 16, 17
Cuba: "black belt" of, 14; and conditions for emigrants in 1930, 29; difficult economic circumstances in, 71, 183; economic and political developments in post-1959 revolution, 67–72; economic isolation of Cuba by the US, 72; expulsion of foreign workers (1921), 12; food rationing in 1962, 73; foreign labourers unwanted in, 11–13; foreign policy toward liberating African countries from colonial rule, 76;

Cuba (*continued*)
hardships in, and requests for repatriation, 84; hearsay of easy money in, 52–53; law forbidding employment of foreigners (1936), 29; military service mandatory in, 117–18; modes of transport from, 184–85; new political framework and land division provided by 1976 constitution, 75; price decline and surge of sugar prompted run on banks (1920), 11–12; provided economic opportunity for migrants, early 1900s, 9; racial inequality in, 14; repatriation from, 28–31; Revolution of 1931, 10–11; socialist state, 75; social services provided by government, 153, 159; and the Soviet Union, 74–75; standard of living in, 172, 186; travel policy for children, 71, 72; troops deployed to Angola, 77; United States influence in, 8–9; use of Caribbean airports for transport to Africa by, 76; West Indian community in, 53

Cuba, childhood memories in: Pablo Atwell, 169–70; Colbert Belgrave, 116–17; Isabel Deane, 111; Pedro Hope Jústiz, 160–62; Nelson Goddard, 87–88; Graciela King, 103–4; Yolanda Nelson Springer, 132; Ofelia Nicholls, 53–54; Frank Philo, 60–61; Josué Ramírez Nelson, 140–41; Gilbert Rowe, 94–96; Maria Thomas Ferrier, 126; Roberto Trotman Brown, 174–77; Juana Yearwood, 152–53

Cuba-CARICOM Day, 81

Cuba post-1959: complications for West Indians with multiple identities, 193; political conformity enforced in, 68–69

Cuba, the Caribbean and Africa (Carlos Moore), 75–77

CuBajan identity, 191–95

CuBajans, 4; Maxwell family as, 85; stories of, 86

Cuban Barbadians: applications made to Barbados embassy in Cuba for birth certificates and citizenship by descent, 82; discussion of, with Isabel Deane, 115; interest in returning to their roots in Barbados, 82–86

Cuban fishermen accused of espionage (1964), 73

Cuban grit, 158–59

Cuban military transport *Columbia*, transport of repatriating emigrants via, 31

Cuban missile crisis (1962), as catalyst for foreign policy shift for Cuba, 76

Cuban resentment of West Indian labourers, 10

Cuban Revolution (1959), 67–68

Cuban sugar estates: Barbadians recruited by agents of, 39; first Barbadian labourers in 1919, 21

Cuban sugar industry, 3; 1920 surplus and price decrease, 21; production during WWI, 9

Cuban towns with people of Barbadian ancestry, 175–76

Cuban workers and retirees at US naval base, fate of, 74

Cubana Airways Flight 455, bombing of (1976), 81–82, 185

Cubans of Barbadian descent as facilitators in the Primary Spanish Programme, 6, 7

Cummins, Dr Hugh (premier of Barbados), 69

Curaçao, 51; Barbadian emigration to work in oil-refining industry, 50

Daily Gleaner, 33; reports from the Royal Commission under Lord Moyne (1939), 48
Dance of the Millions, 11
De cara al campo (student field work programme in Cuba), 111
de Céspedes y Quesada, Carlos Manuel, 11
Deane Commission's report (1937), 48
Deane, Isabel, *110, 112, 113,* 110–15, *194;* arrival in St Lucia, 113; childhood in Guantánamo, 111; children, 115; confronting stereotypes regarding Cuba, 114; departure from Cuba,184–85; family in Cuba, 115; identifies as Barbadian, 195; left Cuba for St Lucia at nineteen, 112; marriage and move to Barbados, 114; never returned to Cuba, 192; parents, 110, *111, 112;* received private English lessons in St Lucia, 113; retired life, 114–15; siblings, 111, *112,* 113; summer vacations spent in programme De cara al campo, 111; work experience in Barbados, 114; work experience in St Lucia, 113
Deane, Sir George, 48
Decree 1404 (1920), mandated expulsion of foreign workers, 21
Decree 2232 (1933) forced repatriation, 12
Democratic Labour Party, achievements of, 50
discrimination in Barbados against citizens born abroad, 109
domestic workers, female migrant workers as, 50–51

Dominica, 184
Dominican Republic, 27; protectionist laws in, 13

Estern Caribbean, Cuban diplomacy in, 76
economic factors leading to 1937 rebellion, 46
Education Act (1878), 19
education in Barbados, 100
education, contribution of CuBajans to, 5
Edward VIII, 35
Eisenhower, President Dwight D., partial economic embargo imposed on Cuba by (1960), 72
Emancipation Act (1834) and apprenticeship system, 19
emigrants in Cuba left destitute, Barbadian government discussion concerning, 29
emigration: de-emphasized after the 1960s, 20, 50; demographics of, 20; lack of Barbados government support for workers on Panama Canal (1883), 27; linked with building of Panama Canal (1904–13), 26–27; sanctioned by Barbados government in 1863, 26; as solution to lack of employment opportunities for returning WWI veterans, 38–39; as solution to overpopulation, 49
emigration agents, Barbadian laws governing (1864), 26
emigration legislation (1873), allowing certain classes to emigrate, 26
Empire Societies' War Hospitality Committee, gifts to Barbadian servicemen sent through, 41

English-speaking West Indians and integration into Cuba, 69
Erisman, H. Michael, 74
Esso and nationalization by Cuba, 72
estate owners in Barbados, complaints of labour scarcity by, 25

Facebook in Cuba, 146
false advertisements regarding work conditions in Cuba, 21
Fanon, Frantz, 99
Forde, Donna, Barbadian ambassador to Cuba, 82
foreign labourers in Cuba: expulsion of, 12; obligatory repatriation, 12
Francis, Ephraim, financial assistance for repatriation from the Dominican Republic, 27
franchise, exclusions to the, 20

Garvey, Marcus, visit to Barbados in 1937, 45
George VI and Queen Elizabeth, 35
Germany, surrender of, and Barbados celebrations, 42
Giovannetti, Jorge, 18
Gmelch, George, *Double Passage: The Lives of Caribbean Migrants Abroad and Back Home*, 36–37
GMR International Tours, 101
Goddard family: and departure from Cuba and mode of transport, 185; in Vásquez, 175–76
Goddard, Ethelbert Beresford (father of Nelson Goddard), 84, 186; relearned English, 88–89; repatriated to Barbados in 1970, 84
Goddard, Nelson, 87, 91, 87–93, 183–84; Barrow and government financing responsible for repatriation, 92–93; children, 88, 89, 91; early years in Cuba, 87–88; grandparents, 88; immigration status affecting visits to Cuba, 91–92; importance of family for migration to Barbados, 186; importance of owning a home in Barbados, 190; impressions of Cuba when visiting, 193; life in Barbados as a CuBajan, 92–93; migrants not accepted as Bajan, 191; repatriation in Barbados (1970), 84, 88; siblings, 87, 186, 194; siblings remain in Cuba, 92
Godson, Francis, 31
Gómez, President José Miguel, 3, 9
Grand Cayman, 167
Grantley Adam International Airport, 77
Grau San Martín, Ramón, 11
Great Depression and overproduction of sugar and unemployment in Cuba, 10
Greaves, M.M., 41
Grenada, Bajan Town residents from, 132
Griffith family in Chaparra, Cuba, 176
Griffith-Watson, Wendy (former chief education officer), 177, 179
Guantánamo, new Cuban province of, 75; West Indians in, 162
Guantánamo City, Guantánamo, hometown of: Isabel Deane, 110; Maria Thomas Ferrier, 125; Pedro Hope Jústiz, 160; Graciela King,103
Guantánamo Bay, water supply cut (1964), 73
Guantánamo Teacher Training University, 188; Pedro Hope Jústiz a senior lecturer at, 163
Guatemala, protectionist laws in, 13

Guyana, 163, 165; agreement with Cuba for airport use in, 76; Cuban planes to Africa refuelled in, 77

Haggard, Godfrey, 15
Haiti as source of labour for Cuban sugar industry, 9
Haiti, migrant labourers in Curaçao oil-refineries from, 50
Hamilton, Governor, 26
Harding, George P., 21
Hart, Richard, 46
Hawthorn Methodist Church, Barbados, 114
Heads of Government Conference, Trinidad and Tobago (1972), CARICOM announced diplomatic relations with Cuba at, 81
Hendrickson Providence, Winifred (mother of Juana, Florencia and Ernesto Yearwood), 152, 157; worked on a dairy farm, 153
Hewanorra Airport, St Lucia, 113
Hinds, Burton, 82
Hollifield, James F., 5, 192
home, as a site to reclaim place and identity for returning migrants, 188–89
Hope Jústiz, Pedro, 77, 160, 162, 164, 166, 160–68, 194; annual visits to Cuba, 167; childhood memories of Cuba, 160–63; choir conductor, Christ Church Girls Primary School, 166; comparison between Guantánamo and Barbados, 164–65; Cuba during the Special Period, 163; daughters Yeneisy and Aimara, 163, 167; difference between Barbados and other English-speaking Caribbean islands, 165; difficulty finding employment after migrating, 188; difficulty of sending remittances to family in Cuba, 167; discussion of local English, 165; earned master's degree at Cave Hill campus, 163; English language abilities and work in tourism, 163; father worked at US naval base in Guantánamo and played piano, 160–61; first impressions of Barbados, 186; Haitian grandmother (maternal), 161; identifies as CuBajan, Cuban, Bajan, Haitian, and Caribbean, 168, 195; immigrated to Barbados in 2000, 164; maternal grandfather, 161, 168; member of Jagüey dance company, 163; quality of life, 167–68; received secondary and tertiary education in Cuba, 162–63; returned to the land of his grandfather, 189; siblings, 160–61; student of languages, 161, 163–64; tales of Barbados in Cuba, 161–62; teaching employment in Barbados, 165–66; wife, Sharon Marshall, 164
Horst, Heather, 188
housing accommodations for migrants in Cuba in segregated neighbourhoods, 15
How Europe Underdeveloped Africa (Walter Rodney), 99
Hoyos, F.A., personal account of Bridgetown riot, 46–47
Hurricane Janet (1955), 62
Hutson, Dr John, nominated as Barbados representative to Coronation celebration in London, 29, 36

immigrants from Cuba not accepted as Bajan, 191

Immigration (Amendment) Act (1970), debate on, 79–80
Immigration Act, cap. 190, 90
immigration to Cuba: increased as a result of WWI, 9; reasons for, 183
immigration legislation, Cuba (1917), 10
Indian Ground, St Peter, branch of UNIA at, 45
internet in Cuba, 146
interviewees, 4–5

Jamaica, 97, 105, 112, 142; agreement with Cuba for airport use in, 76; Bajan Town residents from, 132; migrant labourers in Curaçao oil-refineries from, 50; Old Peoples' Home in Panama run jointly by governments of Barbados and, 83; as source of labour for Cuban sugar industry, 9; Eunice Willie's parents from, 111
Jamaican government, support of emigrants working on Panama Canal, 27
Jamaicans: in Baraguá, 96; in Cuba, 53; returning from the United Kingdom, 188–89
Jaworsky, Nadya, 191

Kennedy, President John F., broadened ban on trade with Cuba, 73
King George V: death of, 32; memorial to, 33–35
King, Graciela, *103*, *105*, *107*, 103–109, *194*; arrival in Barbados in 1973, 105; *carnaval* time in Cuba, 104, 108; childhood in Cuba, 103–4; children, 108; communicating with Spanish speakers in Barbados, 107; departure from Cuba, 185; family in Cuba, 108; first impressions of Barbados, 185–86; identifies as Cuban, 109, 194–95; learning English in Barbados, 106; migrants not accepted as Bajan, 191; mother, 104, *105*; new life in Barbados, 105–6; return visit to Cuba, 108; siblings, 105, *105*, *107*, 108–9, 127, 185; teaching Spanish in primary schools, 107–8; work experiences, 107

labour disparities at US naval base at Guantánamo Bay, 73
labour in sugar industry in Cuba, 9
labour movement in Barbados, 45–46
labour surplus in Barbados, discussion of in the *Herald*, 24, 25
labouring class, Barbados, dire living conditions for, 19; insufficient wages for, 48
labour rebellion of 1937, 46; changes resulting from, 49
Le-Roy y Cassa, Dr Jorge, 14
Leverick, Percy Sinclair, 37
Levitt, Peggy, 191
Ley Morúa (1910), 14
Little England, Barbados referred to as, 42
"located labourer" statutes, 19
London Financial News reports "Cuba Rapidly Returning to Prosperity", 21
London Transport, Barbadian labourers recruited by, 51
Lord Kitchener Memorial Fund, 38

Machado, President Gerado, 58; overthrow of (1931), 10, 11
macro-level approach to migration research, 5
Manatí, Las Tunas, hometown of the Yearwood siblings, 151

Manatí, Rincón de Manatí, Barbadians, Jamaicans and Haitians lived in, 176
Manley, Michael, ended diplomatic isolation of Cuba, 81
Marshall, Sharon (wife of Pedro Hope Jústiz), 100, 144, 164, 177
Masonic Lodge, Cuba District Grand Lodge No. 1, 17
Maxwell, Mrs Josephine, repatriation of family of, 84
Maxwell family, citizenship for, 85
McLeod, Marc, 17
Member of the British Empire, Barbadians awarded, 43
Menocal, President Mario, 9–10, 11
merchant seamen, difficulty of securing employment during war years by, 44–45
Mérida, Mexico, 97
Methodist Church, 114
Mexico, 105; post-1959 Cuba continued relations with, 74
micro-level approach to migration research, 5
migrant labourers in Cuba, 3–4; Cuban decree allowing free entry to Panama Canal workers (1913), 9; difficulties encountered by, acknowledged by the *Herald*, 23; suffered with sugar price crash of 1920, 22
migration: as a complicated process of transnational integration, 191–92; experience of "simultaneous membership in two societies", 192; and modes of transportation, 183; to Panama and Cuba, 50
migration from Barbados, reasons for, 20
migration of Barbadians to the United Kingdom (1955–66), 51

migration research, 5
migration to Barbados: families separated with, 186–87; kinship and family networks as important factors with, 186; life changes as a result of, 185–88; reasons for, 153
Mikoyan, Deputy Premier Anastas, 74
Miller, F.E., 70
monument to those killed in Cubana Airways bombing, Payne's Bay, St James, 81–82
Moyne, Royal Commission under, 48
music, contribution of CuBajans to, 5

National Cultural Foundation (NCF) of Barbados, 121
National Health Service, Barbadian labourers recruited by, 51
National Insurance Scheme, 81
National Union of Public Workers, 4
nationality, concepts of, 194
nationalization of US companies in Cuba, 72
Nelson family in Vásquez, 176
Nelson Springer, Yolanda, *131, 135, 138,* 131–39, 177, 144, *194*; author of textbooks, 139; Barbadian traditions celebrated in Cuba, 132, 133; childhood friends in Cuba of West Indian descent, 132; childhood in Bajan Town, 132; employment in Barbados, 188; family of, 131–32; father of, 17, 133; identifies as Barbadian and Cuban, 139, 195; immigrated to Barbados without family, 136–38, 187; importance of family for immigration to Barbados, 186; life during 1993–94 in Cuba, 136; mother of, 133–34, 136; recalled gatherings with West Indians in Cuba, 133;

Nelson Springer, Yolanda (*continued*)
siblings, 71–72, 131, 177; son Josué, 72, 136, 137, 138; stories about Barbados and Panama from her mother, 134; studied at Alexander Ivanovich Herzen University, 134; taught in various locations in Cuba, 135; tertiary education in Villa Clara, 134; time in the Soviet Union, 75, 134–35; worked at Salvador Allende Pedagogical School for the Training of Teachers, 135; mother of Josué Ramírez Nelson, 144

Neto, Dr Antonio Agostinho, 76

Newton, Velma, 27

Nicholls, Ofelia (née Parris), 51, *52*,*56*, *57*, 52–58; arrival in Barbados, 54; education in Cuba, 54; emigrated to Curaçao, 56–57; family of, 52–53; never returned to Cuba, 192; Ofelia Parris married Clyde Nicholls in Curaçao in 1952, *56*; parents, 52, 53, 54; personal account of 1937 riots, 47–48, 55; reflections on Cuban politics, 58; religious upbringing in Cuba, 54; resided in Glebe Land, St George, 58; return to Barbados (1936), 54; story of the storm (1932), 53; work experiences, 55–56

Nicholls family, departure from Cuba, 184

Niles, Nathaniel (father of Graciela King), 104–5, *105*; friend of Gerald Ethelbert Thomas in Cuba, 125; migration to Barbados based on economic decision, 186–87

Nipe Bay Company, 9

O'Brien, Governor Charles, 14, 38; 1923 press notice regarding repatriation, 28

O'Neal, Dr Charles Duncan, founder of the Barbados Democratic League, 45

Official Gazette, 27, 40; details of memorial service for King George V held at St Michael's, 32–33

oil refineries owned by US and nationalized by Cuba, 72

Old Peoples' Home in Panama, 82–83

Order of the British Empire, Barbadians awarded, 43

overcrowding in Barbados, tempered by emigration, 20

overpopulation, 26; in Barbados since the 1860s, 20; emigration as solution to, 49; and low wages, 25; as prime cause of 1937 riots (Dean Commission report), 48

Palma, President Estrada, 9

Panama, 116; Bajan immigration to, 7; protectionist laws in, 13

Panama Canal Zone, 52; administered by Americans, 98; Social Security benefits in, 83

Panama Canal, Barbadian labourers on, 27; retired workers responsible for construction of, 83

Papiamento, 56

Partido Independent de Color (1908–10), 14

Payne, Clement, deportation of, 46

Payne, D.S., 41

Payne's Bay, St James, monument to those killed in Cubana Airways bombing erected at, 81–82

Peach, Ceri, 51

Peebles, Major Herbert Walter, 33–34, 49; chairman of the rehabilitation committee, 43

Pereira Rocha, Elaine, 13

Pérez, Louis A. Jr, 72
Philo, Frank, 51, 59, 63, 59–63, 183, 194; children and grandchildren, 62–63; Cuba and *tiempo muerto*, 61; death of mother (1945), 62; departure from Cuba,184; emigrated to England, 62; family in Cuba, 63; identifies as Barbadian, 195; life in Cuba, 60–61; marriages, 62; maternal family in Cuba, 59; mother of, emigrated to Cuba, 60; niece Janet in Cuba, 192; paternal grandfather from Antigua, 60; personal account of 1937 riots, 48, 62; returned multiple times to Cuba, 63; returned to Barbados, 61, 62; siblings of, 60; Spanish spoken, 61; standard of living in Cuba and Barbados, 62; strong ties with family in Cuba, 192; work as bus driver, 62
Phosphate Mining Company, 50
Pile, Deputy Speaker G. Douglas, 49
plantation owners, political influence weakened, 49
plantations, attacks on during 1937 rebellion, 47
planter class, Barbados, exploitation of workers by, 19–20
Platt Amendment, 8
plumbing: indoor, in Cuba, 61; outdoor, in Barbados, 62
political consciousness of middle- and working-class Barbadians, 45–46
political protest, 1937 rebellion as, 46
Population and Housing Census, Barbados (2010), 85
poverty as prime cause of 1937 riots (Dean Commission report), 48
Princess Margaret Secondary School, 98–99

Probyn, Governor Sir Leslie, urged elite Barbadians to employ returning veterans, 38
Progressive League (Barbados Labour Party), formation of (1939), 49
property qualifications widened (1944), 49
protectionist measures during 1930s, 12–13

quarantine of British West Indians in Cuba, 14
Queeley, Andrea, 69
Queen Elizabeth and George VI, 35

race war in Cuba (1912), 14
racial discrimination, WWI soldiers experienced, 38
Ramírez Marino, Jacinto (ex-husband of Yolanda Nelson Springer), 135; (father of Josué Ramírez Nelson), 144, 194
Ramírez Nelson, Josué, 140, 144, 140–50, 184; 2006 visit to Cuba, 150; Alchino, close friend in Barbados, 147; Andwele, close friend in Barbados, 147; Aunt Adela, 144; Aunt Gloria and cousin Osvaldo, 142–43; Aunt Olivia "Mami Beba", 142, 144; Barbados Community College and media studies, 148–49; childhood with extended family, 141; comparison of life in Baraguá and Barbados, 145; considers Barbados home but also feels like a foreigner, 192–93; cousin Arabeisy, 142; departure from Cuba, 185; discussion of "height privilege", 148; early memories of Barbados, 143–45; father of, migrated to Barbados from Cuba, 140; half-brother Julier, 142, 146;

Ramírez Nelson, Josué (*continued*)
identifies as Bajan and Cuban, 145; identifies as Cuban but also estranged from the culture, 149–50; interned with Caribbean Broadcasting Corporation (CBC), 149; journey from Cuba to Barbados, 142; left for Barbados in 1999, 141; life in Barbados more disciplined, 147; with the Marshall family, 144; raised by aunts in Cuba, 140; remains in touch with Cuban friends and family, 145–46; reunited with mother in Barbados, 142; taught English by his mother and Auntie Juliette, 143; visits to Cuba, 146; Yolanda, mother of, migrated to Barbados from Cuba, 140

rebellion of 1937, 46–50

Reclaiming Place: The Architecture of Home, Family and Migration, (Horst), 188–89

recruitment of Barbadians to Cuba compared with emigration on own volition, 29

Reed, C.A. (acting colonial secretary), 33; introduction of resolution regarding repatriation by (1936), 28–29

refugees out of Cuba, 70

rehabilitation committee for returning veterans (1945), 43

relief for Barbadians in Cuba (1970), 82–83

relief funds for West Indians in Cuba remitted to the Foreign Office (1958–60), 69

remittances from Barbados, importance of for family in Cuba, 187

remittances from Cuba, Panama and the United States, Barbados reliance on, 21, 23, 25

repatriation of Barbadian seamen from Great Britain, Appropriations Bill financing, 45

repatriation of Barbadians from Cuba, 28–31; during 1969–72, 82; experience in Cuba when permission granted for, 96; government assistance with (1938 and 1939), 27; requests from those who emigrated to Cuba around 1913, 83; requests from Barbadians in post-1959 Cuba, 70–71; routes travelled from Cuba to Barbados, 97, 105

Republic of Cuba (1902), 8

Returned Soldiers Committee (WWI), 38; financed passage to Cuba for veterans, 39

return migrants to Barbados, harsh conditions for, 83–84

Reynolds, Tim, 73

Richardson, Bonham, 19

Roberts, Clarence: memories of opening King George V Memorial Park from, 34; personal account of 1937 riots, 48

Roberts, G.W., 20, 25–26, 27

Rodney, Walter, 99

Rowe family: bonds between Cuba and Barbados, 97; departure from Cuba, 185; and migration, 186; reside in St Philip, St Andrew, and United States, 98

Rowe, Gilbert, 70, 94, 94–102, 183; arrival in Barbados, 98–99; attended University at Cave Hill, 99; Barbados Jazz Festival and GMR International Tours, 101; Cuban identity, 101–2; family in Cuba, 102; father, 96, 97; first impressions of Barbados, 185; friend of Yolanda Springer Nelson,

132; grandfather, 97, 99, 101; importance of owning a home in Barbados after house in Cuba disposed, 190; identifies as Cuban of Barbadian descent, 194; learned English while in Cuba, 98; memories of Cuba, 94–96; migrants not accepted as Bajan, 191; recalled father's return to Barbados, 70–71; reflections on elders in Cuba discussing Barbados, 95–96; resided on Six Roads "University of the Square", 99–100; strong ties with family in Cuba, 192; taught school, 99
Rubik's Cuban (Josué Ramírez Nelson's podcast moniker), 145

Sandals Resorts International, Jamaica, 165
Santa Cruz, Yearwood family in, 153
scholarship for Cubans to study in Soviet Union, 75
schooner *Annie Eudora*, wreck of, off Bonaire, 28
schooner *Blomidon*, 27
schooner *Lillian Barnes*, 27
second-generation Cubans in Barbados, 127
self-help organizations, West Indian migrants established, 16
Shell oil and nationalization by Cuba, 72
slang, 150
sleep-in maids (female migrant workers to Curaçao), 50–51
Smith, Sir Frederick, 50, 61, 76, 81, 82
social clubs, West Indian migrants established, 16
social mobility, opportunities for, in post-1959 Cuba, 69
socio-economic policies, improved living conditions through Cuban revolution's, 68
South Africa, Cuban troops in Angola promoted anti-apartheid in, 76
Soviet Union and Cuba, 74–75
Spanish language in primary school curriculum, 6
Spanish-American War of 1898, 8
Special Period in Cuba (1993–94), 72
Special Period in Time of Peace (era of economic hardship in Cuba, post-Soviet period), 75
Springer, Clotell (mother of Yolanda Nelson Springer), 17; difficulties of travel out of post-1959 Cuba, 71–72
Springer, Hugh, secretary of the Barbados Workers' Union, comment on lack of employment opportunities for merchant seamen by, 44–45
St Croix, Barbados emigration to (1863), 26
St John, Bernard, debate over citizenship for foreign husbands, 79–80
St Lucia, 110; as possible repatriation site for returning Barbadian emigrants, 31; Barbadian emigration to, 50
St Philip parish, site of King George V Memorial Park, 33
St Vincent: Bajan Town residents from, 132; Barbadian emigration to, 50; repatriation of Barbadians from, 27
steamship service between Bridgetown and Cuban ports, 21
Stuart, Freundel (former prime minister), 99
Stubbs, Sir Edward, 49
sugar cane technology, Cubans observed Barbadian achievements in, 81
sugar factory: in Baraguá, 132; in Cuba, 152

sugar industry in Cuba: Charles Enrique Willie worked in, 110; success of, tied to prospects for migrant employment in, 21
sugar production, falling price of during Great Depression, 10
sugar, Cuban, as source for international market, 9
Surinam: Barbadian emigration to, 50; repatriation of Barbadians from, 27
Sutton, Constance, 85
Szulc, Tad, 74, 77

Talma, Edwy, against gender discrimination in 1952 Immigration Act, 79
Tappin, Arturo, *100*
Texaco and nationalization by Cuba, 72
Thomas Ferrier, Maria, 125–30; childhood in Cuba, 126; close to Uncle Everton and Aunt Phyllis in Barbados, 128–30; Cuban and Barbadian identity, 130; daughter Maritza, 126; daughter Niurka, 127; employment in Barbados, 187–88; engaged in university studies while working, 126; extended family on her father's side lived in Barbados, 126; father, 125, 126–27; five grandchildren, 130; homeowner in Black Rock, St Michael, 128–29; identifies as half-Cuban and half-Barbadian, 195; importance of family for migration to Barbados, 186; importance of owning a home in Barbados, 190; large family in Cuba, 125; marriage and family, 126; met family in St Lucy, Barbados, 127; migration of family to Barbados occurred in stages, 187; mother, 125; parents in Barbados, 126–27; relocated with family to Barbados in 1994, 127–28; siblings, 125, 127, 130; visit to Barbados for father's funeral, 127; visits to family in Cuba, 130; work experiences in Barbados, 128
Thomas-Hope, Elizabeth, 191–92
Thorne, Stanley (planter and assemblyman), opposed to emigration, 24, 31, 39
Trade Union Act (1939), 49
Trinidad, Bajan Town residents from, 132; Barbadian emigration to, 50; planters in, 25–26
Trinidad and Tobago, agreement with Cuba for airport use in, 76
Trinidadians in Barbados, 107
Trotman Brown, Roberto, *174, 182,* 174–82, 184; ability to travel, 181; Barbados culture in Cuba, 175; childhood in Cuba, 174–77; Cuba feels like home, 181; discrimination against foreign-born in Barbados, 180–81; employment in Barbados, 178, 188; family in Barbados and Cuba, 192; grandparents, 174, 176; identifies as Bajan as well, 182; immigrated to Barbados in 2002, 177; joined the Primary Spanish Programme, 179; migrants not accepted as Bajan, 191; a recorded musician, 182; taught English in Cuba, 177; teaching at University of the West Indies, Cave Hill, 178; visits to Cuba, 180; worked with Jeannette Allsopp, Caribbean Multilingual Research Centre, 177–78
Trotman, Adolph (father of Roberto Trotman Brown), 174; left Barbados due to economic hardships to work in cane fields, 176; tutored in English, 176

Tudor, J. Cameron, 69

unemployment: and surplus population post-WWII in Barbados, 42; discussion of repatriation and, 30–31
unionization at US naval base at Guantánamo Bay, 73–74
United Fruit Company, 3; housing segregation under, 15; wages paid in vouchers by, 15
United States: banks provided financial assistance to Cuban government in 1920, 21; Barbadian migration to, 50; emigration from Cuba to, 69; influence in Cuba, 8–9; investment in Cuba, 9; marines sent to crush 1912 Cuban revolt, 14; organized crime in Cuba, 67; residents of Panama Canal Zone and benefits through the, 83; severed ties with post-1959 Cuba, 74
universal adult suffrage (1951), 20, 49
Universal Negro Improvement Association (UNIA): chapters in Barbados, 45–46; West Indian migrants supported, 16
uprising in Barbados (1937), 46–50
US naval base (Guantánamo), difficulties receiving pension from, 183; Nathaniel Niles worked at, 105; pension paid in pesos if received in Cuba, 111; source of employment for West Indians, 73, 110

Vansittart, Robert, 16
Venezuela, protectionist laws in, 13
veterans given preference by Cuban sugar recruiters, 39
voyage between Cuba and Barbados, Ofelia Nicholls description of, 54

wages for labourers, Barbados (1909–10), 20
wages, insufficient for labourers, 48
Walcott, E.K., 13, 27–28, 35, 41–42; concerning repatriation, 29–30
Wanderer III (steamship between Bridgetown and Cuban ports), 22
war effort, private citizens and Barbados Legislature contributed to, 37–38
Webster Steamship Company: offices of in Bridgetown, 21; *SS Remelik* returned with workers from Cuba, 1922, 22
Webster, S.C., 29
Welles, Sumner, 11
West Indian community in Cuba, 53
West Indian hospitality towards migrants in Cuba, 17
West Indian labourers in Costa Rica, 13
West Indian labourers in Cuba, expulsion (1921) and quotas (1926), 12
West Indian migrants: British commercial and financial interests in Cuba took precedence over, 16; British subject status of, 18; employed by Baraguá Sugar Company, 16–17; in Cuba, 10, 13–17; self-help organizations established by, 16
West Indian planters, fear of loss of effective labour force by, 25
West Indians as British subjects, 15
West Indians in Cuba, Barbados government increased relief funds in 1961 for, 69
Wilkinson, J.H., 43
Williams, Dr Eric, 100; ended diplomatic isolation of Cuba, 81; rejection of Cuba's use of Trinidad's airport by, 77

women, as migrant labourers to Curaçao, 50–51

women, discriminated against in 1952 Immigration Act, 78

working-class, improved economic conditions for, 49–50

WWI soldiers returning to Barbados, lack of opportunities for, 38

WWII veterans from Barbados, higher standard of living experienced during war by, 43

WWII war measures in Barbados, prohibition of use of imported fertilizers as part of, 41

Xavier Rumeau Line, steamship service between Bridgetown and Santiago de Cuba, 21

xenophobia experienced in Barbados, 180–81, 191

Yearwood, Ernesto, 77, *151*, *152*, 153, 157–58; Barbados as the Promised Land, 189; employed in the merchant marines and in the thermo-electric field, 157; employment in Barbados, 187; employment in Barbados benefits his children, 158; identifies as Cuban and Barbadian, 158, 195; immigrated to Barbados in 2003 for economic reasons, 158; wife, daughter Onilet, and son Israel, live in Cuba, 158

Yearwood, Florencia, *151*, 153, *155*, 155–57; Barbados as the Promised Land, 189; connected with Barbadian relatives, 72; correspondence with Aunt Itha (Ethel O'Neale), 156; employment in Barbados, 157, 187; happy to live in Barbados, 157; importance of family for migration to Barbados, 186; issues involved with immigration to Barbados, 156; migrated to Barbados in 2000, 155; son Yanier, 72, 156

Yearwood, Juana "Jenny", *151*, *152*, 151–54, 158–59, *194*; children, 153; describes achievements of the revolution, 193–94; discussion of identity as Cuban and Barbadian, 154; employment in Barbados, 154, 187, 188; importance of home ownership in Barbados, 190; migrated to Barbados in 2000, 153; relocated to Harrises, St Lucy, 153

Yearwood family: maternal grandparents from West Indies, 152; separated when migrating to Barbados, 187

Yearwood Smith, Vivian Israel (father of Juana, Florencia, and Ernesto), *152*; cut cane in Cuba, 154; failing health and death of, 153, 158; received a national order for work with the Ministry of Education, 152; unsuccessful in returning to Barbados, 189

Young, Governor Sir Mark, 30, 32, 36; memorandum on unemployment issued by, 48

Zayas, President Alfredo, 12, 12, 21

www.ingramcontent.com/pod-product-compliance
Lightning Source LLC
Chambersburg PA
CBHW021839220426
43663CB00005B/313